ASHES UNDER WATER

"Good-bye Everybody," from *A Modern Eve*, published by T. B. Harms Co., New York (1912), courtesy Chicago Public Library

ASHES UNDER WATER

The SS Eastland *and the Shipwreck That Shook America*

MICHAEL McCARTHY

Guilford, Connecticut
Helena, Montana
An imprint of Rowman & Littlefield

Lyons Press is an imprint of Rowman & Littlefield

Distributed by NATIONAL BOOK NETWORK

Copyright © 2014 by Michael McCarthy

British Library Cataloguing-in-Publication Information available

Library of Congress Cataloging-in-Publication Data available

ISBN 978-0-7627-9328-0 (hardcover)

♾™ The paper used in this publication meets the minimum requirements of American National Standard for Information Sciences—Permanence of Paper for Printed Library Materials, ANSI/NISO Z39.48-1992.

Laus Tibi Domine

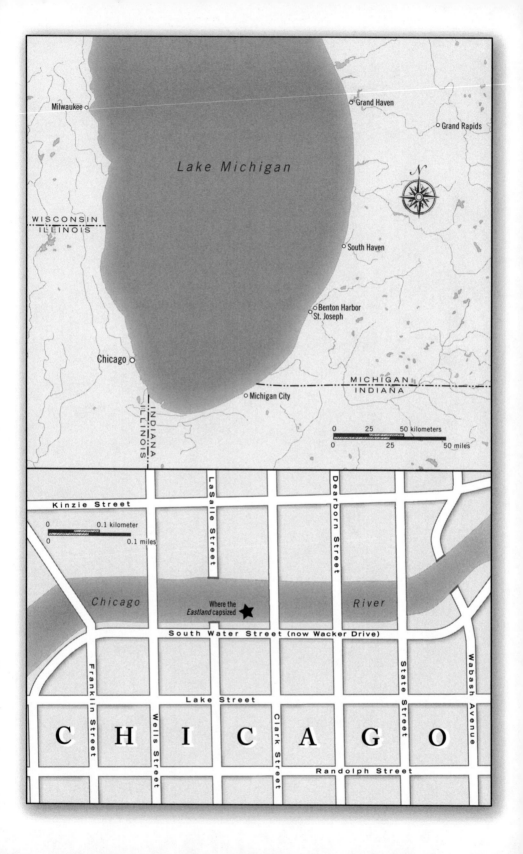

CONTENTS

Author's Note

This is the true account of America's most notorious ship, the country's most famous attorney, and how the least likely of heroes, an immigrant sailor nicknamed "Slim," connected them.

Perhaps like most people, I had never heard of the SS *Eastland* before. Then one day in 1999, a companion at a restaurant along the Chicago River mentioned that a steamship had tipped over nearby in 1915, killing more passengers than had perished on the *Titanic*.

I had lived in Chicago for years. How could I never have heard of this? The cause of such an unimaginable disaster, I would learn, was still a mystery, even as theories had piled up for four generations. I began what would become a decade-long quest to get to the bottom of it.

In time, I discovered a parable of miserable inequality and injustice, an untold national horror:

That a grand steamship, still tied to its dock, rolled over in the middle of a great city, quickly drowning 844 poor people—infants, women, twenty-two whole families—most trapped on the ship's underside.

That efforts to bring the prosperous, guilty shipowners to justice were thwarted by, of all people, the iconic lawyer Clarence Darrow.

That the brute skill Darrow used to suppress a confession and other damning evidence had kept the truth about the *Eastland* from coming out for a century.

§§§

The advent of the steamship in the Machine Age brought splendor and stupendous size. Steamships became the largest moving objects civilization had ever made, and passengers, who numbered in the hundreds on sailboats, mushroomed into the thousands. Steamers became floating factories. Ticket sales soared, as did the cost of errors.

The *Eastland* victims were mostly immigrants from the Old World, European factory hands who perished so quickly, in a scene so macabre, that hard-bitten Chicago policemen wept.

From President Woodrow Wilson down to local dockworkers, the whole country mourned. After the nightmare coursed through the nation's newspapers all summer, the syllables "*Eastland*" would stir shivers for a generation. Then following a great war, they would go silent.

Ships as long as city blocks don't simply capsize in calm water without some criminal negligence. Someone did something wrong.

In the treasure chest of the National Archives, I discovered revealing court testimony about the *Eastland* disaster that has never been published before. It went a long way toward explaining just how that ship could have capsized: that wealthy businessmen knew, despite their denials, that the *Eastland* had troubling stability problems.

Before the tragedy, the ship's managers had even discussed repairing the fatal mechanical flaws, but, cutting corners, they postponed the work. After the tragedy, one of the *Eastland* owners hired armed guards to keep the police from capturing him; the other described himself in sworn testimony as an "angel."

In a grave twist, those two owners would end up being defended by Darrow, who was only trying to prevent them from turning Slim, the innocent engineer, into the scapegoat for the tragedy. Darrow's slippery work in the courtroom may explain why he never breathed a word about the *Eastland* in his memoirs and why his role in this case has remained a dark hole in his otherwise famous biography. But I did find a revealing, heartfelt letter Darrow himself wrote about the *Eastland*, previously lost to history.

In 2001, I was fortunate enough to meet one of the last known survivors of the *Eastland* disaster. Libby Klucina Hruby was only ten on that calamitous July day in 1915. By the time I met her, she was nearly one hundred and rather frail. She nodded and smiled more than spoke. She appeared at a small memorial at the Chicago Yacht Club. We listened to an audio recording of her account from her more lucid days.

Afterward, I approached her, and I passed on my sympathy for her ordeal, as such a young child. Then I reached out and shook her hand, eager to touch, to connect with someone from the *Eastland*, someone who lived that day.

Some days over the past decade, I would go to the riverbanks in Chicago where the *Eastland* sank and sit and listen.

In rolling toward the great city, Lake Michigan roars when its waves gather and tumble over. And when those white waves, the remnants of a long gone ice mountain, settle into a sheen on the clearest of nights, the blue still-ness speaks in glacier-whispers.

Follow the shoreline along Chicago, into the riverbanks, past where the first fort stood, along the old Water Street. There, near the Clark Street Bridge, within the shallows of the Chicago River, stirring perhaps even still, the last cries and breaths of multitudes churned one drizzly summer morning in one vast drowning.

It is for these, the lost voices of the river, that we must speak.

Michael McCarthy
Chicago and South Haven, MI

Cast of Characters

THE *EASTLAND*

Joseph Erickson—The chief engineer of Norwegian descent, charged with conspiracy to operate an unsafe ship and criminal negligence

Harry Pedersen—The captain, a Norwegian immigrant, charged with conspiring to operate an unsafe ship and criminal negligence

James Novotny—A Bohemian immigrant and factory worker for the Western Electric Company who brought his whole family aboard

THE COMPANY MEN, 1903

Leander Leighton—The lake captain and original investor in the *Eastland* who met a suspicious demise

Sidney Jenks—The architect and designer of the *Eastland*

John Pereue—The lake captain who ordered the *Eastland* and had it built for an unusually shallow harbor

THE COMPANY MEN, 1915

George Arnold—The longtime *Eastland* owner, charged with conspiracy to operate an unsafe ship and criminal negligence

William H. Hull—The general manager, who, charged with conspiracy and criminal negligence, hired armed guards to avoid being arrested

Walter Steele—The secretary and treasurer, who, charged with conspiracy and criminal negligence, told investigators he was an "angel"

THE CITY OF CHICAGO

Charles Healey—The chief of police, who had a canny nose for damning evidence

Peter Hoffman—The city coroner, who ran a public autopsy of the tragedy

THE INSPECTORS

Ira Mansfield—The Chicago man whose early, troubling look at the *Eastland* would haunt him to his deathbed

Robert Reid—The Michigan man who licensed the *Eastland* in 1915; charged with conspiracy to operate an unsafe ship and criminal negligence

THE SWEETHEART

Florence Reid—The steamboat inspector's daughter whose untimely romance drew criminal suspicion

THE PROSECUTORS

Charles F. Clyne—The lead attorney for the prosecution who boasted he would not let the guilty escape justice

Maclay Hoyne—The zealous Illinois state's attorney whose hesitation allowed federal authorities to take over the case

THE DEFENSE TEAM

James Barbour—The powerful Chicago attorney who routinely sideswiped prosecutors

Clarence Darrow—The godsend of a defense attorney, in the valley of his career, who would achieve later fame in the Scopes "Monkey Trial"

Charles Edward Kremer—Nicknamed "The Admiral," the admiralty law expert who eviscerated prosecution witnesses

THE JUDGES

Kenesaw Mountain Landis—The fiery Chicago jurist, who would go on to become the first commissioner of Major League Baseball

Clarence Sessions—The judge who presided over the *Eastland* extradition trail from the bench in Grand Rapids

Prologue: Steamer, Sailor, Lawyer

In the teeth of the late summer sun, the captain pointed his pistol at his men.

The SS *Eastland* had been gliding through Lake Michigan's sparkling blue, the black smoke of burnt coal unfurling in twin columns high above its double smokestacks. It was the *Eastland*'s maiden season, 1903. The majestic steamship's bright white and ebony black paint was only three months old. Captain John Pereue was on the bridge, watching over the massive steamship, bowsprit whistling northeast.

The ten-story skyscrapers of Chicago had shrunk behind. The Michigan shoreline was hours ahead. All anyone looking forward could see was blue.

Passengers felt the rumble of the powerful engines on the planks below their feet as they made their way along the promenade deck. Women with shirtwaists, ankle-length skirts, and parasols ambled along, resting here and there on wooden folding chairs, each engraved with the name *Eastland*. Mothers and children took shade on settees under frilly awnings. On either side of the towering smokestacks, there were two writing salons, one for men, one for women. In the fog of the smoking room, men lounged on upholstered divans.

Then suddenly the passengers felt the engines go lifeless. The dull vibration at their feet, gone. The breeze on their faces, fading. The ship was slowing, stopping. Within minutes, it began to roll, listless. No land in sight, just waves of blue trickling far below on the hull.

The block-long ship was stuck out in midlake, with 550 passengers and crew in peril.

Captain Pereue ran from the bridge to the main deck, calling for Richardson, his first mate. The two officers, boots clanging down the stairway, met a band of six crewmen, arms crossed, standing defiant at the bow of the *Eastland*.

"What's the matter with you fellows?" Captain Pereue shouted.

They objected to the meals they were being served aboard and refused to work until they were given "suitable food." The captain shouted at them to return to work. They stood stock-still. These six were the men who fired the ship's coal burners, the firemen. Without them, the ship was inoperable.

Flustered, Pereue and Richardson left the men. Within minutes, the captain returned with his own band of men and a revolver.

"This boat has already been delayed forty minutes through this affair. There must be no more delay," Captain Pereue squawked, pointing the pistol their way. He gave them an ultimatum: return to work in three minutes, or be arrested and charged with mutiny.

Hearing this, the six mutineers retreated farther forward in the ship, farther away from the boiler room, where they were supposed to be firing up the coal to power the engines.

First Mate Richardson leapt at Glenn Watson, the ringleader for the mutineers. Watson drew back, but with the help of a couple of officers, Richardson strong-armed him away from the others, hurried him through the ship, and handcuffed him to a stanchion. It took four officers to overpower and handcuff another mutineer, William Madden. The others were apprehended and dispatched to their quarters, where a guard watched them until landfall.

When the *Eastland* arrived a couple hours later at its home port in Michigan, the six men were taken from the ship in chains. "We'll get non-union men to run the boat," shouted Captain Pereue to the crew, as the men walked off.

The captain, covering his tracks—for reasons not yet clear—invented a colorful tale, and the press ate it up. The men had refused to work, he told newspaper reporters, because the ship's cook would not serve them mashed potatoes. The crew rejected boiled potatoes, he said; they would only accept mashed. The newspapermen gullibly reported on the Mashed Potato Mutiny. For leaving their work between ports, a conviction for mutiny would saddle the men with long penitentiary sentences.

A mutiny on the Great Lakes? In this day and age, people must have wondered, when modernity was flush with the first zeppelin, the electric razor, the escalator, the vacuum cleaner, the neon light? Why, working men could now afford to *ride* on grand steamships. A Michigan man named Ford had just started a company that could make several motorcars in a single day. In the near future, many people truly believed, every home would have its own telephone.

§§§

His nose burned. After a few days, his throat ached. And the sneezing. Joseph Erickson coughed and coughed, blew his nose. "An awful cold," he would later remember.

It was his first introduction to America. He had made the several-day trip aboard the steamer *North Point*, arriving in Philadelphia with a duffel bag and sniffles, from London, in March 1903. He had arrived in England weeks earlier, leaving behind the cliffs and craggy fjords of Norway, where he and his mother and a few siblings lived just outside Christiania, the large city to the south (later Oslo). His mother had a thriving garden of berries, which Joseph loved, and a deep voice; she sang tenor in the church choir.

He was twenty and dreaming of the seamen's life in America, of working his way up to becoming an officer: the men under his command, the fine collared shirts and pressed jackets that ship engineers wore ashore, the respect of the crew.

Erickson had gray eyes, like stormy autumn clouds, and was surprisingly sickly. As natives of high latitudes, Norwegian sailors were normally known as hardy stock, braving frigid winds and ice, whistling sea shanties at winter's worst. Erickson had sailed since he was fifteen, and by the time he arrived on America's shores, he had worked on ocean steamers in Norway, France, England, Germany, Sweden, Holland, and Belgium. Throughout, he was unwell.

"Perhaps nature has not been as kind to me as to others," he would later write to a companion, "but I am not complaining at my lot, as I am not responsible for being brought into this world, nor the work of nature."

It took Erickson more than a week to recover in Philadelphia. No sooner had he gotten better than he was on a steamer bound for the tropical paradise of Havana, Cuba, to pick up mounding tons of sugar and fine-hewn mahogany.

Odd jobs, he knew, weren't going to get him ahead, so he sought out a more permanent position, and American citizenship. Various laws forbade foreigners from serving as officers on US steamships, and though they were often loosely enforced, he didn't want to take any chances.

Erickson took a junior crewman's job on tugboats running between New York, Boston, and Portland, Maine. He was an oiler, a dirty, greasy job keeping ship machinery lubricated in stinking engine rooms.

He filled out his Petition for Naturalization in the Common Pleas Court of Baltimore and paid the four-dollar application fee. His date of birth: March 28, 1883. He then checked the correct boxes, reassuring the immigration authorities that he was not importing any of the ills that concerned them that spring of 1903.

No, he was not an anarchist. Or a polygamist.

No, he did not even believe in the practice of polygamy.

Yes, he was attached to the principles of the US Constitution.

Yes, he renounced all allegiance and loyalty to his homeland, Norway, and its king, Haakon VII.

Yes, he could speak English.

Yes, he wished to reside permanently in the United States.

In truth, Joseph Erickson felt there was nothing for him in his homeland, which he had left as a teenager. For the past five years, he had lived on the sea. When briefly ashore, he checked into seamen hotels. Maybe he could find a home in America.

§§§

The Chicago police were overwhelmed by the crime wave of 1903. Holdups were routine, and street crime went airborne. So many acrobatic burglars scaled brick walls and drainpipes that a new term gained currency: porch climbers.

Danger was everywhere, even the sky above. One woman strolling along the department stores of State Street fractured an arm and leg when a gigantic newspaper billboard shook loose overhead from the wind. The woman, Mary Spiss, sued after being pelted by debris from the largest sign ever erected in the city, a seventy-five-foot glittering monstrosity that spelled out the *Chicago American* in three thousand electric lights. A jury awarded her eight thousand dollars, penalizing the Hearst newspaper empire for its negligence in suspending such a massive sign over a busy walkway.

An attorney tried to get the woman's award thrown out on appeal, downplaying the fact the corporation had precariously installed a billboard that weighed a ton over a bustling street. The appeal failed. The attorney hadn't yet become a celebrity in 1903, hadn't yet become the trial lawyer of the century. His name was Clarence Darrow.

And in little over a decade, through very different paths, Joseph Erickson and Clarence Darrow would find themselves drawn into a federal courtroom by a calamity on the *Eastland*, both seeking to save their careers and their lives.

Part I:
Ahead Strong

CHAPTER ONE

Worshipful Master

Having survived the bullets and bayonets of the Civil War, the two men were not about to lose their dream: their own shipping firm.

In their beloved South Haven, Michigan, they wanted to operate one of the splendors of the age, a powerful state-of-the-art steamship, manufactured in steel, long as a football field.

The two lake captains were rushing to raise money and place an order for a massive steamer that could run tons of fruit from Michigan's fragrant fields to the large and gleaming metropolis of Chicago, seventy-seven miles across the lake. They would also carry passengers in nicely appointed cabins for day trips.

The captains, one named Pereue and one named Leighton, became anxious because word was the Dunkley-Williams Company, which operated a lucrative docking operation and ran some smaller boats out of South Haven, was aiming to do the exact same thing: order a gigantic new steamship, same route, fruit, people, all of it. The steamship business was fairly new, and to many it just seemed that if you built a ship, passengers would arrive, money would flow. You'd soon be living the comfortable life of a capitalist.

To lure passengers away from the Dunkley-Williams ship, the two captains decided to appeal to civic pride and name their ship after its home city, the *City of South Haven*. Dunkley-Williams already had the *City of Kalamazoo*, its namesake a town in Michigan about an hour east of South Haven by train. And other companies similarly tugged at the heartstrings of the locals, with names like the *City of Racine*, the *City of Detroit*, the *City of Sheboygan*. While they never publicly announced it, the Dunkley-Williams men, unbeknown to the two captains, also planned to name their ship the *City of South Haven*.

There obviously couldn't be two ships with the same name. Someone was going to lose out.

§§§

The chief proponent of the new Michigan Steamship Company was John C. Pereue. He had served in the Civil War on a transport on the James River. Pereue was born in Greenwich, Connecticut. He descended from French shipbuilders; his father and grandfather owned and sailed vessels on the Atlantic and immigrated to the colonies during the Revolutionary War. After the Civil War, he moved to Michigan, where timber was abundant, and where he and a brother began building wooden ships on the Black River in South Haven.

Over the years, Pereue was captain (or the more commonly used "master") of two schooners, stately sailboats named the *Early Bird* and the *Hummingbird*, and two steamers, one of which was named for his then twelve-year-old daughter, the *Hattie B. Pereue*. He had master's papers to sail on the Great Lakes and the oceans, freshwater and saltwater. He had married Frances Elizabeth Stufflebeam in December of 1869, and their marriage would last sixty-two years.

Having successfully built wooden ships in South Haven, he had gone into retirement in 1901 and that winter decided to take a voyage with Frances and friends on his personal yacht, the *Clifford*, whose cabin was finished out in rare mahogany and sycamore. He took them on a cruise down the Mississippi River, along the Gulf Coast, around Florida, and up the Atlantic Coast. They planned to reach New York in the spring and navigate the Erie Canal to Buffalo. En route they would see cities and sites, stopping as long as they pleased in each port.

By May, the *Clifford* had traveled five thousand miles, and when they arrived back in South Haven, Captain Pereue was restless, eager for another adventure.

He had seen grand steamships all over the country, packed with people, and he wanted one in his hometown. Imagine the civic pride. If it had its own steamship, South Haven would stand above the other harbor towns dotting the Lake Michigan shoreline.

Pereue figured he'd find a natural accomplice in Leander Leighton, one of the most prominent men in South Haven. Born in Maine in 1840, Leighton came to the small town of Otsego, Michigan, at age twenty, first as a store clerk. Ten years later he would arrive in larger South Haven, quickly gaining a reputation for exceptional business skills. His entrepreneurial bent and his staunch Republicanism were both so impressive that the midwestern man was known even in New York financial circles. Over the years, he was a merchant, ship carpenter, shipowner, and lake captain. He was a leader in the Freemasons, worshipful master of Star of the Lake Lodge No. 78.

In 1870, he constructed the Leighton Opera House, which drew crowds to nightly shows, political meetings, and lectures by senators and visiting opera singers from Chicago. For leisure, he sailed the small steamers *Cupid* and *Adrienne*.

In South Haven, the Leighton name was everywhere. A prime street downtown was named Leighton Block. On it was Leighton's Dollar-Saving Department Store, whose motto was "Quick Sales and Small Profits," and another shop called Leighton & Warrick, which advertised "Groceries, Crockery, Glassware, Wall Paper, Curtains, &c, &c."

Leighton was intrigued with Pereue's idea, a massive fruit shipping business to Chicago. It would certainly raise the stature of his beloved town on the shore. In 1902, South Haven's business scene was aged, stagnant.

There were 213 resorts and rooming houses, all running ten miles north and south, most along the shoreline. One of the most popular in town was Snobble's Restaurant and Boarding House. The resorts drew visitors, many from Chicago, driving up passenger traffic at South Haven a remarkable 17 percent in just two years, to 150,000 people.

South Haven's population had more than tripled to five thousand since 1890. It was blessed with the lake and with rich soil, which combined to make ideal growing conditions for fruit. Lake Michigan kept the climate temperate: not too hot in the summer, not too cold in the fall. The lake also generated frequent rain to water the crops. Strong winds in the fall of 1902 tore the red-and-white stripes on flags toward their forty-five stars.

Fruit production began in earnest as the lumber business faded. Vast new groves of fruit trees were coming into bearing, and within three years fruit production would double: peaches, pears, plums, grapes, and apples. And blueberries, a festival of blueberries. Someone was going to have to move all that produce.

As the two old captains talked it over, Leighton didn't appear to give much thought to one troubling development with his partner. One of the ships Pereue had built, the one named for his daughter, had sunk just a few weeks earlier. In September of 1902, the *Hattie B. Pereue*, filled with a cargo of hemlock lumber, foundered at the entrance to the Ludington harbor, 120 miles north of South Haven. The 105-foot steam barge rested on the bottom of Lake Michigan, blocking the harbor until it was later raised and repaired.

Leighton and Pereue decided to give the contract for their new steamer to a cargo-ship builder, the Jenks Ship Building Company in Port Huron, Michigan, 230 miles east of South Haven. It was quite a coup for Jenks, its first passenger steamer. The two men went to Port Huron, on the shore of Lake Huron, to discuss details, and by the first week of October, the ship order was ready. They were on their way to bringing their *City of South Haven* home.

One week after the contract was signed, the *Hattie B. Pereue* sank again, a second time on Lake Michigan. Its crew of fourteen survived by swimming to a nearby pier. This time it sank for good.

§§§

Superstition among Great Lakes sailors ran strong into the twentieth century. The crew on the large lake freighter *William E. Corey* declared that the ship was "hoodooed," or jinxed, ever since the man in whose honor she was named left his wife for a young vaudeville actress. The ship then had three accidents in three months, including crashing into the docks on the Chicago River. At her launching, she slid away from her moorings too soon. The young woman who was to break the bottle to christen her became so flustered she spilt the champagne into the water and forgot to say anything. During the launch of a new ship, any mishap was seen as an omen.

To some sailors on the lakes, too many As in a ship's name was bad luck, as was a name with thirteen letters. Changing the name of a ship, particularly, was inviting trouble. Never, ever change the name.

§§§

The ship's contract, dated October 7, 1902, ran five pages, typed, double-spaced. For $235,000, the Jenks Ship Building Company of Port Huron, Michigan, was to build a steel passenger steamer 275 feet long, with its beam, or width, thirty-eight feet. In terms of rating, the new craft would have as high a rating as any vessel on the Great Lakes and an ocean classification that would allow her to go upon the high seas without reinspection.

Terms also called for four boilers and two engines, each the state-of-the-art "triple expansion" type. Delivery was to be in time to get her on her route out of South Haven by June 1, 1903, "unless detained by fire, labor strike or lock outs."

The paperwork made it clear that Pereue and Leighton were concerned about speed for their *City of South Haven*. Fully half the contract terms addressed how breakneck the ship would be. They set a target of twenty miles per hour, fast as anything on the lakes. Great Lakes sailors measured speed in miles, not knots. And the South Haven men offered incentives to soup the ship up. The Michigan Steamship Company would pay Jenks twenty-five hundred dollars for every quarter of a mile the ship could make exceeding twenty miles per hour. The builders stood to make a twenty-thousand-dollar bonus solely if the ship could make twenty-two miles an hour on an ordinary run. The builders would have to forfeit twenty-five hundred dollars, on the other hand, for each quarter mile below twenty miles per hour.

This was so important that Pereue and Leighton added a provision, the seventh article, allowing them to refuse to keep her if she did not attain a speed of at least nineteen miles per hour. The ninth article even gave the new shipowners sixty days after taking delivery to test her and refuse to keep her if she trailed nineteen miles per hour.

Fast ship, or no ship.

The contract was signed by Captain Pereue and Angus M. Carpenter, the secretary for Jenks. The only other signature was that of the witness, C. E. Kremer, a high-powered admiralty law specialist from Chicago who was an amusing after-dinner speaker and an amateur painter. He taught at the University of Chicago. His signature was the most decorative on the contract.

Another thing about the extravagant Charles E. Kremer: He had an unusual and distracting habit of doodling while defending marine men in court.

§§§

Dunkley-Williams was flabbergasted. Formed the previous March by merging two South Haven rivals with interests in ships, docks, and canning operations, Dunkley-Williams was the big shipper in town. It ran four small steamers, the *City of Kalamazoo*, the *H.W. Williams*, the *Petoskey*, and the *Glenn*. The managers had been considering buying or building a much larger ship, a queen of the fleet, to boost its business carrying passengers and fruit. How had they been beaten? How had someone else ordered a new steamer for South Haven?

Dunkley-Williams had been hesitant to build a bigger ship for good reason. All shippers were having fits trying to maneuver their ships around South Haven. Its harbor was more like a shallow pond. The Black River, home to the docks, was more of a creek. Just after the Civil War, the river was only seven feet deep. After some dredging, it ran to about twelve feet, dead center, but was shallower near the banks.

Twelve feet, or two fathoms, was safe water to river men, a level they called "mark twain," adopted incidentally as the pen name of the famous author. But that was when steamboats were smaller and much lighter. On a Monday night in September 1902, the *Petoskey*, whose back end tipped eleven feet three inches into the Black River, dragged on the bottom and crashed into the pier. "I felt I had gotten off cheaply," said J. M. Mitchell, the captain of the steamer, "for I had narrowly escaped being driven into the Midway pavilion."

Quarters were cramped too. There was a turning basin, where ships entering the channel would nose around and exit back into the lake. It was so tight that it had been dug wider over the years by propellers scooping its edges.

And then, that sandbar. A single grain of sand could not stop a rowboat, but several feet of sand could bring an immense two-thousand-ton steamer to a dead halt. *Bam.* Stuck.

When the fall storms came each season, the channel just outside South Haven harbor was frequently blocked by a stubborn sandbar. Annually, nature piled up a little underwater mountain; then shippers dug under water and hauled the top of it away. Then nature did its thing again, and so on. It was a costly, confounding back-and-forth. Even the larger Dunkley-Williams lacked the funds to dredge a channel deep enough for clear passage of the larger steamships.

And the whole problem started with human intervention, "development." To get around the problem of very shallow shorelines, South Haven, with help from the Army's Corps of Engineers, built long parallel piers, one north, one south, each jutting seven hundred or more feet into Lake Michigan. Out that far, the lakebed deepened quickly, from mark twain, to mark three, which is eighteen feet, to twenty-six, to thirty-two, to what sailors called with great relief "no bottom."

The glitch at that harbor, though, was very fine sand, dusty as ashes. Currents, wind, and waves easily swept the light sand under water into enormous piles. Nature seemed to like to shoal the hazardous sandbank right in front of the man-made double pier, the doorway to the harbor.

Sailors in South Haven came up with tricks to "jump the bar." Some revved the engines and, when it worked, simply powered through "Ahead Strong," the fastest speed, in Great Lakes jargon, a ship could muster.

The *Petoskey*, the largest ship in the market at 171 feet long, found it had to load very lightly. Though she could carry 770 tons of cargo, she was under orders to take on no more than five hundred tons in or out of South Haven. Because of the sandbar, Dunkley-Williams had to forgo 30 percent of its revenue each time the *Petoskey* went out.

Stuck, Dunkley-Williams appealed to Uncle Sam. R. W. Crary, a vice president for Dunkley, wrote a lengthy letter to General George Lewis Gillespie, who was in charge of the Army Corps of Engineers, begging him to make the harbor and river at South Haven more navigable. Crary wanted the channel in the Black River dredged to eighteen feet of depth. He wanted the piers extended out into deeper water, to help avoid the bars that formed at the harbor's entrance. He wanted the turning basin widened considerably.

"Owing to the shallow water in the river," he wrote, "we have . . . found it impossible to properly steer the vessels and in consequence have collided with piers and docks and schooners lying at the docks, causing no little damage."

He made his case with statistics, showing how the tons of shipping cargo in the South Haven area had more than doubled between 1898 and 1901. He talked up the larger swarms of passengers coming to the summer resorts year by year. He pleaded:

> *The increase in the passenger business and the prospect for still further increase with improved service has rendered it imperative that larger and swifter boats be placed upon the Chicago route to accommodate the thousands who desire to take their outings in the heart of the peach belt of Michigan.*

As Crary composed his letter, right there on the wall in his office were blueprints for the ship his firm planned to name the *City of South Haven*. It would be nearly ninety feet longer than the *Petoskey*'s 171-foot length, which dipped, at most, 12.2 feet in the water—puny, by going standards.

In appealing to General Gillespie about the growing importance of the South Haven–Chicago route, Crary made a stunning admission: "We are ready to place a larger boat upon the run, but a boat of the dimensions needed for this business would draw more water than is to be found in the South Haven Harbor."

In other words, too much ship, too little water. And the Michigan Steamship Company, unbeknown to Crary or General Gillespie, was planning a ship even larger.

General Gillespie kicked the issue to Charles Keller, the Army Corps of Engineers regional chief in Grand Rapids, for help. Keller understood the problem but was no friend of industry. He preferred a conservative approach when scarring the earth for profits.

Keller thought dredging the Black River to sixteen feet would be sufficient for the harbor traffic in South Haven, he wrote to General Gillespie. And he thought one of the Army's new fleet of hydraulic dredge ships would be perfect for that. When the snow globe at the lake bottom finished its stirring each year, only some one hundred thousand cubic yards of sand were deposited in front of the South Haven piers. Keller knew the Army Corps' hydraulic-suction ships could easily get in front of that.

The first one of those dredge ships would be named to honor the leader of the Army Corps: the *General Gillespie*. Born in Tennessee, Gillespie still kept loyal to the Union, receiving the Medal of Honor for carrying dispatches through enemy lines under relentless fire to General Sheridan at Cold Harbor, Virginia. After the war, Gillespie oversaw harbor improvements at Cleveland, Chicago, Boston, and New York. He was in charge of ceremonies at President McKinley's funeral in 1901.

Against sharp opposition by private marine dredge operators, General Gillespie argued that the federal government should take a greater role in ensuring that the channels of the nation were navigable. Keeping ships moving was both a matter of industry and of national security.

As more ships ran aground, pressure grew on Washington to act. With approval from the War Department, Gillespie commissioned the construction of several of the dredge vessels. The suction-dredge ship, basically a floating vacuum cleaner, would inhale the sand from the depths, clearing away the shoals. His namesake ship, the *General Gillespie*, would work solely on Lake Michigan, the only one of the Great Lakes entirely within US borders. And soon it would need junior crewmembers.

One of those who applied was Joseph Erickson. After a year in America, mostly on her waters, he was developing an attachment to the nation. He would later write, "I would be glad to serve my Country on Uncle Sam's ships."

CHAPTER TWO

"He Could Attend to the Rest Himself"

Dunkley-Williams did not know where things stood. It was early October and they still hadn't heard back from General Gillespie. But they dared not wait for word; the rival Michigan Steamship group was moving, ahead strong.

One week after the Michigan Steamship contract was signed, the directors of Dunkley-Williams met on a Saturday morning in mid-October and quickly voted to order a new steel steamer to run between Chicago and South Haven. It would be 260 feet long, with a forty-foot beam, all steel, and four boilers. The ship would have staterooms and capacity for two thousand excursionists. The inside was to be finished out in mahogany. A dining room was set for one hundred people.

Crary wrote back to General Gillespie, pointing out that now two immense ships were being built for South Haven, both much larger than any ship in the market. They needed room to move around.

Dunkley-Williams wanted to have the pride of South Haven. They had already selected the Craig Ship Building Company, in Toledo, Ohio, for their grand plan and sent along blueprints for the new steamer. As soon as the vote concluded, they wired a telegram to Toledo: STEP ON IT. They then let the press know their plan to name their large, all-steel ship the *City of South Haven*. To get things moving quickly, both namesakes of the company, S. J. Dunkley and H. W. Williams, arrived at the shipyard in Toledo that day.

Galled to learn that Dunkley-Williams was planning to take the name *City of South Haven*, the Michigan Steamship Company suggested a gentlemen's agreement with its rival. Whoever launched their ship first won rights to the name. The loser would have to select another one. Given that Dunkley-Williams was a week behind in ordering and had a mid-June completion date, the Pereue team felt confident. Dunkley-Williams accepted the duel.

By Thanksgiving of 1902, the Pereue team seemed to have the race locked up for *City of South Haven*. The *South Haven Daily Tribune* noted that the ship was on course to be launched in early March, months ahead of Dunkley-Williams's June delivery. The paper noted one other thing: "It will have a double-bottom hull, with four feet of air space in between, making her almost impossible to sink."

§§§

As the winter began, the competing *City of South Haven* projects were emerging at shipyards 121 miles apart in Ohio and Michigan. From their keels, skeletal scantlings at first, then plate-by-plate, rivets turning, they were shaping up into immense steamers casting block-long shadows. After the first of the new year, 1903, Dunkley-Williams vice president R. W. Crary rushed out to Toledo to check progress.

He found some six hundred men working on the ship, and wherever he went in the machine shop, or the foundry or the joiners department, the work was buzzing. Welding sparks flew like fireflies. The frames were up, the deck beams were in place, and several plates were installed. They were clearly ahead of schedule.

Captain Pereue hurried northeast to Port Huron to see where his project stood. He had reason for concern. There was one small matter: The firm had never built a passenger ship before.

As a shipbuilder, Jenks had emerged perfectly situated for the late nineteenth century. Demand was enormous for strong wooden hulls in the fast-growing ship business, and any place that had a bounty of hardwood timber was well positioned to capitalize. Port Huron was in St. Clair County, which was blessed with forests of oak and pine and a location central to the Great Lakes region.

Throughout that area, every shipyard was backed up with work. No sooner had a new ship been launched than the keel blocks for the next one were laid. The Toledo Shipbuilding Company could complete a five-hundred-foot freighter start to finish in less than four months. When the *Smith Thompson* was launched, there was no ceremony; the shipbuilder was too busy. When the *Thompson* left the ways, another keel was immediately laid, and construction of the next five-hundred-foot monster was underway.

§§§

New yards had come with the new century, in what was to be the most important decade in Great Lakes shipping history. In 1901, it was Ship Owners Dry Dock Company in Chicago. The next year, Columbia Iron Works and the Great Lakes Engineering Works, both in Michigan. In Wisconsin, the Manitowoc Shipbuilding Company in 1903. Within ten years, nearly three hundred massive new steamships would be built, a record.

In Port Huron, Michigan, Orrin Jenks had made the Phoenix Iron Works one of the best foundries in Michigan, producing steam engines for the *Eugene C. Hart*, among other well-known ships. It was named Phoenix because it was built after the prior factory had burned down. Orrin and his father, William, had started the business, though William died suddenly in 1902, two weeks before Captain Pereue's rushed visit.

William Jenks had been the powerhouse of the family, and all were surprised by his death; he was still going strong at eighty-four, having outlived two wives. Two days before his death, he helped one of his employees saw some timber with a crosscut saw.

Newly ambitious, Orrin and his sons, William and Sidney, decided to try shipbuilding themselves. They were already manufacturing steel boilers and engines for wooden ships, so why not the whole ship? In December of 1890, the Jenks Ship Building Company was formed with Orrin as its guiding light and president.

Sidney Jenks, grandson of the company founder, studied engineering out east, attending Cornell University. He was charged with designing their first passenger ship, the one for Captain Pereue. And his mission on Day One: How to jump the sandbar? Essentially Pereue had ordered a ship that was too big for its home port.

Quickly, Jenks seemed in over his head. Now thirty, and out of school for years, he repeatedly went out to visit his old naval engineering professor at Cornell to figure out just how to build an immense ship that could draw only ten to twelve feet of water. At least twice, Jenks talked over designs with Professor George McDermott, shuttling between Port Huron and Cornell, in Ithaca, New York.

Then he and his old instructor had a sudden falling out. "He was huffy at my attitude," McDermott would later write, "packed up the [design] which he had drawn out, and, leaving, said he could attend to the rest himself."

At his drawing board back in Port Huron, Sidney Jenks attended to the rest himself. And his design deep in the bottom of the ship was dreadful.

§§§

It was just after New Year's Day of 1903 that Captains Pereue and Leighton learned they were in trouble. In a stroke of luck, the Craig shipyard in Toledo was able to quickly construct the rival Dunkley-Williams ship because it had a lot of material on hand that had been ordered for other ships whose plans fell through. They simply reused plates and girders and framework already constructed.

That meant Dunkley-Williams was going to get its ship into the water first and snatch the name the *City of South Haven*.

The Michigan Steamship Company was handed its first defeat and was going to have to change its ship's name; according to superstition on the lakes, it would be a cursed vessel.

To regroup, Pereue and Leighton decided they needed to find a different way to generate buzz in town for their ship. They needed a *name*. They needed a way to make people in town still feel like they were partners in the new steamer. How about a town-wide naming contest? Pereue published a statement in the South Haven newspapers in late January:

> *We will give the person who suggests a name that is acceptable by the Company $10 in cash and a season pass for the ship. Name can't exceed eight letters. It may be an Indian name, or a name suggestive of speed, comfort or beauty. Names should be taken or sent to the Citizens State Bank, South Haven, with the word "suggestion" plainly written on the envelope, which must be sealed. The contest closes at 1 p.m. Monday, Feb. 2, 1903.*
>
> *Michigan Steamship Company*
> *J.C. Pereue, Treas.*

The contest electrified the town, from old to young. For two weeks, the envelopes arrived at Citizens State Bank, each one sealed and marked "suggestion." They were addressed in blue and black ink, pencil, even crayon. There were 563 suggestions submitted by the deadline, and nearly three hundred afterward that were dismissed. There were ten suggestions for Michigan, twenty-two for Hiawatha, eight for Pokagon, and thirteen for Majestic.

One letter, from an eight-year-old girl in Muskegon, Michigan, read:

DEAR SIR: I read in the paper about you wanting a name for your new boat. Mama said maybe I wasn't too little to write you, but she laughed when she said it so maybe I am. . . . I wish you would name it Quinnipac because it is in a story mama read to me and I thought it so pretty. I am sorry there are 9 letters but maybe you can squeeze in the other one.

§§§

March was going to be tough for the Michigan Steamship Company. Dunkley-Williams announced it was going to launch its ship, the *City of South Haven*—their *City of South Haven*—in just a few weeks. They also announced plans to have state-of-the-art technology on board. They would offer telephone connections so passengers in their rooms could make calls to South Haven residents when in that port and to Chicagoans when the ship was in the large city, an operation never attempted on a steamer before. And they planned a daily newspaper, the only one printed on Lake Michigan, which would be published aboard the steamer during her sailing season, with the latest news and sports scores.

At this point, Michigan Steamship's vessel was nameless. There were no imaginative plans for telephones or newspapers. Still smarting from the loss of the name they really wanted, Pereue and Leighton huddled, looking for some other way to trump their rivals. Why should anyone ride their ship? What would captivate people enough to pull large numbers away from the *City of South Haven*?

Soon they would come up with a gimmick so shrill, so brassy that the Chicago police would be called in to investigate it.

CHAPTER THREE

"Steady as a Church"

Feeling the Michigan Steamship Company had fallen behind, Leighton decided to become the front man, starting friction with Pereue that was not to end well. That spring, Leighton opened a temporary office in one of his windows on Center Street along Leighton Block. Not helping the partnership was a glowing article in the *New York Financial Review* about the prospects for the Michigan Steamship Company, largely because of Leighton's leadership. "His experience and recognized conservatism in business would prevent his entering into a project of which the future was even dubious," the paper gushed.

When rumors started to circulate that the new Michigan Steamship vessel would have a bar on board, and all the attendant nastiness that can come with inebriation, it was Leighton, not Pereue, who issued a statement to the press. "There will be a bar," he wrote, "but I desire to state further that no intoxicating drinks will be dispensed over it, for we do not expect to carry any passengers but those who can live four or five hours on *soft* beverages."

§§§

Then, finally, a good sign for Michigan Steamship. The *City of South Haven* was scheduled to be launched in Toledo on a Saturday in March, but the launching had to be postponed because of wind gusts and low water. Lake superstition held that any glitch in a launch was an omen.

The following Monday, a drizzly morning in Toledo, the launch party held umbrellas, and President Dunkley's daughter Pearl christened the *City of South Haven*. As the foam from the champagne bottle colored a spot on her bow, the ship dropped into the water.

Dunkley-Williams sent a telegram back home to South Haven to be splashed across the front pages, one sure to make blood boil over at the Michigan Steamship offices.

TOLEDO, OHIO, MARCH 23—TOOK MY FIRST PLUNGE AT 11:05 TODAY. EVERYTHING IDEAL. SEE YOU NEXT JUNE.

STEAMSHIP CITY OF SOUTH HAVEN

Pereue and Leighton had been one-upped. Discouraged, the directors of the company met and moved forward with one decision for now. They chose as the winning entry in the naming contest the suggestion of Mrs. David Reid of South Haven; their ship would be called the *Eastland*.

§§§

In Port Huron, the massive *Eastland* became part of the skyline in early 1903. Over the months, townspeople had watched every stage of progress as the ship emerged from its most skeletal form. The whole town made plans to attend the launch, celebrating Jenks's first passenger steamer. "No parent watched with more pride over the development of his offspring than did the townspeople over the progress of a ship evolving on the stocks," recalled Dorothy Marie Mitts, who grew up in Port Huron.

The launch was set for the first Tuesday in May. Students would be dismissed at noon, and most of the stores and offices in town announced that they would be closed, to allow salesclerks and other employees to attend. A platform had been built at the bow of the *Eastland* for the launch party, which would include men and women from Jenks and the Michigan Steamship Company.

Finally, at 1:50 in the afternoon, more than a month after the *City of South Haven* was launched, the Stars and Stripes were winched into the wind, and a roar went up from the crowd of more than six thousand people. They had lined the banks of the Black River, packed onto the Grand Trunk Railroad bridge, climbed trees, and sat on top of buildings, anywhere where they could get a view.

Suddenly, whistles blew in the factories, on steamers and on tugboats.

Church bells and school bells pealed. The tintinnabulation, the roar of the crowd, the festive sounds welled up unabated as Frances Pereue, wife of the captain, struck the steel bow twice with a beribboned bottle of champagne and christened her the *Eastland*.

The ship started down the ways, side-launched in Great Lakes tradition, struck the water, and sent large waves over the riverbanks, dousing the crowds nearby and pushing them back. She dropped about two and a half feet into the water, then rolled over about forty-five degrees.

"And she came right back up," recalled Sidney Jenks, the *Eastland* designer, "just as nice and steady as a church."

CHAPTER FOUR

The Flower Ship

Mrs. Reid was so proud that her choice of the name *Eastland* had won the contest that she hired a horse-drawn coach to ride her around the streets in South Haven in pomp. She waved as the horse clip-clopped along Center Street, Superior, Huron, Erie, Michigan, Ontario, Eagle, Phoenix, and St. Joseph.

Even as the *Eastland* floated on the Black River in Port Huron, her first baptism by water, the boilers and engines had yet to be installed. That fitting-out work would take several more weeks, and the days were lengthening. The summer season was nigh, and Pereue and Leighton still didn't know how fast the *Eastland* would be on the water. Their whole business plan was banking on outrunning the *City of South Haven*. Would the *Eastland* make the nineteen-mile-an-hour mark? Would she be faster? If she did not make nineteen, they could walk away and leave Jenks stuck with the ship. The press was already hailing the *City of South Haven* as "The White Flyer." As they contemplated their rivalry with the *City of South Haven*, the pair knew they still had one hope.

§§§

Just after seven in the morning on a Thursday in June, the whistle at the pumping station gave a ten-minute blast. Everyone in South Haven knew why: The *City of South Haven* was approaching. Its big white hull was draped in waving, colorful flags. Several ships steamed out to meet the *City of South Haven* about a mile offshore, including the *Peek-a-boo*, the *Nydia*, and the *Phylida*, which had been chartered by the city council to carry the roller-skating rink band.

As she steamed closer into view, people could make out the names on the twirling streamers, the neighboring towns of Kalamazoo, Battle Creek,

Saugatuck. Hung from the Black River bridge was a sixty-foot banner that said WELCOME TO THE CITY OF SOUTH HAVEN.

The *Eastland*, which was supposed to be delivered by then, was sitting at her fitting-out berth 230 miles away on Lake Huron, still a work in progress.

§§§

The summer season was half over by mid-July, and Pereue and Leighton were anxious. They were so eager to get the *Eastland* out to South Haven that they demanded to know the soonest possible date they could take possession of the ship. When they were told July 16, Pereue personally took the wheel in the dark at 2:30 that morning at the Jenks shipyards. Since the *Eastland*'s speed hadn't been tested, Jenks kept possession of the title at that point and provided engineers to staff the cruise under Pereue's command. But the Michigan Steamship men finally had their ship.

It was a Thursday, and the plan was to show it off in South Haven for an hour or so and then dispatch it on its first trip to Chicago. In a publicity stroke, Leighton offered a free ride on the *Eastland* back to South Haven to anyone who paid his or her own train fare out to Port Huron. About 250 people bit.

The *Eastland* steamed north, past Thunder Bay, arriving about two in the morning the next day at Mackinac Island, at a spot where Lake Michigan and Lake Huron kiss. Hovering offshore, Pereue tried out the powerful new three-thousand-candlepower searchlight from the pilothouse perched atop the ship, allowing everyone aboard to see the island in twilight.

Nosing into Lake Michigan for the first time, the *Eastland* hugged the curving shoreline, southbound for South Haven. About four o'clock on Saturday morning, the fire whistle at the pumping station blasted, awakening the town. Despite the hour, hundreds of people ran toward the docks and the riverbanks.

After the streets filled, they stood and sat on rooftops, climbed hills, elbow to elbow, men in white shirts and ties, suits, and bowlers, women in long skirts and shimmery blouses. Boys in knickers fidgeted around, jockeying for a view. New telephone poles and lines followed the streets, as heads craned to spot the oncoming ship. By the time the *Eastland* reached its dock astride Maple Street on the Black River, people were flocking from all directions.

The maiden voyage was perfect.

Hundreds came aboard to inspect the *Eastland*. They walked up and down the grand stairwell, which seemed to draw everyone. With elaborate curving banisters and spindles, it connected the main deck to the cabin deck. They circled the ship on its promenade deck, which ran six feet wide and an eighth of a mile around. They stepped into some of the four hundred state-rooms, each fitted out in mahogany and white enamel, with running water and Pullman blinds. In the main saloon, the walls were adorned in mahogany and silk.

At a ceremony aboard, a South Haven dignitary read a forgettable sing-song of a poem titled "The Maiden Trip of the *Eastland*." And there were solos played on the piano and on the violin. Two vocalists sang solos. A few young men were rehearsing for a blackface minstrel show.

And then the spectacle really began. The crew fired up the calliope, a keyboard instrument that uses steam whistles to produce notes. *Toot, toot, toot,* the calliope sounded from the top deck. It was monstrously loud, fasci-nating to watch. As a note was played, steam puffed from the rows of pipes, like teakettles whistling. A chord produced several puffs at once, and each individual note sent a little blast of steam into the air.

People surrounded the calliope, transfixed, as Professor Charles Little, the instrument's "manipulator," faded in and out of view in misty clouds of steam. Ragtime, requests, popular tunes—he played them all. In the coming weeks, the *Eastland* would make its way around the Lake Michigan shore-line, and, as the shrieking contraption could be heard ten miles away, people came running from villages all along the way.

It was a page from Barnum & Bailey, the loudest show on water: a mas-terstroke of showboating, the calliope. And the *City of South Haven* did not have one.

Impatient to make headlines in Chicago, Pereue, still learning how to maneuver the powerful twin propellers, ordered the *Eastland* to be towed back out. As they were underway, one of the *Eastland*'s lines got caught in a propeller. It took some time to disentangle the mess. Finally, it was towed out into the harbor, and about 10:30 in the morning, behind schedule, it steamed off, thick smoke trailing, to Chicago, where the Press Club was awaiting the new ship.

For that first run, the *Eastland* had an immense flower arrangement on board. To commemorate the ship's arrival in its home port, W. A. Hartman, who ran a greenhouse in South Haven, created a replica of the *Eastland* out of flowers. It was three feet long, sixteen inches wide, and twenty inches tall. He wired together two thousand daisies, five hundred carnations, and one hundred roses, the hull and smokestacks composed completely of daisies.

CHAPTER FIVE

Stuck on the Bar

Out of Chicago that first summer, the *Eastland* ran daily at 9:30 in the morning for one dollar roundtrip. Saturdays it left at two in the afternoon. The company's docks were on the northwest corner of Fifth Avenue and South Water Street, just opposite the Chicago & Northwestern train depot. The docks were in one of the best locations in the city, with tens of thousands of Chicagoans daily shuffling to all the elevated and surface electric rail lines.

The first week the *Eastland* operated in Chicago, it began racing the *City of South Haven*. By contract, Pereue and Leighton had ninety days to stretch its legs, to discover its top speed, and possibly walk away from the purchase. Timed to the half-minute, races were great for publicity and bragging rights.

In their first Chicago–South Haven race, in late July, the *City of South Haven* finished eleven minutes in front of the *Eastland*. On the return trip, the *Eastland* trailed by five.

This was demoralizing for Michigan Steamship and Leighton, who was one of the most notable of South Haveners. For one thing, the *Eastland* used twin propellers, while the *City of South Haven* had only one, and the *Eastland* was specifically built for speed. After handing the *Eastland* back-to-back defeats, President Dunkley crowed that he would bet the spectacular sum of five thousand dollars with any ship that wanted to race the *City of South Haven*. No one dared take the bet.

The two ships did race again the next week, though. The *City of South Haven* made the crossing from Chicago, arriving home in three hours and fifty-five minutes. The *Eastland* took four hours and nine minutes. The *City of South Haven* started hanging broomsticks on its portholes, signaling victory.

Only one month into operations, Leighton was having second thoughts about Pereue as master of the *Eastland*. When the firemen called the mutiny in mid-August over rotten food on the ship, and Pereue tried to dismiss the whole thing with a cockamamie tale about mashed potatoes, Leighton had had enough.

On the last Saturday of August, nine days after the mutiny, Leighton replaced his partner. He ordered Pereue to step down from the bridge and meet his replacement, Captain Frank Dority. It was a huge surprise in marine circles around the lakes. Among other things, Pereue was a large stockholder in the Michigan Steamship Company.

But the word getting around was that Leighton thought Pereue was not up to scratch, outmaneuvered by the powerful twin-screw propeller ship. Pereue could not consistently rev the *Eastland*'s speed up. Also, at one point, he had run the *Eastland*'s stern end into a docked tugboat in the Chicago River, swamping the tug.

Leighton talked the matter over with Robert Roe Blacker, a lumber baron from Manistee, Michigan, a major investor in Michigan Steamship. Blacker had once been the mayor of Manistee. Quite wealthy, he had homes throughout Michigan and in Chicago.

Blacker agreed: Pereue had to go. While Pereue had had no experience with double-propeller ships, Captain Dority, an experienced master of railroad car ferries on Lake Michigan, was said to be one of the most skillful handlers of twin-screw ships around. The *Eastland*, though, would quickly prove a trial.

§§§

In the off-season, the *Eastland* headed back to winter over in Port Huron. The interior of the ship had been stuffy in the heat of the first summer, and it still was not running fast enough for Leighton and Blacker, who started taking greater interest in the ship. Jenks agreed to install a new air-conditioning system to improve ventilation and make other modifications to rev up her speed.

In Grand Rapids, Michigan, the grand jury had a busy docket in early November, with a post office robbery, a counterfeiting ring, a moonshine operation, and the *Eastland* mutiny. The sailors on trial had legitimate grievances. "For some time we had been unable to swallow the stuff put before us," Glenn Watson reported. "We were literally starved on board the *Eastland*, given meat not fit for a dog to eat, and potatoes black with soot.

"We found out that our meals were gleanings from the passengers' tables. We could stand it no longer, and, when the meals came in dished up in a worse state than usual, the men refused to work until suitable food was given to us."

After hearing the evidence, the jurors decided to issue no indictment against the ship's firemen. Charges were dropped. And Pereue was gone.

§§§

All spruced up, with new wooden letters seven and a half inches tall spelling EASTLAND in red with gold leaf, the ship returned to South Haven—poorly. The *Eastland* struck the bar in the harbor the first day back and could not break loose. Captain Dority tried reversing the engines; it backed up a bit, then wedged in worse, about two hundred feet from the piers.

Looking out from the lighthouse keeper's home, Captain James Donahue could not have been surprised to see the *Eastland* stuck. He had watched as vessels switched from sail to steam, had watched ships grow to sizes unimaginable only a few years earlier.

He was an old salt, one of the ghosts of the Civil War limping at ports all over the Great Lakes. He carried out his duties, ambling down from his house on Michigan Avenue to the South Pier, on a wooden leg and crutches. At the Battle of the Wilderness, a Minié ball struck his left leg. Donahue had fought on the Union side in Fredericksburg, Antietam, Vicksburg, and finally he lost his leg in intense fighting near a little stream in Virginia called Mine Run.

The one-legged lighthouse keeper was a legend in South Haven for his heroic rescues. Before 1900, he had saved at least fifteen people from drowning. He plucked a sailor named Tom off the south pier one night, after the man had fallen off a scow, using his crutch to retrieve him.

Captain Donahue worked miracles to be sure the lantern always stayed lit on the old wooden lighthouse. One night during a severe storm with fifty-mile-an-hour winds, spray dashing clear over the white lighthouse, Donahue crawled out to the light at 12:30 in the morning, with his lantern between his teeth, on his hands and knee. Singular, knee.

The captain outlived two wives, had six sons and a daughter, and was fond of a good horse. He interspersed the lighthouse logs with facts about his personal life. One entry: "Rain and Cloudy wind Moderate S the Lake

Smooth the Night dark the Weather Warm—my Wife Died this Afternoon at 4 P.M. of Lung Deease."

The next day he wrote, "Foggy Wind Light the Fog thick all day the Lake Smooth The night dark I Berryed my wife to day at 4 P.M."

Captain Donahue oversaw the rescue operation of the *Eastland*. The tug *Mentor* was dispatched and it took the *Eastland's* starboard bowline, but as it tried to free the ship, the line snapped. They then tried a new, heavier line on the starboard back. The little tug heaved and swung side to side, while the steamer's propellers alternated forward and backward, stirring up sand underneath. Eventually, the *Eastland* pulled backward off the bar, swung around, and nosed into its dock two hours late.

The *South Haven Daily Tribune* had an alarming editorial:

> *The danger to this valuable vessel in her home harbor, especially if the sea had become rough, and the great difficulty for handling by both the* Eastland *and the* City of South Haven, *should persuade the people of South Haven of the need for the contemplated harbor improvement. Something must be done.*

Either the winter repairs at Port Huron or the new captain made a difference, or both, but the *Eastland* found its stride. On Friday, July 1, 1904, it made its fastest crossing, pier to pier, Chicago to South Haven, three hours and thirty-eight minutes. It was a sprint enjoyed by 1,705 passengers, including the Young Men's Club of St. Columkill's parish. The *Eastland* passed the *City of South Haven* at noon in midlake and came in several minutes ahead of her.

In South Haven, the resort business was bursting. People lined both piers each time they heard a faraway whistle, waving hands, waving handkerchiefs. Horse-drawn carriages, with frilly tassels on top and the name of a resort emblazoned, sat waiting at the docks along the Black River. Voices called out like carnival barkers: "This way for Variety Fruit Farm!" "Fern Glen Bus!" "Sleepy Hollow Bus!"

The resorts competed for spaces near the dock with farmers, with wagons loaded with crates of fruit and produce. Eventually, South Haven figured out how to profit from this scarcity. The town sold a one-dollar badge, resembling a policeman's. Anyone wearing it could move to the front of the lines at the dock.

§§§

Two years earlier, Captain Pereue had warned the designer at Jenks Ship Building, Sidney Jenks, about the shallow harbor in South Haven, the shallows of the Black River. Until the harbor was properly dredged, Pereue said, "We'll be on the bottom most of the time, striking bottom coming in and out probably."

Jenks thought about it. He decided to put a double bottom in the *Eastland*, with air between the two sets of hull plates, four feet apart. That way, he would later say, if it "would strike a rock or anything of that kind, and open her bottom, why of course, she would not sink, because it would only fill that compartment."

That protected the hull, sure enough. But to change depths quickly, that was going to be a real problem. The ship would travel most comfortably, with its greatest stability, when she displaced the water by about fourteen feet. The South Haven bar and river only gave clearance for about ten feet to twelve feet.

In most ships, some weighty material was carried in the hold to make the ship steadier, to adjust a crucial point in buoyancy called the center of gravity. Ballast material could be solid, principally iron, stone, or gravel; or liquid, water.

To jump the bar, Jenks decided to use water, not unusual on large lake ships, because it could be emptied and refilled, allowing greater maneuverability to float higher or lower in changing depths of water. Under his design, pipes were filled through a single port, called a seacock, which could be opened to let water gush in and increase the weight of the ship materially. The hole was ten inches around.

And once Lake Michigan started pouring in with a whoosh through the seacock, it splashed into a large rectangular pen, like an aquarium, that had six pipes. Those fed into other holding tanks on the sides, port and starboard, and the front and back, or fore and aft, of the ship.

By directing the water from the manifold into one of the tanks, the engine-room men could raise the ship up and down, and lean it, or rotate its hull slightly to port or starboard. In other words, they could tip the ship any direction they wished, using tons of the incoming water. They used pumps to empty the compartments quickly, spraying it back into the lake.

Jenks's ballast system would allow the engineers on the *Eastland* to adjust for heavy wind and wave conditions, easing her deeper into the water for extra stability. Then they could lighten her up by emptying the tanks when she needed to clear the bottom in shallow water.

At the time, Jenks's designs called for seven-inch-diameter pipes to feed the water-ballast tanks on its largest ships, 440-foot freighters. That was perhaps too large for a ship under three hundred feet long, the size of the *Eastland*, Jenks thought. Six-inch pipes would suffice, he decided, and would save on material costs.

Larger pipes, of course, would allow the engine-room men to stabilize the ship more quickly. But what difference could an inch make?

CHAPTER SIX

Faints, Curses, and Screams

The warning letter came within hours of the mishap, a narrow escape from a capsize on Monday morning, July 18, 1904. It was addressed to R. R. Blacker, president of the Michigan Steamship Company. It came from the Steamboat Inspection Service office in Chicago. And it was unequivocal in its gravity.

"We expect to receive satisfactory assurance of your immediate attention to this matter," wrote local inspectors Ira Mansfield and Roy Peck, "or we feel that we shall be compelled to put the steamer out of commission until such time as changes have been made to render a recurrence of this listing impossible."

The inspectors were threatening to pull the *Eastland* from service the morning after it nearly capsized, outside South Haven. By bizarre coincidence, and much to the misfortune of Michigan Steamship Company, Inspector Mansfield happened to be on board the *Eastland* and personally observed the bucking bronco of a ship.

Consulting, the two steamship inspectors explicitly blamed some malfunction by the water-ballast equipment. They were sure of it, they said. The letter added: "This condition absolutely must be remedied at once."

It was a Sunday night, a little after six, and there was a huge crowd aboard, 2,270 people, including a large group of Chicago postal employees. Captain Dority piloted it over the bar at the mouth of the harbor, and the *Eastland* sped up, running ahead strong, for about five minutes, putting it a mile and a half out. Suddenly, it tilted sharply to the left, or port, about fifteen degrees.

In the engine room, the portly chief engineer William Eeles started running water into the ballast tanks to correct the incline, which began to worry passengers. He ordered his men to fill the starboard tank, on the high side, away from the dangerous tilt.

As the minutes passed, a few women, their balance off, their footing slipping, suddenly began to shriek. Then others joined them, elbowing and pushing.

To save themselves, many rushed to the high side of the ship, and the *Eastland* suddenly began to flip around, rotating the other way and even more severely, a nauseating twenty-five degrees to starboard.

Passengers below decks began screaming when they saw water rushing through the lower gangways, drenching them and forcing them against the cold hull of the ship. There was a rush to grab life preservers, which were passed hand-to-hand. Passengers fastened the straps. Some people grabbed chairs, crates, anything within arm's reach to float on.

"There was a terrifying sound of rushing water, and I reached for a life preserver, feeling sure that the end had come," one Chicago passenger, H. H. Kenard, recalled. "Women fainted, men cursed and children screamed. It was terrible."

"It seemed that we must surely capsize. Even the crew were frightened," recalled another Chicago man, Mr. Kierle. "One woman near me wanted to jump overboard, and a man near me just grabbed her in time."

Captain Dority left the helm to his first mate and ran down to the engine room to consult with Eeles. He clanged down the ladder with difficulty, as it was leaning with the ship. In a frenzy of questions and answers, the engineer told the captain he had been having trouble stabilizing the *Eastland* but thought he had finally gained control. Dority ran back up to the hurricane deck to reassure the crowd: The ship's tilt is being corrected, he said, but you can help speed matters up by heading down to lower decks.

"For God's sake, captain," cried Henry Welch, a postal superintendent, "why don't you turn the boat back, even if you think it is safe. Think of the women and children on board."

Many were afraid to budge, thinking they'd be trapped below in a sunken ship. They clung to the upper rail on the sideways ship. At that point, two crewmembers grabbed a fire hose and sprayed it at the crowd, forcing them down the stairs in a chaotic scramble. John Harrington, a postal clerk, recalled the indignity of getting doused by the spray and the rush of women below, with their dresses or shirtwaists wet.

The *City of South Haven* was nearby, preparing to steer over if passengers were flung overboard. After watching, its captain saw that the *Eastland* had righted itself and was holding steady, and the *City of South Haven* decided to keep its course.

After about twenty-five minutes of rolling topsy-turvy out on the lake, the *Eastland* seemed to have found its footing. Despite the protests of passengers, Captain Dority ordered the ship onward, and less than three hours later the skyscrapers of Chicago appeared over the bow of the ship.

When they arrived at the dock in the Chicago River, many of the women on the *Eastland* were ashen, still clinging to life preservers strapped over their dresses.

CHAPTER SEVEN

River Afire

The *Eastland* parked itself on a Chicago River that had confounded the city throughout the nineteenth century. Chicago only became the magnificent glittering metropolis it did because it overcame two things: fire and water. The Great Fire of 1871 raged over three days in early October, leaving at least three hundred dead and leveling more than three square miles of the city. In the aftermath, city fathers had an opportunity to rebuild, and, looking upward, they invented the skyscraper.

Conquering the Chicago River would require one of the greatest feats in engineering ever. Along the river's more than thirty miles of branches and forks, Chicago rose on its banks to become the most populous and wealthy city between the two coasts. The population, growing a half-million people every decade, overwhelmed the river, polluting it beyond recognition. It gained derogatory nicknames: a bog, a ditch, a sewer. For a few days, it might run north, then, for no apparent reason, turn south. Many days it stagnated, scum-brown.

On the South Fork, the legendary slaughterhouses dumped cattle innards that rotted under water, then bubbled up in methane. The surface toughened with grease, stank, and came to be called Bubbly Creek. Legend was, head-bobbing chickens would prance across the top of the water.

The stockyards, which accounted for nearly a quarter of all the industrial production in Chicago, were feeding a country that was growing more prosperous and demanding more meat on dinner plates. The slaughter factories attracted the attention of an enterprising journalist, Upton Sinclair, who would reveal the gory facts of meat production in his book *The Jungle* so graphically that the public would recoil.

The busy river brought all manner of entrepreneur with crazy schemes and inventions, some left buried in the mud twenty or more feet below the water's surface. One man tried to pilot the river depths with a rudimentary submarine, something nearly unheard of in the city. On its first run, the craft sank. It came to be called the Foolkiller.

The filth of the city and the machinery all along its banks left the river slick, kaleidoscopic with oil. The river became an occasional cauldron. It sometimes combusted. Across the surface of the twisting Chicago River on any given night, one could see blue flames dancing.

A severe storm in 1885 caused the Chicago River, which flowed into Lake Michigan, to flood the lake with sewage, pollution, even dead cats. Something had to change. Plans were made to reverse the flow of the river by dredging out an immense canal, which was completed in 1900.

Dredging out twenty-eight miles of main channel, some through solid rock, took thousands of men who cleared enough total dirt to make an island a mile square and twelve feet tall. Bubbly Creek, the stockyard cesspool, began flowing when the locks were opened to reverse the river's direction. Crowds downtown watched in awe as the river, coffee-color their whole lives, turned clear blue.

Outfoxing the river with a shovel, the city kept digging. Starting in 1900, Chicago dredged out freight tunnels under streets all over downtown, with branches burrowed through the blue clay connecting into building base-ments. The tunnels were designed to leave the streets clear for commuters, trains, and horse carriages. Below ground, and in some cases underwater, the tunnels were meant to be unimpeded channels for telegraph wires, and later, telephone lines.

They also gave space for deliverymen to haul in coal, merchandise, and other supplies and to haul away garbage and ash. But men and women with darker hearts turned them into a shadowy underground highway for booze, opiates, and stockinged bodies. These unholy tunnels would one day provide quite a nice scapegoat for the *Eastland*.

§§§

Crime was boiling over in Chicago. There were charges that the city police were corrupt and useless, their pockets lined with boodle. The streets were open game. Three men in their early twenties, gaining notoriety as the

Car-Barn Bandits, murdered eight people in six months. Police were baffled. Then when the trio was tracked down at a farm, they fled from fifty armed policemen by hijacking a train, killing a brakeman, and forcing the crew to aid their escape. Within a year, each would hang.

Shootings were brazen. When one customer refused to pay for an extra cup of coffee with his fifteen-cent dinner late one night, the restaurant owner shot him dead. Months later, as one woman tried to defend her dye shop from two unarmed thieves, one of the men threw acid on her, disfiguring her face and hands. They got away with fifty-seven dollars and an overcoat.

The streets, above ground and below, were unsafe for children. Youngsters called "night children" sold gum, candy, and newspapers in clubs and saloons well past the mandatory, and often ignored, closing time of midnight. In the darkness of the streets, the child vendors came into contact with prostitutes and vile men and all the vulgarity of gutter life. Boys as young as ten were employed at saloons, some paid two and a half cents a game to set up bowling pins in the alley late nights.

There was no haven for youngsters. Leering men fondled and pawed at young girls in candy shops and ice-cream parlors behind purposely placed curtains, screens, and hidden rooms. Underfed, anemic children arrived at the Juvenile Court, charged with stealing food.

Helping avoid the police were lookouts, also called "lighthouses." They were hired men who stood in front of saloons. Whenever an officer approached, the man would press an electric button concealed in the woodwork or behind a beer sign. They also used hand signals to tip off the cops' approach.

Suspicious of the police, citizens groups formed, with names like the Law and Order League and the Chicago Women's Club, started up by a reformer named Jane Addams, who was gaining a nationwide reputation for ministering to fallen and broken women.

A commission of aldermen began to take testimony. There were shocking tales of slavery, protected gambling, and con men running "brace games." There was much discussion of the Everleigh Club. Housed in a palatial mansion downtown on Dearborn Street, the infamous brothel had six perfumed parlors named for different flowers and a staff of thirty "butterflies," or courtesans.

Prince Henry of Prussia made a point of stopping by while in the United States. A Chicago lawyer named Edgar Lee Masters, who fiddled with poetry in his spare time, was a frequent client. Masters would form a law partnership later that year with a well-known attorney in town, Clarence Darrow.

Mayor Carter Harrison vowed to clean the city up. He took a few well-publicized steps to give the impression he was knuckling down, such as revoking the license of a saloon with crooked gambling in the rear, belonging to a powerful gentleman called Mushmouth Johnson.

Most Chicagoans got by as they could. Newsboys. Bootblacks. Hash slingers. Ash haulers. Horseshoers. Sempsters. Billposters.

One woman, named Bertha Lebecke, alias Bertha Miller, alias Bertha Siegel, made still another name for herself through colorful hornswoggling. Approaching a well-dressed man on the street, she would "faint" into his arms and during the commotion, as people circled around, heads craning, she would slyly bite off diamonds and jewels from his stickpin or shirt studs, or just pickpocket his wallet. She came to be called Fainting Bertha.

CHAPTER EIGHT

Distant Voices

After Thanksgiving Day every year, the Clark Street Bridge turned festive. Parked right below the bridge, there in the Chicago River, was the same beautiful three-mast schooner. Chicagoans lined up every year since 1887 to cheer on the arrival of the Christmas Tree Ship, which sailed in from Lake Michigan, made the turn west into the Chicago River, and tied up to her berth below Clark Street.

The scent of pine hovered above her cargo, three to four hundred tons of fragrant spruces from the Wisconsin woods. The trees lined the top deck, alongside the immense spindled ship wheel, which was as tall as a man. Trees in 1904 ran seventy-five cents for a full-sized one and one dollar for a bristling showstopper.

Some Christmases, Captain Herman Schuenemann, a jolly lake man with a shaggy mustache, brought an extra surprise for the children: once a bear, another time an eagle.

The ship was formally called the *Rouse Simmons*. Captain Schuenemann's young daughter, Elsie, who had goldenrod curls, helped her father on board. As a young girl, she had played with toy boats, rather than dolls.

§§§

By 1904, Clarence Darrow was tossing and turning through life. He was forty-seven and had emerged on the national stage as a labor lawyer, coming to the aid of striking coal miners two years before in Pennsylvania. Yet he still couldn't quite decide what he wanted to do in life. He had divorced his wife of nineteen years, then second-guessed that decision, then was smitten by an aspiring Chicago newspaper reporter named Ruby Hammerstrom, sixteen years younger than he. Surprising most of his friends, the two married in secret in the summer of 1903 and took a cruise ship to honeymoon in Europe. The romance with Ruby started a Darrow fascination with female reporters that wouldn't end with her.

Darrow's family consumed his thoughts in 1904. That was the year his father died and Clarence published a semi-autobiography titled *Farmington*, a nostalgic portrait of growing up in small town America. He began life in Farmdale, Ohio, east of Cleveland, and had been practicing law since the late 1800s. He later moved to Chicago, wrote literature reviews, and dreamed of being a man of letters.

He briefly considered running for mayor of Chicago, but instead ran for and won a seat in the Illinois state house. As an associate of newspaper baron William Randolph Hearst, Darrow seconded Hearst's nomination as Democratic candidate for president of the United States. At one point, Darrow took a job with the city of Chicago, as special counsel for traction affairs, to help the city beat injury claims from streetcar and train victims.

Darrow was discovering that he loved the pulpit—anywhere—and, as his audiences grew, his thoughts turned more extremist. Among his heroes were Leo Tolstoy, the Russian literary giant, and John Altgeld, a onetime governor of Illinois who strengthened child-labor and workplace safety laws.

A hero of the Progressive Movement, Altgeld wrote an 1890 book called *Our Penal Machinery and its Victims*, which included a detailed statistical portrait of justice in Chicago. It found, for instance, that the police arrested 32,800 people in 1882 alone, but ended up releasing fully a third of them because they had done nothing wrong.

Charging that prisons were overcrowded, Altgeld blamed poverty, poor upbringing, and "labor-saving machinery" that allowed companies to save production costs, but left many men idle and desperate. He argued for a penal system that emphasized rehabilitation over punishment. Darrow devoured the book.

"There should be no jails," Darrow announced one day, speaking to applauding prisoners at the Cook County Jail. "They do not accomplish what they pretend to accomplish. If you would wipe them out, there would be no more criminals than now. . . . They are a blot upon any civilization, and a jail is an evidence of the lack of charity of the people on the outside who make the jails and fill them with the victims of their greed."

As 1904 opened, Darrow drew himself into a tragedy at the self-advertised "Absolutely Fireproof" Iroquois Theatre. During a full matinee at the theater in Chicago's Loop district, an arc lamp shorted out. Flying sparks ignited a tall muslin curtain. In minutes, the three-story theater was aflame, trapping crowds fighting for the exit doors, which were unmarked. There were no smoke alarms. Salvagers would pull some six hundred bodies out of the ashes.

The horrible deaths led to indictments of Mayor Harrison, one of the theater owners, and others. As the city raged at the men for the atrocity, Darrow, who had theater-business clients and a cozy relationship with men in city government, published an extraordinary letter in a Chicago newspaper, recommending, of all things, forbearance.

"This terrible tragedy was the direct result of an effort to save money at serious risk of human life," he acknowledged. Still, "to send anyone to prison for this dire disaster could not bring back one of the dead. It would be vengeance pure and simple, and the fruits of vengeance are always evil."

No one was ever found criminally responsible.

§§§

Chicago moved on, and thrived. One particular company, Western Electric, even outgrew the city's business district as a manufacturer of telegraph equipment, commercial typewriters, and incandescent lamps. An early product was fire alarms; after the Great Fire of 1871, the company profited smartly from them. Over the years, the firm began branching into other electronic devices and eventually found its way into telephones.

In 1903, with sales of more than thirty million dollars, Western Electric was running near round-the-clock shifts, pumping out as quickly as it could the tall, slim models called candlestick phones. And demand was phenomenal. Telephone lines were being strung all over the country. Coast-to-coast calls were on the drawing board. Businesses were beginning to print phone numbers on their stationery and advertisements.

The world was changing. Ring in the new. This was a revolution in the industry of transportation, conveying for the first time the human voice, the music of the soul.

A kind of fragmentation of the person began to take shape, a voice for the first time divided, at long distance, from a body. It seemingly brought people closer, yet put them at greater remove. This unnatural division, this disembodiment, would reshape lives for generations to come.

Western Electric was poised to become the sole manufacturer of telephones for the whole country. The firm set aside several million dollars for a new factory on the outskirts of Chicago and purchased 113 acres of prairie land west of Chicago. That area was already home to thousands of immigrants, who had poured in from all over Eastern Europe, some who mispronounced the city's name as *SHICK-ago*. They took whatever jobs they could find, at whatever hours. Men shared boardinghouse rooms, sleeping two to a bed, head to toe. Men would fall asleep next to one fellow and wake next to another who had come off his shift.

Western Electric couldn't meet demand with immigrants alone, so it began hiring schoolchildren to help as clerks and for other positions. Builders speculated on property surrounding the factory, surmising that hundreds of new homes would be needed.

By 1904, Western Electric had broken ground for the new factory: the Hawthorne Works. That same year James Novotny, a youthful cabinetmaker from Bohemia, married another Bohemian émigré. He and his wife would soon have two children, and the growing family would bring him looking for a new job at the factory.

CHAPTER NINE

"A Little Heaven Afloat"

Construction on the *General Gillespie*, the largest dredge ship ever built, was completed, and she began running around Chesapeake Bay in August 1904 testing her machinery. The Army was set to send her to work in Boston Harbor first, then out to the Great Lakes, with Joseph Erickson on board as an oiler.

Having arrived only a year earlier from Norway, Erickson had never seen the Great Lakes, never been that far inland. Like other Europeans, he couldn't have imagined how immense they were—nor how violent. The second largest of the Great Lakes after Superior, Lake Michigan was one hundred miles across and triple that in length. It was 279 feet deep on average but could drop to nine hundred feet. And it was ice-cold. "On hitting the water, even in the summer," said Earl Parsons, who worked as a deckhand for years on steamers, "you will think a thousand devils have you."

Sailors joked that there were three seasons on the Great Lakes: July, August, and winter. Squalls came out of the blue. Suddenly the waves and winds had all the force and madness of a sea. They called it heavy weather. In an instant, day turned to night.

One November storm raged on Lake Huron and Lake Superior for an unrelenting sixteen hours, winds howling at sixty miles per hour. When it was over, the drowned bodies of Captain W. A. Black and other crewmembers of the *Charles S. Price* were found wearing life belts with the name of another steamer, the *Regina*, on them. Searchers puzzled over what had happened. The two ships may have collided, they thought, and sailors who were thrown or jumped onto the *Regina* fastened themselves with the nearest life belts at hand. The *Regina* sank with no survivors, and the *Charles S. Price* was found floating upside down in Lake Huron, her twenty-eight crewmembers drowned.

On the *General Gillespie*, Erickson wrote letters to his mother back in Norway, in the twilight in between watches. Afterward, he would drift off into the night in his bunk to the throb of the engines. Some nights the crew quarters were so hot, the men on the lakes slept in the night air, stars twinkling above.

Erickson's fellow crewmen might have crabbed about duties during games of cribbage, their favorite off-duty pastime. Watches ran six hours on, six off. It was common courtesy on the lakes to show up a few minutes early to relieve a companion. If you were late, among the less foul of cursing one might get was "Fury and snakes!"

Erickson needed a good recommendation from the *General Gillespie* captain, Daniel French, for his citizenship application. He would have to keep whatever objections he had to himself at this point, but he was less reticent about the hard life on the lakes when writing to a confidante.

"I am going ashore this morning as I could not go yesterday or the day before," Erickson wrote. "I don't get no time off, only six hours, and in that time I have had to eat and sleep a little, when the bedbugs don't drive me out, like the other night: had one hour sleep before going on watch at midnight."

Some of Erickson's crewmates had previously served on the Great Lakes; they could have passed on cautions about shore leave out there and the rascals at certain ports.

On payday, gamblers and prostitutes hovered. In Cleveland, you'd want to look out for Elephant Bill, Mother Lovely of Third Street, Chicken Smith, and Hickory Nut Mary, all of whom would pickpocket you one way or another. In Chicago, particularly in the blocks north of the Chicago River, in an area called the Sands, the price for a roll with a hooker: two Liberty Head quarters.

You really needed to watch yourself in years gone by at a variety house in Wakefield, Michigan, that had to be accessed through a back door at Bedell's, a respectable emporium. The wilder club had a red-capped monkey that scampered curly-tailed through the audience during the vaudeville show. The Wakefield monkey was trained to pickpocket patrons' wallets and watches.

§§§

The trip from Baltimore to Ludington, Michigan, by way of the St. Lawrence River and the Great Lakes, took exactly one month. The *General Gillespie* had a dark hull and polished brass that twinkled in the sun. Her single smokestack was black, tilted slightly back toward the stern, a leaning tower of Pisa. At night, the lanterns attached to the forward mast glowed.

Erickson was eager for a commendation from Captain French, and his nationality was in his favor. At ports across the country, mariners from Scandinavia, Norway particularly, were coveted. Great Lakes captain Arthur H. Clark loved sailing with a crew of Scandinavians, but decidedly not Irishmen, whom he decried as "a species of wild men . . . wallowing in the slush of depravity." Norwegians, on the other hand, "clean, willing and obedient. . . . A vessel with a whole crew of these strong, honest sailors was a little heaven afloat."

At the end of the last century, Norwegians, sailors included, flocked to America. By 1890, they reached twenty-two thousand in Chicago alone, a number that would more than double over the next two decades. In time there would be not one but two Chicago dailies in Norwegian, the *Skandinaven* and the *Norden*.

Norwegian sailors flocked to America for the higher wages, $1.75 a day versus three dollars a month in Norway. Years later, so many light-haired immigrants were employed by the Coast Guard that it came to be nicknamed the "Norwegian Navy." By 1890, Norwegians threatened to take so many jobs from Americans that William Windom, the secretary of the treasury, issued a ruling. All officers on vessels under the American flag *must* be citizens of the United States.

§§§

The journey from Norway was neither easy, nor short, at nearly four thousand miles. Stretching along the Atlantic Ocean, the Arctic Ocean, and the North Sea, Norway offered its natives few options for work beyond farming and the hazardous life at sea. But the ocean had been in their blood since at least the Viking Age.

There were a half dozen states, mostly midwestern ones, that Norwegians settled in. The sailors often arrived in New York and moved via Buffalo and the Great Lakes to Chicago. Over several decades, the people of Norway who followed their countrymen made homes on Chicago's North Side, in the Sands district.

There was something more than money driving sailors from the ocean to the Great Lakes: homesickness. To seamen accustomed to long voyages, working apart from their families for years at a time, lake service allowed shorter trips and more time in their home ports with wives and children. A steamer could run from the eastern end of the Great Lakes in Buffalo, New York, to its western front, in Duluth, Minnesota, in three and a half days. The Norwegian émigrés were rebelling from the long-standing tyranny of work's dictating life; there was a growing feeling that leisure was a part of living.

"In sailing on the ocean as Norwegian seamen, we had to sign an agreement to stay with the vessel for two years," recalled Harry Gresholdt, who sailed the schooners *Newhouse* and *Lizzie Setsner* after settling in Wisconsin. "I desired to find a place where I could enjoy home life. I decided to go to America. I came to Manitowoc, where I built me a home and began to sail on the lakes."

Home life would loom large, as well, for Joseph Erickson.

CHAPTER TEN

Dragon Breath

Most of Erickson's colleagues on board the *Gillespie* were smart fellows, high school or college graduates. As newcomers to the sea, they started as deckhands and soogey men, rinsing, swabbing, sweeping the deck, often covered in ash and ore dust.

Jokes broke tension. The job of oiler was dangerous, particularly in the lower ends. With his years at sea, Erickson would not have been taken in by the pranks typically played on cub sailors. One surefire joke: sparks watch. The new deckhand was told to keep a close eye out for any sparks coming out of the smokestacks. (Here and there, they routinely did flicker up harmlessly, like fireflies.) As soon as you see any, the innocent man was told, find the captain right away, and even if he's asleep, wake him up to alert him.

Normally, Erickson, as oiler-in-training, would feel the machinery with one hand to see if it was getting too hot, a cup of oil in his other at the ready. Oil was precious. A spilt cup would mean he would not have enough to finish his watch. When he felt any bearings getting hot, he would feed the equipment some oil, to take the temperature down.

In the engine room, a tinderbox of machinery, it was a constant vigil against overheating, for both machines and men. Erickson's small stature made him a natural for the cramped room. As the ship rolled, the suffocating quarters down there, the stink of metal and oil, the feverish and stagnant air, it was easy to get seasick.

Wheels called eccentrics and other rotating machinery would turn up to ninety times a minute. Amid a deafening roar of engine thunder, in tight space where commands needed to be shouted, Erickson would approach the lower ends, the part of the engine where the pistons drove the crankshaft, with his boss, the third assistant engineer.

With his supervisor looking on, he learned to take the temperature in this treacherous spot of the engine room. Erickson had to learn to stretch out his arm, timing his reach to avoid the spinning crank. He would synchronize his body to the rotation, then when he thought the timing was just right, reach his hand behind the one-ton crank, feel quickly, then dodge the crank on its return rotation. It took split-second timing.

In the hold, there was gallows humor whenever a newcomer was training as an oiler, the jokes being about the going-cost for replacement cork arms.

From the bowels of the *General Gillespie*, firemen emerged blinking into daylight so soiled with ash and oil that they came to be called the "black gang," as did other crews working below. As an oiler now, Erickson did not miss his work on the gang. Before he arrived in America, he was a fireman on four different oceangoing ships, shoveling coal on runs between Norway, France, Germany, Sweden, Holland, and Belgium.

Back in the days of sail, men had piloted and powered the ship on the top deck, in the open air, wind whistling through the rigging. Steamships submersed the power below the waterline, into the belly of the ship for the first time, and men had to climb down a series of steep metal ladders to reach this dark, steamy-wet new world. When they came up for fresh air, they always had a sweat towel around their necks and bright eyes peeking out of coal-dusted faces.

One Great Lakes fireman, Richard Hallett, vividly remembered the moment the fireboxes opened: "There were sounds of low thunder, blobs or orange-colored flame that crisped my lashes and breathed the hair off my arms with dragon-breath."

Worse, getting ground up in the brutal equipment wasn't unusual, as when Charles McDaniel, the night engineer on another ship, the *Independent*, was standing his first watch. A sand-sifting machine caught his clothes and dragged him into the spinning pinions. He was crushed to death in the gears.

§§§

Exhausted, Erickson and the other junior oilers would climb out of the engine room in their grimy overalls, up the iron stairway (the ladder, they called it), boots clattering to the deck. Instead of the herring or the porridge called *Grøt* Erickson was accustomed to in Norway, the typical lunch on the

Great Lakes was sausage, mashed potatoes, pork chops, peas, bread and butter, jam, tea, and pudding: all the food you wanted. With coal dust floating in the air from the boiler room to the engine room, the men working lake ships would dig into their suppers, which sometimes included a dusting of ash sprinkled from their arms. They forked it in, ash and all.

To learn how the engines operated, Erickson and the oilers on the *General Gillespie* helped engineers repair all the machinery aboard. After a year as an oiler, a man had a shot at any job in the engine room. But even that had its own hazards. The chief engineer of the steamer *Sylvania* was cleaning a cylinder one day when a piston rod dropped accidentally, cutting his hand off.

Erickson started making about forty-five dollars a month, along with board on the ship, working regular six-hour watches. After a year, if he impressed the chief engineer Emmet J. Phillips enough, he would be allowed to take an exam with the local officer of the Steamboat Inspection Service.

If he passed, he would be given a spot as third assistant engineer. His pay would nearly double, to about eighty-five dollars monthly, including board. His first paycheck at the new level would be eye-popping, making anyone in his shoes feel like a capitalist.

Erickson had his eye on the final prize, chief engineer, the man in charge of all the machinery, the steam boilers, the engines. Pay ran as much as $175 a month, and the title would make him the second most powerful officer on board any ship, after the captain.

The chief engineer was fully in charge of his own department. He had to have a license issued by federal government inspectors after he passed a strict examination. There were no classes to take, no college to attend. It was learning on the job, and book learning. Erickson was going to have to pore over texts like Roper's *Catechism of High Pressure or Non-Condensing Steam Engines.*

And when he was ready for his examination, he didn't know for certain which inspector he would face. Some were easier than others. Eventually, Erickson would stand before one of the harshest inspectors on all of Lake Michigan.

§§§

On the Chicago side, anyway, the *Eastland* was beloved. Two songwriters memorialized the Chicago–South Haven cruise with a song titled "A Sail in the Summertime." One verse went:

Sailing, sailing isn't it joy sublime,
To go to South Haven and spend all your "saven,"
With your baby mine. Sailing, sailing,
Go o'er the Michigan line,
On the *Eastland* so grand,
the best boat in the land,
For a sail in the summertime.

All along the Chicago River downtown, the workers in offices knew the *Eastland*, as did those on trains passing the billboards for coffee, cheese, and Quaker Oats, as did those in the department stores. Some had ridden on it; many more had simply heard it.

That July, Chicago merchants and manufacturers were fed up with a troubling trend. Every day when the mammoth *Eastland* steered through the Chicago River and its calliope blasted its musical mayhem, their employees would rush to the windows to watch it pass. Untold hours were lost, they figured. Businessmen started calculating the loss of productivity from such daily distractions, twelve thousand dollars annually, all told. They turned their grievance over to the Chicago chief of police, who turned a deaf ear, ruling the calliope was noisy, but lawful.

Later that summer, the *Eastland* and the *City of South Haven* staged a well-publicized rematch. The booty: coveted bragging rights. The championship ring had gone to the *City of South Haven* in their initial 1903 season. The *Eastland*, with a new captain and some mechanical revisions, took the title the following year. This season was up for grabs.

With passengers packed on both ships, the *City of South Haven* had a ten-minute head start, as the *Eastland* cast off its lines in Chicago and nosed toward Lake Michigan. In short order, the *City of South Haven* steamed well ahead and kept expanding its lead, smoke trailing from twin smokestacks. Out on the lake, the *Eastland* and the *City of South Haven* looked remarkably similar, nearly identical in length, width, and height. Both had two smokestacks; both looked more like ocean-liners than lake steamers.

Trailing badly, the *Eastland* needed to do something. Chief Engineer Eeles had a thought. Consulting with Captain Dority, he ordered the ship's fires "cleaned" and the ashes removed from its boilers to get a fresh start. Within a half hour, the ash expulsion seemed to be working. The Michigan shoreline coming within sight, the *Eastland* had pulled within a mile of its rival, a half mile, several hundred feet. The *City of South Haven* couldn't break farther ahead, the *Eastland* matching her foot for foot. Then, at two hours and fifty-four minutes into the race, the *Eastland* suddenly outfooted the *City of South Haven.*

As the *Eastland* pulled out in front, crowds cheering on both decks, Professor Little took to the calliope at the rear of the ship, blasting the popular tune "The Girl I Left Behind."

It was a hot day, but hundreds of people crowded the bluff and piers at South Haven, cheering the *Eastland* as it arrived in first place, broomsticks on its portholes. The *Eastland* made the trip in three hours and forty minutes, averaging 21.5 miles per hour. The "White Flyer" had fallen to the "Greyhound of the Lakes."

After the race, G. P. Cory, general manager of Dunkley-Williams, declared that the *Eastland's* 3:40 time was nothing to crow about. Why, he pointed out, it did not compare with the *City of South Haven's* record of three hours and thirty-one minutes. He held out hope for a rematch, saying, "The *South Haven* will give the *Eastland* a race at any time, for marbles or money."

Barrel-chested after their win, Leighton and Captain Dority decided to up the ante. They put the word out that the *Eastland* would race the *City of South Haven* again, for a five-thousand-dollar pot.

Steamboat inspector Ira Mansfield was not happy. From his offices in Chicago, he issued a warning to both shipping companies: Under no circumstances would they be allowed to race, as it was against government rules for steamboats on the lakes. No longer could they endanger the lives of passengers for such sport, he said.

§§§

Out on Lake Michigan, the *General Gillespie* was at work on the bar outside South Haven. It was a three-week chore. Off watch in the engine room, Erickson stepped up on deck, looked out, and saw in the distance a large steamer he'd never seen before. It looked like the oceangoing ships he'd worked on running out of Europe. Its hull was tall and sleek and white, like two slices of wedding cake leaning together.

Erickson would not set eyes on the *Eastland* for another ten years, for better, for worse.

CHAPTER ELEVEN

Too Late, the *Messenger*

The thief, an amateur, must have amused Erickson and his mates. While their ship was docked in St. Joseph, Michigan, Harry Gordon, a deckhand on the *General Gillespie,* was caught shoplifting nine pairs of ladies' gloves. It was exactly this kind of shenanigan that Erickson needed to avoid, if he hoped to win citizenship. His mates would go into town and get drunk, provoke fights, and stir dustups with the law. He could not afford such indulgences, and they didn't really suit him anyway. He was a straight arrow, and puny, not much of a fighter. And he had worked hard to keep his record clean. Before the *General Gillespie* headed out, Erickson often used his time in port to write letters to his mother in Norway, a few lines about where his ship was going, how much he liked the work, and then signing off, "With love, from Joseph."

The *General Gillespie* was making headlines in towns all over the Great Lakes as it worked its marvels that summer. At Grand Haven's harbor, its massive suction pipes sucked a seventy-five-pound boulder up from the lakebed thirty-five feet down. The twin pipes drew sand from the bottom of the harbor and emptied it into the *General Gillespie*'s hold. Once it was full, the dredge steamed out to the lake and emptied the sand into the depths.

Sailors couldn't help but notice that the *General Gillespie* didn't look like the typical dredge ship, which was more of a flatboat or a scow. The *General Gillespie* really looked more like a warship, and she was in fact on a sustained campaign to subdue the nation's waterways. A colossal industrial kingdom had begun to spring up on the shores of the Great Lakes, fueled by cheap shipping, an army of immigrant laborers, and bountiful raw materials, particularly iron ore. In just a few years, coal mines, limestone quarries, steel mills, factories, railroad yards, shipbuilding yards, and docks dotted the shorelines of the nation's interior.

The industrial hub of America had moved from the East Coast to the Midwest. The ports in cities around the Great Lakes emerged as the greatest manufacturing region ever seen. The heart of the continent had become the crucible of America's twentieth-century industrial boom.

By 1900, with shipments reaching twenty-two million tons, iron ore surpassed all other cargo on the Great Lakes. Year after year records were set and then broken. Six years later, the Great Lakes accounted for only one in ten vessels in the United States but carried 43 percent of the freight in tons. Ore was feeding the steel mills in the Midwest, which in turn were helping fuel the shift from wood to steel for many building materials and even household appliances. The ore rush was on.

Freighters shuttled fortunes, port to port. Entrepreneurs started hauling cargo with anything that would float: cigar-shaped whalebacks, splintering schooners, monitors, turtlebacks, turret ships.

Colonel Orlando Poe, the legendary superintendent of the Soo locks, observed, "The wildest expectations of one year seem absolutely tame the next."

The Soo locks, which allowed ships to rise from Lake Huron to the height of Lake Superior, became clogged with traffic, and it was not unusual to wait hours to get through. Delays came with great cost. While waiting for the lock one July day, Richard A. Justin, an assistant engineer on the steamer *St. Clair*, decided to repair some pipes; the engine turned over and the air pump beam caught him, crushing his head, killing him almost instantly. Only thirty-two, he left a widow and small child.

§§§

Great Lakes shipbuilders had stretched the limits of materials and marine engineering to create larger and larger ships: longer, wider, taller. Ship lengths reached an astonishing five hundred feet. And the richest men in America were fronting this enormous expansion.

Having already made his fortune in oil, John D. Rockefeller broke ground in the iron business in Michigan and Minnesota in the late 1800s. As mining grew in the region, he began his own shipping company to control transport costs on the trips to mills in Ohio and Pennsylvania. He initially ordered twelve ships larger than anything ever seen on the Great Lakes, and he eventually grew his operation to a squadron of sixty.

Nervous that he would be edged out, Andrew Carnegie formed the Pittsburgh Steamship Company and bought six ships of his own. In 1901, J. P.

Morgan bought out Carnegie and formed US Steel, which had interests in 104 mines, five railroads, and 112 freight ships on the Great Lakes. The armada, all with red hulls and silver smokestacks, came to be called the Pittsburgh Fleet, or the Tin Stackers. It was the largest fleet on the lakes from 1901 on. At one point, it was the world's largest single group of freight steamers, for which it gained another, more scornful nickname—the Steel Trust Fleet.

Many shipping companies couldn't build vessels fast enough and shopped overseas for freighters. It took ingenuity to fit ocean-size ships through the bottlenecks in the waterways on the East Coast leading out to the Great Lakes. Bringing immense cargo freighters from abroad sometimes involved chopping them in half, yanking out their mid-bodies, then welding the bow and stern sections together. The ship would then proceed through the tight locks with the middle section in its cargo hold. Once a ship was through, welders would fuse the middle back in place, restoring it to its original full length.

In 1906, the first six-hundred-foot-long ship appeared. In less than two decades prior, the number of passengers carried on the Great Lakes skyrocketed from 2.2 million to fourteen million.

The fates of towns all along the lakes rose or fell because of the shipping craze. Dredging channels to allow hulls to sink deeper could steal port traffic from a neighboring town. In the Chicago River, the Great Lakes Dredge and Dock Company began widening the turning basin on the south branch of the Chicago River because larger ships simply could not turn around anymore.

Expansion simply begot more expansion. Knowing the turning basin was being stretched out in Chicago, Dunkley-Williams made plans to lengthen the *City of South Haven* by sixty feet.

This all kept the *General Gillespie* very busy. Erickson was one of a thirty-man crew, which had a payroll of two thousand dollars monthly. Hours were long, and the ship, even as a new vessel, was repeatedly taxed. It broke a rudder on a Friday morning in September 1905 and was anchored in the harbor at Frankfort, Michigan. Nearby, Erickson and his mates heard urgent splashing. A boy of eleven, Romaine Vancolen, had been trying to rig a sail on his dinghy when he plopped into the water and began drowning. First Mate Harry Levins immediately lowered the ship's launch, *The Messenger*, and furiously paddled to the boy. Levins did not arrive in time. The men of the *General Gillespie* carefully took the body aboard.

The boy's mother, they later learned, had given her son permission to stay out of school that day to go sailing.

CHAPTER TWELVE

A Lingering Hat

Across the lake in the spring of 1905, a Chicago wedding made headlines. THE LARGEST OF YESTERDAY'S SOCIAL AFFAIRS, screamed the *Chicago Record Herald*. The bride was Mary Eveline Steele, the eldest daughter of Julius and Ida Steele. The service brought a large gathering of South Side society to the Kenwood Evangelical Church. The bride's brother, Walter Steele, was first usher.

The Steele family prominence was built on the success of the fifty-six-year-old patriarch, Julius Steele. Born in rural Michigan, he moved to Chicago as a child, was educated in Chicago public schools, and afterward showed an affinity for business. After several years with Atwood & Steele, manufacturers and importers of grocers' sundries, Steele had recently become its treasurer. The firm's offices were smack in the center of the Loop, right on the main highway of commerce, the Chicago River. Outside its doors, Chicago was a large and hungry city, and his firm provided food. Steele was a Republican, a Congregationalist, and a member of the elite Chicago Athletic Club.

And in March, there was the prominent announcement of the wedding of the first of the four Steele children. It had one paragraph solely on bridal apparel, including the tulle veil, held to the bride's hair by a coronet of orange blossoms. The article referred to three of the Steele children. If the youngest son, Blair, were there, the story made no mention of him.

The previous May, Blair had lost his legs under the screeching wheels of a streetcar. According to news reports, the boy of ten was showing off for a companion, playing a dangerous prank called "flipping a streetcar."

But his father, Julius, did not care a button about the news reports that blamed his son. The day after his daughter's wedding, he filed a sixty-thousand-dollar lawsuit in the Superior Court against Northwestern Gas Light and Coke Company of Evanston. According to the Steele claim, the boy was playing in the street and tripped over an obstruction thought to have been left by the gas company in front of an electric car, which cut off both of Blair's legs.

And now his father was demanding someone pay.

§§§

The *Eastland*'s third season, 1905, was coming to a close, and the ship, while fast, was struggling financially. Being unable to jump the bar, the *Eastland* each day kept roughing up its durable hull, made of riveted plates of solid carbon steel. It scraped its propellers, sucking sand into its bearings and snapping twenty-eight propeller blades off in one season alone. Within the company, one thing should have been clear: The ballast system was not nearly responsive enough to help with the troublesome sandbar. Expenses were running up, at one point more than fifty thousand dollars of damages and repairs, and bills were going unpaid.

Worse, the *Eastland*'s reputation in South Haven was mud. P. S. Staines, a South Haven doctor, was with his wife on the pier that day in July 1904, when the *Eastland* teetered toward capsizing. "Although the Michigan Steamship Company tried to have people feel that the boat was safe," the doctor recalled, "many people refused to cross the lake on it, feeling that it was top-heavy and liable to capsize."

Passengers had been spooked, and ticket revenues sank. The steamer company ran low on cash. Then it faced a claim of $1,591.50 for life preservers brought by the Armstrong Cork Company of Pittsburgh. By late December 1905, the Michigan Steamship Company had to close its doors.

With Michigan Steamship itself unable to pay, the lumber baron R. R. Blacker, a founder and lead financial backer, capitalized on the situation and personally bought the *Eastland*, picking it up at a bargain, one hundred thousand dollars cash, roughly a third its original price.

Within months, he would sell the ship, for what must have been a tidy windfall. With the proceeds, he had blueprints drawn up for a new home, in Pasadena, California, that would cost a stunning $83,230. Every detail of the Blacker House would be handcrafted in the so-called Arts and Crafts style. That movement was a revolt against furniture and housing materials mass-produced in factories, in favor of wood, metal, and glasswork painstak-ingly brought to life by the hands of skilled artisans.

As it turns out, when Blacker unloaded the speedy *Eastland*, he sold it to the last company anyone would have expected, the last one Pereue or Leigh-ton would have wanted. Blacker sold it to the enemy, Dunkley-Williams.

§§§

Maybe his heart gave out, or he was merely dizzy. That was the going specula-tion of his family and friends. Maybe it was his final surrender to the ship he had battled so passionately.

The fall after the *Eastland* was sold, Leander Leighton, the man behind the line of retailers along Leighton Block in South Haven, stepped aboard the *City of South Haven*, his rival for more than three years.

At the dock in South Haven, Leighton boarded and proceeded directly to his stateroom, Parlor A, forward, on the port side. His mustache was bushy, gray, and the hair at his temples was as white as his collar.

He left his traveling bag and his overcoat. He walked up to the hurricane deck, paced back and forth opposite the pilothouse. He stopped periodically to exchange a few pleasantries with the captain.

Captain J. M. Mitchell, who knew Leighton, thought it odd, how quiet Leighton was—out of character.

About 11:30 that night, a cabin boy saw Leighton leaning against his stateroom door, hat in his hand. It was the last time anyone saw him.

The next morning, with the *City of South Haven* docked in Chicago, another cabin boy went to check in on Leighton and found his room empty, his bed still made. They searched the entire ship, all the decks, the engine room. He was nowhere.

Eventually, they did find one trace of Leighton on the promenade deck, near where the captain last saw him, his hat.

The mysterious news was in the newspaper later that afternoon. There were more questions than answers. South Haven was shocked by the disap-pearance of one of its luminaries. The man who built the Leighton Opera House, the man behind the *Eastland*, apparently plunged into Lake Michi-gan somewhere in the middle of the night and quietly vanished.

CHAPTER THIRTEEN

April Fool's Day

The suction motors on the *General Gillespie* had thundered for thirteen hours, from 4:00 a.m. to 5:00 p.m, day after day, every day of the week. The roar could be heard more than a mile away, on the docks, on the shore, that much louder aboard. The crews' bunks rattled, leaving them sleepless.

It was dredge work. The ship had been clearing a sandbar outside Muskegon, Michigan, for several weeks. During dredging, the bellow-howl of vacuuming was relentless, inescapable.

The earsplitting ship moved a little south in the succeeding weeks and finished up the season in Holland, Michigan. There, several steamers of the Graham & Morton line had run aground while trying to reach their docks, another case of ships' being too large for the lakes. And more were on the way. Great Lakes transportation companies were preparing to launch a fleet of thirty new vessels in the coming season, 1908.

Dunkley-Williams, now running both the *Eastland* and the *City of South Haven,* renamed itself the Chicago & South Haven Steamship Company. It soon became apparent that there was not enough traffic between those cities to justify operating two large steamers.

An investor group out in Ohio, looking for a steamship, took interest in the *Eastland.* Their plan was to run passengers from Cleveland, a growing industrial city of nearly four hundred thousand people, to a large amusement park sixty-odd miles west on Lake Erie called Cedar Point. Early investors in the *Eastland* included Cleveland politician Newton D. Baker, who would later serve as secretary of the War Department.

As negotiations began, tragedy struck at the Jenks shipyard on a Wednesday morning in March 1907. A fire broke out and several new machines recently installed were damaged. Jenks was at a disadvantage already. The

Black River at Port Huron was narrow—it was a tight fit to build ships even fifty feet wide. But shipping companies started ordering vessels wider than that.

There were ten competing shipyards in Michigan alone; six in Ohio, including the large yard in Toledo. There was more than four thousand dollars of damage, and Jenks, which hired four hundred men at its peak, decided to close its doors. In its sixteen years in business, the yard had built twenty-six ships. The *Eastland* would be the last passenger ship that Jenks built.

§§§

Five days after the fire—on April Fool's Day—the men in Cleveland signed a deal to purchase the *Eastland* for $275,000.

Cedar Point was a sprawling newfangled carnival for a new century, and for a country with leisure time as never before. An early roller coaster, called The Racer, ran in a figure-eight at the breakneck speed of ten miles per hour. Children and their parents spun around on a twirling water swing. A twelve-hundred-seat Opera House offered two shows a day, a dime each. The new Hotel Breakers had six hundred rooms, most overlooking Lake Erie, and a glittering Tiffany chandelier in the lobby. Self-billed as "the Atlantic City of the Great Lakes," Cedar Point was glamorous and decadent by day, all neon and sparkle at night.

The men operating Cedar Point knew how to promote and had plans to plug the *Eastland* into the show. The *Eastland*'s debut on Lake Erie came the first week of June 1907. Promoted as the "Aristocrat of the Lakes," the *Eastland* had been overhauled with a four-thousand-square-foot marble dance floor and its own dance band, the Eastland Orchestra. The waft of hamburgers sizzling was in the air as the ship made its way along. Elsewhere, there was a battery of slot machines. For the children, there was a wheel of fortune that awarded chocolates to the luckier patrons. Later, musical accompaniment came from Tom King's twenty-eight-piece concert band, which played ragtime and marches.

It all started so well, so wonderfully in fact, that the owners of the Lake Shore Navigation Company would puzzle over just why so many people, so quickly, became scared to set foot on the *Eastland*.

CHAPTER FOURTEEN

Swallowing the Anchor

As the 1907 season opened in June, the new captain on the *General Gillespie*, E. L. Evans, had a big headache: his chef quit. William Love was hired on as chief chef of the ritzy Brevoort Hotel in Chicago. The finest hotels and city restaurants on the Great Lakes often vied with the steamers for talent, men who could run a round-the-clock kitchen, while rolling. Sailors were paid wages, but board was a big part of their compensation: a berth of one's own and three meals a day, free. The firemen and coal-passers, the Black Gang, in particular, required heavy food.

So each spring, captains competed with one another to secure the best cooks they could. It wasn't unusual for one captain to swipe an outstanding chef from another ship. Port to port, sailors were gossips. Word spread quickly if the food was scrumptious or god-awful. A reputation for poor meals often meant troublesome turnover; men simply wouldn't show for the next run. And, of course, in the worst of circumstances, men might mutiny.

Captain Evans had other preoccupations. Port authorities in St. Joseph were puzzled to find thousands of fish floating around their water intake, and the *General Gillespie's* earsplitting dredge became their top culprit. They charged the ship with environmental harm, suspecting that the fish in the proximity of the rumbling suction pipes were being sucked in with the sand and killed.

Even more pressing for Captain Evans was keeping his men out of the hoosegow. Fireman William Morton had just been paid when he arrived on a Friday night at a bar in downtown Muskegon. Within hours, he was arrested drunk on the sawdust of the saloon floor in the levee district and locked up at City Hall. He appeared before the judge the next morning, paid a three-dollar fine for public intoxication, and was released in time to make the *General Gillespie's* departure.

As the fall winds were turning chilly, John McCourt, a deckhand on the *General Gillespie*, was swept up with a group of drunken sailors and thrown behind bars below the stairs at City Hall. He managed to weep his way out of the charges. He blubbered remorse at his hearing, promising in his deep Irish brogue never to be caught intoxicated again.

By comparison, Erickson, the rising oiler in the engine room, was sober, quiet, reliable—in short, a model for the character references he would very shortly seek. A letter of recommendation from a lake captain was gold. In many towns, a captain was the most respected and wealthiest man around. In Grand Haven, for example, where the *General Gillespie* wintered, the home of Captain William R. Loutit, built in 1894, had cavernous rooms with high ceilings, several fireplaces, a ballroom, a game room, and living quarters for servants.

But Loutit built it in the days when captains were part owners of ships. The growing heft of vessels meant great sums had to be amassed to finance them. Ships were simply being pushed out of reach of individuals into corporate ownership. The position of master of a steamer typically drew bold and sharp men, who, sensing the changing times, quite easily veered into other lucrative careers.

What that meant for Erickson, who was putting finishing touches on his final application for American citizenship, was that he was going to have to impress another man, and quickly. Before the 1907 season ended, Captain Evans quit to study law at the University of Michigan in Ann Arbor.

Lake men had a saying for when someone retired from the sailing life: He swallowed the anchor.

§§§

About thirty-five miles from the *General Gillespie*, they finally caught the pirate.

He was slinking outside Frankfort, Michigan, while the dredge ship was outside Manistee, one town down the shore. The *Tuscarora*, a maritime law-enforcement speedboat, fired one shot across the deck of the getaway vessel that Saturday afternoon in June 1908. In a final dash to catch the pirate, the *Tuscarora's* boilers steamed so blistering hot that her center-ship smokestack burned all the paint off.

The chase actually began earlier in the month, when a Lake Michigan skipper named Dan Seavey came aboard the schooner yacht *Nellie Johnson* at

Grand Haven, Michigan. The story is, he brought a large amount of liquor aboard, got the crew drunk, and threw them overboard. Somehow he managed to commandeer the vessel with his own crew, planning to sail it to Chicago to sell off its cargo of cedar posts from the Lake Superior region.

Alerted to the theft, the US Revenue Cutter Service, the government's marine police, sent its speedy *Tuscarora* after Seavey. Seavey decided to change ships to evade capture, and he commandeered the two-masted *Wanderer*.

"We had a good description of the *Nellie Johnson* and the *Wanderer*," Captain Preston Ueberroth later told news reporters. "He had a good start, and it was an exciting race, but we finally overtook Seavey and ordered him to lay to."

Ueberroth brought Seavey to Chicago in irons. He had caught him seven miles southwest of Frankfort, Michigan, not quite in sight of the deafening *General Gillespie*. He sent armed deputies aboard with a warrant charging piracy.

§§§

The new captain of the *General Gillespie* was Donald McDonald, born on one of the Thousand Islands, which straddle the US/Canada border. McDonald was of Scotch descent, blunt and outspoken. Before the *General Gillespie*, he was captain of the *Search*, a government survey ship that worked all over the Great Lakes.

At the end of the season, Captain McDonald liked what he saw in Erickson. The captain wrote a short recommendation letter.

> *This is to certify that the bearer, Joseph Mallings Erickson, has been employed on the US Dredge "General Gillespie" for four years, and I take great pleasure in recommending him to you as a sober, honest, industrious young man, and I consider him a very desirable citizen of the United States.*
>
> *Very respectfully,*
> *D.A. McDonald*
> *Master, US Dredge, General Gillespie*

Erickson was on his way to becoming an American, clearing the way to become a nautical officer. To prepare for his exam before the federal government inspectors, he studied engineering texts when he was off watch. A classic and well-advertised textbook was *Questions and Answers for Marine Engineers*, a brick at seven hundred pages. It offered the inquisitive engineer-in-training 807 questions and answers, all for two dollars.

Each day, they raised the Army Corps flag on the *General Gillespie*. From a distance its logo was puzzling; it looked like a capital W. Closer in, one could see it displayed a logo the engineering corps had recently adopted, a turreted medieval castle.

As he finished his application and attached the captain's letter of recommendation, Erickson looked at the Petition for Naturalization. On the question, My Place of Residence, he hesitated. The only place he had lived in America for the past five years was on a ship. He wrote in looping, nearly effeminate, script: US Dredge *Gen. Gillespie.*

After all, as one Norwegian proverb put it, every man's home is his castle.

CHAPTER FIFTEEN

A Thousand Balloons

Something happened on the Sherwin-Williams trip on a Tuesday evening in July of 1907; scuttlebutt was that the *Eastland* nearly capsized. Passenger accounts suggested it had acted just like in the close call near South Haven three years earlier, something no one in Ohio seemed to know anything about. On Lake Erie on July 23, the *Eastland* began to tip one way, then frightened passengers ran to the other side, making it topsy-turvy. Nothing made the papers, but the story would linger in Cleveland, only to resurface some years later at a most inopportune time for the *Eastland* owners.

Catching smatterings of rumors about the ship's safety, the *Eastland*'s Cleveland publicists decided to fight back. Newspaper ads promised "A Week's Pleasure in a Day." And, noting that the *Eastland* was all steel, they adopted a clunky slogan of reassurance, "Won't Sink. Can't Burn."

They also began recruiting heavily among corporate and fraternal groups for summertime outings to Cedar Point, including the Sherwin-Williams Company, the Retail Butcher's Association, and the Brotherhood of Railroad Trainmen.

The promoters stepped up the entertainment for men. A wireless telegraph was installed so passengers could get updates on baseball scores. Several "exotic" dancers were hired, including "Little Egypt," who could jiggle her exposed belly in ways not generally seen before in Ohio.

The Lake Shore Navigation Company also came up with a number of incentives to lure hesitant Clevelanders back to the *Eastland*. It ran a lottery, handing out five thousand picture postcards all over Cleveland. About five hundred of them could be redeemed for one free ride. In the final week of the 1908 season, any woman could ride to Cedar Point for free if she were escorted by a paying man. Three days before the 1909 season opened, the company set off a scramble in town when it released a thousand balloons from the roof of the Cleveland Post Office, each one containing a free ticket to ride the *Eastland*.

The *Eastland*'s reputation was on the mend. On July 4, 1909, the ship carried its largest load of passengers since it had been running out of Cleveland, twenty-five hundred. It was a festive day, and the new captain, Merwin Stone Thompson, stood proudly on the docking bridge just after the last of the passengers had boarded. In his dark captain's suit and bow tie, he was thin, angular, tall, in command of the largest ship of his career.

"I was interested in the *Eastland* and secretly had been wanting an opportunity to handle her," he would later write, "so I was delighted to be appointed her master." That Independence Day, he presided over the unloading of Cedar Point passengers at Cleveland, twenty-five hundred getting off, another twenty-five hundred coming on. It would take about forty-five minutes, and as the new passengers were boarding, some prankster thought it would be funny to yell "fire." Thompson, who kept a leather billy club on hand, ran up and whacked him, and officers escorted the joker to the *Eastland*'s detention room to sleep off the Cedar Point beer.

So many passengers on the *Eastland* at once: twenty-five hundred.

Exactly, inspection officials in Cleveland would later conclude. Many too many.

CHAPTER SIXTEEN

Sleeping on a Volcano

As designed, steamships were floating bombs. The problem began when shipyards thrust not only a teakettle under water, but the whole blazing stove too. It tempted fate, to stoke a submerged furnace into a roar. Fire under water simply wasn't the natural order.

Harnessing the power of heated water had already set in motion the Industrial Revolution, with factory machines thundering and steam locomotives chuffing. The steamship followed, and in a single stroke, humanity was no longer limited by waves and wind. Steam paddle wheelers began crowding rivers, swiftly carrying passengers great distances downstream—and upstream. In the early nineteenth century, they were modern marvels.

Then something horrible started to happen.

On a Friday in April 1838, the *Moselle* was steaming away from Cincinnati toward St. Louis when all four of its boilers exploded. The deck blew into the air, leaving the rest of the *Moselle* in splinters. Pieces of boilers and fragments of human bodies bulleted more than a quarter mile, landing on the Kentucky and Ohio shores. Flung three hundred feet, one man was found with his head crashed through the roof of a house.

Between 1825 and 1848, roughly three thousand people were killed or injured by boiler failures. The superheated boilers usually failed catastrophically because of poorly welded seams, patchy metal strength, or cold water splashing on the scorching plates. When the boilers blew on the *Redstone* on the Ohio River in 1852, the explosion could be heard forty miles away. The heat was hellish. Spoons aboard fused together.

The explosions were spectacular and often in sight of shore, horrifying the public. In one account of the explosion on the *Oliver Evans* in 1817, "the deck was strewn with mangled and writhing human beings . . . six or eight, under the influence of maddening torments, had torn off their clothes, to which the entire skin of their limbs or bodies adhered." When the *Oronoko* exploded on the Mississippi River in 1838, the steam tore through the ship with the force of a tornado, killing more than one hundred passengers as they slept.

Mark Twain's brother, Henry Clemens, died after an explosion on the *Pennsylvania* near Memphis in 1858. Twain, still going by Samuel Clemens, had just left the ship himself days earlier, where he worked as a pilot in training. Otherwise, he would have been on the ill-fated steamboat, robbing American letters of one of its great authors.

The disaster haunted him the rest of his life. "Four of the eight boilers exploded with a thunderous crash," Twain wrote, "and the whole forward third of the boat was hoisted toward the sky! . . . A great many persons had been scalded; a great many crippled; the explosion had driven an iron crowbar through one man's body."

Steamboat companies were terrorizing the public; in developing one of the first large technical advancements for the country, they had accidentally created a weapon of mass destruction.

Insurers steered clear. Their life-coverage policies covered many steamboat risks, including "fires, enemies, pirates, rovers, assailing thieves and all other perils, losses and misfortunes." But Aetna life-insurance policies carried a written disclaimer voiding coverage if the claimant worked anywhere near a steamboat.

Convinced the danger was unavoidable, entrepreneurs tried "safety barges," which divided ships in two: the engines placed on one barge towing another barge with passengers at a safer distance. The Swiftsure line briefly operated such vessels between New York and Albany. "Why sleep over a volcano?" one of its ads asked.

§§§

The frightened public begged officials in Washington for help. Federal oversight of private industry hardly existed. No one had a clue how to proceed. Under pressure to do something, Congress reached for a ridiculous approximation: rules for stagecoach and horse-carriage operators. In 1838, new federal steamboat rules were devised based on that preindustrial, horse-and-buggy model. Inspections were haphazard. Shipowners had to pay the inspector five dollars per inspection. The new oversight covered the provision of lifeboats, signal lights, and fire pumps and hoses, among other things.

The new rules quickly proved useless. Congress would take up the issue again in 1852, with the support of marine engineers terrified of their workplace. It effectively created the Steamboat Inspection Service, charged with setting precise standards for constructing boilers and ships. An army of government inspectors would safeguard against unscrupulous operators, test the boilers and their safety valves, as well as license the captains and engineers.

To put an end to the boiler explosions, the Steamboat Inspection Service employed a staff of nearly three hundred nationwide. It split responsibility for ships, with one inspector monitoring hulls, meaning the general structural integrity of the vessel, and the other overseeing boilers, the tinderboxes for disaster, along with all the other machinery aboard.

Each ship had to have an annual going-over at the hands of the government inspectors. Inspectors were also responsible for investigating all maritime accidents and violations of law within their jurisdictions.

For the busy offices, the Steamboat Inspection Service turned to heavily experienced marine men, sailors who intimately knew the local coves, harbors, rivers, and sandbars. The hectic lower eastern shore of Lake Michigan was the responsibility of the office at Grand Haven, Michigan, and the inspector of hulls was an old captain with a stoop and a sunken face, a stern, severe man: Robert Reid.

CHAPTER SEVENTEEN

Judgment Day

Inspector Reid often meted out maximum penalties. When Reid stepped aboard an excursion motorboat one day and counted only twenty life preservers for the thirty passengers aboard, he immediately suspended the license of the operator, charging gross negligence. To inspect the wooden hull of the *Eugene C. Hart*, he got out on a raft in Benton Harbor, Michigan, and circled the ship, marking stanchions and planks that had to be replaced before he would issue her a permit. Later, he went back to ensure they were swapped out.

He insisted so many repairs be made to four steamers run out of Sheboygan, Wisconsin, that the owners would have gone bankrupt making them. The four ships were retired, adding to an aging armada of wooden schooners, vessels no longer economical to run, left to rot in their harbors. Going to splinters, too, were their elaborate figureheads of yore, the seabirds, mermaids, American eagles—the prow ornaments that for centuries echoed the name of the ship and signaled the wealth and clout of the ship's owners.

Reid ordered other ships practically rebuilt stem to stern, to the great frustration of the owners. When the men who owned the *Robert E. Johnson* sued Reid over his repair orders, the court actually agreed that the inspector was being too strict.

The Reid family was well known on Lake Michigan. Reid's father, also named Robert Reid, was a native of Ireland and had sailed on the ocean early in his life. At twenty-two years old, he immigrated to America, making his way to Michigan, where he was a master on lake vessels for three decades. He owned the scow *Granger*, which he ran between Chicago and various ports along Lake Michigan.

An astute businessman, the elder Robert Reid bought some sixty acres of farmland in Saugatuck, Michigan, where he grew peaches, pears, apples, cherries, and quinces. He had two sons, Alex and Robert, both following their father to sea. They both worked on the steam barge *Marshall F. Buttars*.

While the *Buttars* was tied up at Marinette, Wisconsin, in early May 1894, Alex was crushed to death in a lumber avalanche as he directed the loading of the barge. Alex made no sound as two piles of lumber rolled on top of him. It took fifteen minutes to pull the timber off him.

The sole son, Robert, kept working on the *Buttars*, eventually becoming captain, piloting the steam barge between Chicago and the east shore harbors of Michigan. Some years later, Robert moved to Grand Haven, which had an enormous lumber market. He married and had three daughters. The youngest was born on Christmas Day of 1889; they named her Florence.

§§§

By February of 1909, the *General Gillespie* was back again in Grand Haven, and Erickson scheduled an appointment with Reid, the local inspector of hulls. Erickson felt he was ready to take his exam and be licensed as the third engineer, the lowest-ranking officer below decks. It was the first step in a seven-year apprenticeship that would qualify him for the chief engineer's ticket, second in command, and the ultimate aim of every marine engineer.

Working six to seven days a week for nine months, Erickson had learned the practical side of the engine room deep inside the *General Gillespie* from Chief Engineer Emmet Phillips, who had earned his engineer "ticket" on saltwater. During the Spanish-American War, Phillips was chief engineer on one of the government transports that helped shuttle the American army to Cuba. Erickson looked up to him, as a mentor. Later, they would become confidants.

The theoretical side Erickson taught himself with his textbooks. If he passed, he would be licensed to help repair machinery and keep an eye on the pumps, dynamos, and so on. Captain Reid and his partner, Charles Eckliff, the boiler inspector, would grill Erickson for seven days on horsepower, electricity, steam boilers, and preventing explosions.

Erickson showed a firm command of the material, a natural. Reid and Eckliff were so impressed with his grasp of engineering, in fact, that they took the unusual step of bumping him up a grade. He was licensed not in the typical entry-level post of third assistant engineer, but as a second assistant on ships of any tonnage.

Of the engineer candidates that came Reid's way, there was something about Erickson, something special. He would have other plans for the young man.

Erickson, himself, could not yet head into the winter dreaming about his career promotion and what the next season held in store. Earlier in the year, he finally got word from the Department of Commerce and Labor on his petition for citizenship. It was not what he had hoped for. The bureaucrats quibbled with a ship's being considered a residence.

The correspondence was short and to the point: "The Dredge *General Gillespie*, upon which he had been working, did not come under and within the meaning of the Statute. . . . The petition of the said Joseph Mallings Erickson to become a citizen of the United States is hereby denied."

With that denial, he faced deportation. Having relinquished allegiance to Norway, Erickson was a man without a country. Or a home.

Fury and snakes.

CHAPTER EIGHTEEN

"I Can't Do Anything Like That"

The undercover detective stepped aboard the *Pere Marquette*, a grand steamer licensed to carry five thousand passengers, a little before 5:30 in the evening in South Haven. It was a Sunday in late August, and the ship was headed to Chicago. He milled about with the other passengers, a notebook at the ready. Shortly after they were underway, he went below, to the deck with the staterooms. He stood in place as other passengers shuffled past. After a while, he observed four men go into stateroom No. 66. He noted the room number and kept watch. Two girls visited the room during the crossing.

Down the hall, in stateroom No. 61, he saw one girl go in, and counted four different men visiting the room at different times. He made his way to the bar room. About twenty young girls were drinking beer there; five of them were not over twelve years old. One child, eight, was drinking beer with older people.

Such a rumpus afloat. Such dens of sin.

These were among the findings of the 1911 report by Chicago's newly formed vice patrol. Its official title: "The Social Evil in Chicago: A Study of Existing Conditions with Recommendations by the Vice Commission of Chicago." It came at the urging of citizen groups including the Anti-Cigarette League, the Anti-Saloon League, the Chicago Refuge for Girls, and Jane Addams's Hull House.

A year earlier, the commission sent out dozens of undercover investigators into Chicago's streets, brothels, saloons, and movie houses. The Vice Commission wanted to map out where crime was happening and to make a complete census of all houses of ill repute. What the census found was stunning: The city had five thousand full-time prostitutes and 192 houses of prostitution, with 2,343 rooms, 1,012 call girls, and 189 madams or keepers.

The final report would include specific sections on the relation of prostitutes to whiskey, morphine, cocaine, murder, and theft.

The commission estimated that in 1910, in Chicago, prostitution was a $5.5 million industry.

And then there were those lake boats. They were long suspected of debauchery, with easily available staterooms and heaven only knows what behind their closed doors.

Among steamships, the one the vice commission simply called X1044 was "the worst." The names of individuals and particular establishments or vessels were withheld, in favor of cataloguing them with numbers and letters. However, the report imprudently revealed just enough details to identify some offenders. It mentioned, for instance, that X1044 carried five thousand passengers on the Chicago–South Haven run. And it mentioned exact arrival and departure times, helping narrow the possibilities to one: the *Pere Marquette*.

The anecdotes on the steamers piled up. On the afternoon of July 2, 1910, an investigator left Chicago for South Haven on Ship X1050. Two girls and two boys were sitting in front of stateroom No. 20. One of the girls refused to enter, saying, "I ain't no saint, but I can't do anything like that." Later her companions persuaded her to enter the room. They did not come out during the entire trip.

It was clear that an anti-prostitution law passed the year earlier wasn't working. Under it, violators using any watercraft for prostitution faced prison time of one to three years and a fine of up to one thousand dollars.

A stronger provision was needed. Congressman James Mann later that year would sponsor federal legislation to criminalize interstate transportation of women for "immoral" activity. In just a few years, a noted Chicago architect, Frank Lloyd Wright, would become ensnared by the Mann Act. And to rescue him, he would call on Clarence Darrow.

§§§

Mayor Harrison, now in his fifth term, had to acknowledge it: Chicago had become a sewer. The new City Hall building, a majestic pillared building with granite relief panels and marble stairs, was a symbol of government power, the institution that intended to take back the streets.

From the eleven-story building, modeled in classical revival style, the mayor publicly closed the Everleigh brothel, amid protests from some police officials. Eyeing the movie houses that had started up recently, city hall began strictly censoring all films exhibited in Chicago. No film was to be shown without the approval of the general superintendent of police. A city ordinance on candy stores and ice-cream parlors banned owners from allowing males under twenty-one and females under eighteen from remaining in the shops between 10:00 p.m. and 7:00 a.m.

And the sweet shops were further forbidden from having curtains, screens, or partitions of any kind, with fines of five to one hundred dollars per offense. Court records showed that many young girls, according to the vice report, "have been ruined in such places." A Morals Court was about to be formed. In its first year, it would hear five thousand cases, often attended by lurid curiosity seekers.

It was a city in a hurry, with the trains of twenty-six railroad companies chuffing crisscross daily. The air was heavy dark noxious smoke coal dust. There wasn't even a single word for it, but someone would soon coin a short term combining smoke and fog.

Automobiles were beginning to roll onto the streets, horns braying. "Scorchers," or speed-devils, were menacing. "Something must be done about those fellows who run their machines 10 to 20 miles an hour," an angry Mayor Harrison proclaimed. "I'm in favor of compelling the gears of all machines to be not above 8 miles an hour."

A different kind of scorcher was the Western Electric Company. With electricity creeping into daily lives, it was well on its way to becoming the largest employment site in all of Chicago, with some eighteen thousand workers. Since it was on the outskirts of the city, it had to create many services for its large workforce living right nearby. It opened Hawthorne Hospital, staffed with nurses, as well as a library and a building and loan to help many of its working-class employees buy homes. The factory site also had a ballpark, a gym, and its own rail line. It was called the Manufacturer's Junction Railway, and with twenty-seven freight cars it ran supplies in and finished goods out.

The candlestick phone was the company's breadwinner, made from 201 parts that had to be delicately assembled. The company, which had a lock on phone manufacturing, would have seven hundred thousand of them on order in America in 1910 alone. The rest of the world wanted in too, with Italy and China placing orders. Oceangoing freighters carried spools of telephone cable tall as men and emblazoned with WESTERN ELECTRIC COMPANY circled around them.

Given the phenomenal demand for phones, the Chicago company had to scour the globe for materials. Platinum, for telephone transmitters, came from the Ural Mountains in Russia. Silk was from Italy. Iron, for magnets, from Norway. Rubber was Brazilian. It took resources from seven countries to complete a single phone call.

One visitor to the Hawthorne factory described it as "a mad waltz of spindles that whirl silk and cotton threads and copper wires." He added: "Wire is big here. Some is fashioned into fantastic shapes, like absurd sea-monsters, and, are, in fact, the nerve systems of switchboards. Some is twisted into cables with a dozen whirling drums, which is a dizzying sight, as each pair spins in opposite directions."

The world was changing, and it wasn't easy to find work with the old-world handcraft talent of James Novotny, the cabinetmaker from Bohemia. He managed to find a job, though, at Western Electric. He worked in Department 4930, which handled woodworking for the telephone company, under foreman George Goyette.

Novotny's two children were growing, and James moved the family of four into a house on West 24th Place, near enough to the Hawthorne Works to see the black smoke billowing from its smokestacks. He bought the home and started paying toward his total mortgage of one thousand dollars.

Life was grand. And the perks kept coming. The next year the company was going to start annual picnics for all eighteen thousand workers. For the company known for doing even small things in a big way, those occasions would grow so grand that Western Electric would soon need to charter steamboats.

CHAPTER NINETEEN

The Bargain

Out on Lake Erie, meanwhile, the *Eastland* was bleeding money. The ship hadn't made a penny in its nearly four years there. The reputation was poor for the self-advertised "Won't Sink" ship. So the owners decided to address the jinx head-on.

They ordered quite extraordinary half-page advertisements offering in bold capitals a $5,000 REWARD in the *Cleveland Plain Dealer* and the *Cleveland Leader* in August 1910.

The ad, a convoluted essay that ran 286 words, first talked up the *Eastland*'s attributes: all-steel, water compartments that carry eight hundred tons of ballast, two powerful propellers, and on and on.

"The material she is built of," it continued in wooden prose, "the type of her construction, together with the power in her hold, makes her the staunchest, fastest and safest boat devoted to pleasure on the Great Lakes."

For those who stayed with it, the ad then noted that someone had "put into circulation stories to the effect that the Steamer *Eastland* is not safe." It suggested competitors were viciously spreading the rumors.

Some four hundred thousand people had enjoyed themselves on the *Eastland*, the ad noted, "without a single mishap." And it spelled out who could collect the five-thousand-dollar jackpot: "any persons that will bring forth a naval engineer, a marine architect, a ship builder, or anyone qualified to pass judgment on the merits of a ship, who will say that the steamer *Eastland* is not a seaworthy ship."

The ad, of course, omitted a couple things. The *Eastland* had changed owners the prior season, the original group only too happy to unload it to a new investor with railroad interests. And one of the directors of a Cleveland bank had tried in vain to stop the loan for the *Eastland*'s purchase; based on his experience booking steamships in Cleveland, he was convinced the *Eastland* was not seaworthy.

§§§

Life was about to speed up for Erickson, who seemed content to stay with his trusted mentor, Chief Engineer Phillips, on the Army Corps dredge. After all, it was home. Perhaps because of his government service, working for the Army's Corps of Engineers, Erickson was able to appeal his citizenship ruling. It was reversed. He was an American. All was set.

Erickson's ship, the *General Gillespie*, had to rename itself following a new War Department order that no government ship should be named for a living officer. The new name would be the *General Meade*, for the onetime commander of federal forces at the battle of Gettysburg.

The ship picked up a mascot that season, a fox terrier they found bobbing in an unmanned rowboat nearby. He joined another newcomer. With his assistant engineer's credentials, Erickson used some pull to get his brother, Peter, hired on the dredge as an oiler. Joseph had summoned his fifteen-year-old brother from Norway, encouraging him to take up the seafaring life with him. Joseph could teach Peter the ins and outs of oiling. He could take care of his brother as he learned to maneuver the engine room's treacherous lower ends, where the pistons and crankshaft meet.

Joseph Erickson had learned quite a few tricks out on the lakes. The constant vacuuming of sand between piers was punishing on the machinery. When repairs were needed to the *Meade*'s propeller bearings outside Muskegon one day, the crew conducted a maneuver called "tipping ship."

They filled the forward water-ballast compartments below decks with water, plunging the *General Meade*'s nose into the water so low that the propellers were raised above the waterline. Then the engineers could row up close and repair them.

The *General Meade* was at anchor in deep water, standing nearly on its head, its forward deck completely submerged and its stern high in the air. It looked like it was going down by the head.

People out on rowboats and hotels along shore became alarmed, certain the ship was sinking. People started shouting:

"Are you sinking, captain?"

"Jump in and swim for it!"

Small boats came to the rescue from all sides. The crew of the *General Meade* was amused that the repair maneuver had so alarmed people, and went about their duties as if nothing were wrong. In time, the people who had rushed over to help became miffed by the stunt. They rowed away angrily.

As the summer was ending, when blueberry picking in Michigan turned to apple-cider season, the men went ashore one day in Muskegon. The puppy ventured too far away, and they lost him.

The ship's mascot had vanished, and Joseph Erickson was not far behind.

§§§

Her obituary was strangely short:

Ida Walter Steele, wife of Julius, died suddenly Monday morning at Kenwood hotel. Funeral services at the home of her brother, Alfred Walter. Burial private.

This for a woman whose comings and goings, summer vacations to Connecticut and Maine, her bridge club and luncheons, all routinely made Chicago's social columns, like "The Whirl of Society."

She and Julius had been married thirty-four years. Her full, maiden name was Ida Ophelia Walter, and she and her husband used her maiden surname, Walter, for their firstborn son.

In just the past three years, the stature of Julius Steele had risen substantially. He was promoted from treasurer to president of Atwood & Steele, whose reach of products had grown beyond Chicago and Illinois into Michigan and elsewhere.

Steele shepherded a small delegation to Chicago mayor Fred Busse's office to oppose installation of a new streetcar line, which they argued would be noisy and a danger to neighborhood children. His own son, Blair, of course, lost both legs to a streetcar.

Shortly before Ida's death, the Steeles had just begun summering in St. Joseph, Michigan, a sunny resort town on a sixty-foot bluff overlooking Lake Michigan. Returning to his boyhood stomping grounds, Julius Steele bought 105 acres of rich farmland. Along with fruit orchards he had planted for recreation, he had three horses and eight cattle.

Walter, now twenty-nine, followed his parents out there. He did not seem to be interested in his father's business in Chicago, but something about St. Joseph attracted him. Out there he met a local girl, Lulu Mielkie, nine years younger than he. They married in September of 1911. When Julius returned to tend to business in Chicago, Walter stayed.

Walter's oversight of the orchards financed by his father would connect Walter with the big docking operation at St. Joseph, the E. A. Graham docks, run by William Harvey Hull. The two men were interested in the surging fruit business in the surrounding area of Berrien County. In time, they would begin searching for a cargo ship to run out of St. Joseph. They would soon hear there was a bargain out in Cleveland, a ship called the *Eastland*.

CHAPTER TWENTY

Playing with Fire

Four days before Thanksgiving, 1912, on its way to Chicago with more than three hundred tons of spiky cargo, the beloved Christmas Tree Ship sank. The *Rouse Simmons* was off the coast of Two Rivers, Wisconsin, when she went down in a storm. Captain Schuenemann and a partner, Captain Charles Nelson, along with the rest of the schooner's crew, disappeared. Chicagoans were heartbroken.

Within weeks, Captain Schuenemann's widow and his daughter, Elsie, following in her father's footsteps, arranged for trees to be sent by rail to Chicago. They placed them for sale on the schooner *Oneida,* moored at the foot of the Clark Street Bridge, for sale through the Christmas season of 1912. People warmly bought from the surviving Schuenemanns.

That winter, Clarence Darrow had a wreck of his own to contend with. And it distantly involved his mistress. Five years into his marriage to Ruby, he took up with Mary Field, a leftist reporter he met in the spring of 1908. Her radicalism developed from her working with immigrants in settlement houses in Chicago. Sixteen years younger than he, she admired his progressivism, his stature.

That November of 1912, Field was in Indianapolis, reporting on a trial for a socialist newspaper. Darrow was in Los Angeles, on trial for bribing jurors and facing imprisonment. At one point, Field had come out to cover his trial, to console him, but he hadn't seen her in some time. And his outlook was grim.

"I shall not go back out east until this is over, whenever and however that may be," he wrote to her. "I have lived, and life at its best is short. . . . The future will justify us all, but we won't be here."

Darrow had put himself in hot water. He had accepted a union-financed commission to defend two brothers, John and James McNamara, charged with dynamiting the *Los Angeles Times* building in the fall of 1910. Someone planted a suitcase with sixteen sticks of dynamite, and twenty employees died in the terrorist bombing of the notoriously antiunion newspaper.

Labor relations around the country had become a war, with companies routinely hiring private detectives to spy on union organizers, to subvert their activities, even to kidnap them. The brothers in the newspaper bombing, in fact, had been kidnapped by gumshoes hired to bring them to Los Angeles for trial. Some union men felt they needed to resort to terrorist methods, even fatal violence, to even hope to compete against the riches of corporations.

In defending the brothers, Darrow used a favorite tactic: blame something else. In this case, that would mean an alternate reason for the blast. The explosion wasn't caused by dynamite, he said, but by a gas leak. As the trial wore on and the gas theory grew less convincing, Darrow felt he would have to resort to drama. To prove he was right, he vowed to bring into the courtroom a model of the newspaper building for a reenactment to demonstrate just how it exploded.

He ordered a replica of the *Los Angeles Times* building, with a scaled-down printing press, linotype machines, and desks. The defense team spent thousands of dollars making the model, but whenever they blew it up, their experiment proved the opposite, that it probably was caused by dynamite, not gas.

Meanwhile, Darrow grew more dubious about the men he was defending. Facing what seemed to be an open-and-shut case by prosecutors, Darrow persuaded the brothers to plead guilty rather than face the death penalty. The labor leaders who hired Darrow felt betrayed.

Prosecutors weren't satisfied though. They were convinced Darrow had, through an accomplice, attempted to pay off a juror before the men had pleaded guilty. And so they brought Darrow to trial.

By August 1912, Darrow had made a passionate, and unusual, plea to the jury.

"Suppose you thought I was guilty, suppose you thought so . . . would you dare to say by your verdict that scoundrels like [the district attorney] should be saved from their own sins, by charging those sins to someone else?" They played dirty, so why can't I? the lawyer argued. I was just fighting the devil with fire.

Later, he argued, "Here is a contest between two parties in litigation; the prosecution has a right to load us up with spies and detectives and informers, and we cannot put anyone in their office. Now, what do you think of that? Do any of you believe it?"

In his summations for other cases, Darrow would portray his clients, labor or otherwise, with the qualities he admired, traits a jury would warm to: courage and self-sacrifice. Standing before the jurors in Los Angeles, Darrow now reached for that approach to save himself.

"I have committed one crime for which I cannot be forgiven. I have stood for the weak and the poor," he told them. "I have stood for the men who toil."

Against overwhelming evidence of his guilt, the jury ended up acquitting him, apparently swayed by the idea that Darrow's underhanded tactics were no worse than the prosecution's.

Friends and associates suspected that Darrow had beaten legitimate charges; that, in his zeal to defend labor as a grand cause, he justified jury tampering among other improprieties. He was the champion of individuals. He needed to protect them at any cost from the enemy, the vast impersonal institutions constructed by well-heeled industrialists.

His onetime law partner, future poet Edgar Lee Masters, thought Darrow clearly sacrificed the McNamara brothers to save himself. Upon Darrow's return to Chicago, Masters would later write: "I suspected at the time what I afterward was sure from all the facts, namely that he pleaded his client guilty in order to escape prosecution himself. . . . I wanted nothing to do with his case. I did not want my name mentioned with his."

His mistress was circumspect. Field would later admit that she investigated the jury in the McNamara case on behalf of her boyfriend. "As to his 'guilt,'" she would confide to a Darrow biographer, "none of those close to him ever questioned; and it made no difference. Certainly he was not guilty in any larger conception of justice."

Prosecutors in Los Angeles considered bringing Darrow to trial again for misconduct in defending the dynamiters.

He sank further. "What in the hell should I be worried about?" he wrote to Field, from Minnesota, where he was lecturing. "If I went to prison, I would have a room bigger than the very little box that I will lie in for Ever after a very few years."

He quoted a couplet by the poet A. C. Swinburne in the letter:

Even the weariest river
Winds somewhere safe to sea

And then Darrow added, "And the sea is death and annihilation."

§§§

In the smallest hours of his life, the broken lawyer returned home. Darrow had arrived back home in Chicago in 1913 in a hard place. His face never looked older. At age fifty-six, he discovered that he had fewer friends than he thought and even less money. He had been paid handsomely, forty-eight thousand dollars, for the McNamara case, but he spent it all defending himself.

Crestfallen, Darrow decided to leave law behind and spend the rest of his time on lectures and literature. At home in South Chicago, he plopped into a wicker rocker and said nothing to his wife for a time.

"Well, Rube," he finally said, "it kinda looks like our lawyering days are over."

He started using a typewriter, and punched out this passage to a friend: "I have heard a good many literary fellows say that they could write better by using a typewriter; so it had recently occurred to me that this is just what I lacked, so I am practicing on my friends and here goes with you."

An old acquaintance whom Darrow had met at socialist meetings in Chicago came back into his life. Peter Sissman, a Russian immigrant with a lazy eye, heard that Darrow was contemplating quitting legal work. Sissman went to visit him. "You must not," Sissman told his older mentor. "If you remain in Chicago and don't open your office, it is a tacit admission of guilt."

"But I have no practice," Darrow replied.

CHAPTER TWENTY-ONE

A Sickly Daughter

His engineer's credentials burning through his pocket, and no opening in the engine room on the *Meade*, Erickson finally had to look elsewhere. He was a citizen, safe from deportation and clear to proceed up the engineer ranks. There was an opening on the *Ashtabula*, a railroad-car ferry.

Like other freight ships, it was very spacious in the middle, the cargo hold. At 338 feet long and fifty-six feet wide, the *Ashtabula* was nearly double the ship that the old *General Gillespie* was. Erickson took a job as second assistant engineer of the ship known as "The Pride of Ashtabula."

The ship ran a dull route, shuttling back and forth the same forty-seven-mile course between Ashtabula, Ohio, on the south shore of Lake Erie, and on the north shore, Port Burwell, Ontario.

The chief engineer asked Erickson to take an exam to become a first assistant engineer. He passed the test before Inspector Reid, and two days later was promoted to that position. Working his way up, Erickson brought aboard his brother, Peter, again as an oiler.

The news was all over Ohio that fall, that the steamship *Alice* had exploded on the Ohio River, near Glenfield, Pennsylvania. The ship was seven hundred yards from the locks when the boilers exploded, one whistling like a missile fifteen hundred feet through the air, landing on Neville Island. Among the dead were the captain, the mate, the chief engineer, a fireman, a watchman, and a female cook.

The *Ashtabula* returned to its Ohio port town each night, with the docks full of girls and women waiting for their fathers and husbands. Erickson had no one waiting for him. He started looking for another ship for the 1913 season.

§§§

Erickson and his brother switched to the *C. W. Watson*, virtually the same size as the *Ashtabula*. While Joseph's position was the same, first assistant engineer, the *C. W. Watson* was owned by the Tomlinson fleet. With twenty-five vessels, it was a formidable freight shipper, based in Duluth, Minnesota. A job with Tomlinson would mean many opportunities for advancement and much wider travel than pacing the same bitty stretch of Lake Erie.

In March, Erickson took the step he'd been working up to for years. He appeared again before Inspectors Reid and Eckliff in Grand Haven. This time, he was there to take his final exam, the one to become chief engineer. After several days of questions, Reid and Eckliff conferred the coveted "engineer's ticket" on Erickson. He walked away with papers to be chief engineer, "all tonnage, lake, bay and sound." He was finally qualified to head any engine room on the Great Lakes.

The next few months gave way to fall, always treacherous on the lakes, and 1913 was worse than usual. Early November brought what came to be called the Big Blow, which raged across the lakes over four days. Hellish winds of sixty miles per hour blew for hours, occasionally kicking up to seventy and more. In the gales of November, thirty-five ships were demolished, some never heard from again. Wreckage floated to the shores for weeks afterward.

A disaster fund was started for the families of the 254 victims of the storm, mostly officers and crew. The Disaster Fund reached $68,149, largely raised from the thousands of workers who manned freight and passenger vessels. From the *C. W. Watson*, Erickson donated five dollars, the same as the better-compensated captain.

§§§

In his Grand Haven offices, Inspector Reid had now seen this promising young man, Erickson, for three years running. Sometime after Erickson passed his final exam, Reid got to thinking. His daughter was getting up in years, twenty-three. He had been concerned about her. She was short, curly haired, and cute, but sickly. With no man in Florence's life, her parents had sent her off the year before to study at the Muskegon Business College.

Reid would periodically send Florence money with a short letter on Steamboat Inspection Service stationery. Ever cautious, the inspector never enclosed more than five dollars at a time, just in case the envelope was lost or stolen. Sometimes he would include little math riddles, other times updates on the family in Grand Haven. After his own father passed away, the family decided to sell the old farm. "I am painting and fixing up every chance that I get, but it is slow work, a few minutes, night, noon and morning," he wrote to her. "I hope that the place will be sold for I am sick of the thing."

With a matrimonial view, he got to thinking about his daughter and this freshly minted chief engineer. Joseph Erickson and Florence met a few days before Christmas in 1913. Soon after, their love affair would touch off scandal.

CHAPTER TWENTY-TWO

"A Mr. Hull Is on the Line"

By all accounts, the *Eastland* was a rotten business. During its seven seasons on Lake Erie, the "Queen of the Lakes" ran through five captains. The longest tenured was Captain Thompson, whose run with the ship would prove memorable simply because there were no notable mishaps on his watch.

Eventually, Thompson was replaced by George L. Phillips, whose misfortunes were swift. He and the *Eastland* company's general manager were arrested for allowing gambling on board. Caught up in the district attorney's campaign to stamp out slot machines on lake steamers, they had to pay one thousand dollars bail each to avoid being jailed.

In the same sweep, deputy marshals removed sixteen coin slot machines from the *Eastland*. They posted a deputy marshal for the rest of the trip, and threatened to keep one on board all summer to ensure compliance. The marshals shut down a dime-a-turn spinning wheel, with a box of candy as the payout.

§§§

The world had reeled months earlier with the news of the sinking of the *Titanic,* on April 15, 1912. The mammoth ship, nearly nine hundred feet long, had struck an iceberg, and the "unsinkable" ocean-liner foundered in the twilight. About eight hundred passengers and seven hundred crewmembers perished in the freezing Atlantic Ocean. The ill-fated ship, bound for New York on its maiden voyage, had enough lifeboats for only about half of those on board.

Two weeks later, the Steamboat Inspection Service issued an advisory to its inspectors nationwide, recommending they be conservative with how many passengers they allowed aboard vessels in relation to available lifeboats.

Setting appropriate limits on passenger capacity was up to local inspectors and could vary year to year, or even from inspector to inspector. When Cleveland inspectors Thomas W. Gould and James McGrath reconsidered the *Eastland* that year, they decided its current capacity of twenty-four hundred was too hazardous—but not because of the lifeboats aboard.

Rather, they were concerned about the ship's dependence on its water-ballast system. To make the *Eastland* safer, less reliant on its sometimes sluggish ballast equipment, the inspectors decided to reduce its passenger capacity to two thousand. Then Nils Nelson, the supervising inspector for the district, personally spoke with Captain Phillips and Chief Engineer Grant Donaldson, giving them this warning: "Be careful and tend to the water ballast."

The warning seemed to have helped. The following season started quietly enough. Then on July 9, 1913, as the *Eastland* was returning to Cedar Point from Cleveland, Captain Phillips doubled over in pain. Using a wireless radio, the crew notified the port in Cleveland that they were headed back. An ambulance rushed the captain to the hospital. Doctors discovered his appendix had burst. They operated, but the next day the captain passed.

As the season ended, the *Eastland* had run up losses of $175,000 to $200,000 between 1907 and 1913. Running with an unusually large crew, hampered by heavy debt, carrying virtually no freight, the *Eastland* proved unprofitable.

Then the manager of the Eastland Navigation Company in Cleveland heard from a Mr. Hull out in St. Joseph, Michigan. Would they be willing to sell the *Eastland*?

§§§

Only ten survivors of the steamer *Sultana* explosion were able to attend the annual survivors' reunion, in Toledo, Ohio, in April of 1914. In the deadliest maritime disaster in US history, some seventeen hundred people died. They were mostly Union veterans, recently released prisoners of Confederate forces. They were headed home from the Civil War when the boilers blew in late April of 1865.

As the overloaded ship struggled against the current around two o'clock in the morning, the boilers blew, and the *Sultana* was afire seven miles up the river from Memphis. One second the veterans were asleep, the next they found themselves splashing in the freezing Mississippi River.

Usually the name of a ship that had been through such a public disaster would be retired. "Sultana," though, had been an appealing name for sailors. It meant a concubine or a mistress for a sultan. The cursed name *Sultana*, for whatever reason, had been resurrected by the Tomlinson line in 1902, when it built a 353-feet-long, forty-eight-feet-wide steel freighter.

Going into the 1914 season, old man Tomlinson seemed impressed with his first engineer on the *C. W. Watson*, Joseph Erickson. George Ashley Tomlinson, a Minnesota shipping magnate, decided to promote the young man to chief engineer on the *Sultana*.

The shipping line reached out to Erickson, who was wintering in Grand Haven. While there, Erickson had begun courting Inspector Reid's daughter Florence, who was working at the Grand Haven Baking Company. Saturday at the bakery was cream puff day.

The pride of Grand Haven was the Story & Clark Company, an immense three-story piano factory in the downtown district. At its peak, it would employ an army of five hundred workers, in a town of about five thousand. One longtime superintendent of the factory was elected mayor of Grand Haven.

Demand for workers was so high every person in town either worked for the piano factory or knew someone who did: music, to many ears. Keeping jobs filled, though, was a chore. The factory would have no problem, in fact, retaining one man on the payroll even though he faced charges in the wrongful deaths of hundreds of people.

CHAPTER TWENTY-THREE

"Goodbye, Everybody"

About the time Florence Reid and Joseph Erickson were engaged, he had to ship out on the *Sultana*. It was a difficult time for his intended. Beginning in the winter, Florence had found herself short of breath, feverish, wheezing in pain. She was suffering from pleurisy, a painful inflammation around the lungs. Ailing and lonely, she missed her fiancé.

The freight ship was to disappear for months, running on three of the Great Lakes. With Erickson fully in command of the engine room, the *Sultana* ran coal to Ashtabula in Ohio, spring wheat from Duluth, Minnesota, oats to Cleveland. It traveled to the port of Detroit, through the Soo locks over and over and all throughout Lakes Erie, Huron, and Superior.

Erickson was a full officer. Men called him sir—and didn't address him unless he spoke first. His one trapping of the professional class: his own desk.

He had a flawless first year as chief engineer. There were no glitches for the *Sultana*, giving Erickson ample time to instruct his assistant engineers in just how he wanted things run. Like many freight ships recently built, the *Sultana* had a "double bottom," which contained water-ballast tanks.

At any given point, Erickson would have asked his men how full the ballast tanks were, and an assistant would "sound" the tank, using a dipstick. They would then chalk the readings onto a small blackboard in the engine room. Depending on conditions, Erickson could order more water in the forward, aft, port, or starboard tanks. The system allowed the engineer to roll and tilt the ship. A little more in the No. 6 forward, for instance, would be a typical order. Or, bring her to eight feet in the No. 2 tank.

The variable ballast also allowed Erickson to adjust height when loading, whether ore or any other heavy cargo. There was such competition to load quickly and get underway that some crews paid bribes, "beer money," to loaders to hasten things along. In the rush to move freight, too, there were mishaps. When a freight ship occasionally ran into and cracked a concrete dock, it was not unusual for the crew to splash water on the spot quickly. That way the damage did not look new.

There were always patrolmen at the docks, looking for something amiss. Near the Soo locks that year, the patrollers found a bottle with a piece of paper bedaubed with grease prints inside. When they retrieved it, they found that it told of the final moments of the *Henry B. Smith*, which had headed into the terrific storm of the previous November and was never heard from again. The note was signed simply, *Oiler.*

Sunday morning—To the Hagwood company, Cleveland, finder please forward. The Henry B. Smith broke in two, opposite No. 5 hatch about 12 miles east of Marquette. We are having an awful time.

§§§

Hundreds of people clutching their *Eastland* tickets crowded around the E. A. Graham docks as evening approached on July 3, 1914, eager to start their holiday weekend. The ship was supposed to depart from St. Joseph, Michigan, at 5:00 p.m. As the hour neared, no *Eastland.*

The ticketholders milled around the dock, checking their watches, heads craning into the harbor. Eventually, company representatives showed up at the dock to spread the word, the *Eastland* was being repaired; it wouldn't run at all that weekend. The crowds filed away, annoyed, angry, their Fourth of July spoiled.

The company men did not reveal how seriously the *Eastland* had been damaged.

The St. Joseph-Chicago Steamship Company had only owned the ship about a month, and the new managers didn't want the bad publicity of missing the all-important July 4th weekend. They also could not afford to forgo all that crucial ticket revenue. They had already advertised two extra roundtrips that weekend between Chicago and St. Joseph, and the papers in both cities carried ads showing scheduled *Eastland* departures on July 3, 4, and 5.

The managers spent days scrambling to find a substitute ship, but every other one was booked. At the last minute, they had no choice but to walk onto the docks to inform the hapless passengers.

The season of 1914 was to become the worst the *Eastland* had to that point. And the two men responsible for running it, despite being named Steele and Hull, had no idea what they were doing.

Walter C. Steele and William H. Hull, who lived in St. Joseph, had teamed up to buy the *Eastland* in the winter of 1913. They were forced to. The Graham & Morton Transportation Company, one of the largest steamship operators on Lake Michigan, had just decided to defect from St. Joseph and concentrate its business at its headquarters town one mile away, Benton Harbor.

That left St. Joseph, a resort town that billed itself as "the Coney Island of the West," without a steamship serving it. And the hotels and mineral spas in St. Joseph relied on tens of thousands of visitors each summer, primarily from Chicago, sixty miles away on Lake Michigan. In the meantime, there were many farmers who were suddenly left high and dry.

The enmity between the sister towns, separated by the St. Joseph River, was historic. St. Joseph was the smaller of the two, with about seven thousand people. While St. Joseph was a magnet for leisure, Benton Harbor, with twelve thousand people, was a town consumed by manufacturing, with eighteen hundred employed in factories, and many more to follow.

People in St. Joseph derisively called Benton Harbor "Bungtown." Groups of boys meeting out on the river while ice-skating would remove their skates and swing blades at one another in fights. There were fierce baseball games between the Benton Harbor Wolverines and the St. Joseph Mutuals. At one point, St. Joseph sent a delegation to the Michigan capital of Lansing to oppose the granting of a city charter to Benton Harbor.

So when Graham & Morton dumped St. Joseph, it was not a great surprise. But with grave concern all over St. Joseph about their fruit and tourism markets, Steele and Hull saw opportunity. What if they brought St. Joseph its own ship?

For Hull it was also a matter of livelihood. He had married into money. His mother-in-law, Edwina Graham, was rich from her family's connections to the Graham & Morton line. She was part owner of the E. A. Graham docks in St. Joseph, the very ones Graham & Morton left forlorn. Hull had married Edwina Graham's daughter, May Graham, who was a regent of the St. Joseph office of the Daughters of the American Revolution. Through that nepotism, Hull obtained the job of managing the docks at St. Joseph. With Graham & Morton gone, Hull was out of work.

It appears Steele used his father's money to help bring a steamer to St. Joseph. Though he had quite a receding hairline, Walter was only thirty-one years old then and had no record of employment either in Chicago or St. Joseph. Yet he quickly coughed up a stunning thirty thousand dollars to help buy a new ship for the town.

Hull and Steele heard that the *Eastland*, which had been running on Lake Erie, was a bargain, that the bank that financed its purchase was leaning on the owners to sell the ship. Hull went out to Cleveland in 1913 and took a trip on the *Eastland*. He was impressed.

But he and Steele knew nothing about steamships, so they employed a former Chicago harbormaster to inspect it and make recommendations. Walter Scott reported back that the *Eastland* was a fine ship.

Steele and Hull then went out to Cleveland together to look the *Eastland* over. The ship was tied to its dock for the winter of 1913. "It was a fearful day," Hull recalled, "snowing and cold."

They began negotiating. They quickly grew nervous. This was their best prospect, and two other parties were interested in buying it.

The two men from St. Joseph negotiated all winter. Then Steele went out to Cleveland in April and signed papers to buy the *Eastland* for a handsome $150,000. The bank in Cleveland was thrilled; Hull and Steele felt they had paid low. To finance it, they planned to offer $150,000 in bonds. Steele immediately picked up three hundred, or thirty thousand dollars' worth of them, making him the largest shareholder in the new St. Joseph-Chicago Steamship Company, which would own the ship. Hull's wife, May, and her mother each bought 140. Walter's crippled brother, Blair, bought fifty. Julius Steele, their father, had three.

Still, there was a problem. Steele and Hull remained about twenty thousand dollars short. They managed to sign a contract to buy a ship they did not have enough money for. And with the deadline for paying up looming, they faced losing the *Eastland*.

Working with the daily newspaper in town, the two men got a top-of-the-front-page placement for an advertisement. The headline was Mass Meeting Tonight of Vital Interest to the People of St. Joseph. The plan was to throw open the doors to the Tabernacle, an auditorium at the corner of Main and Ship Streets, and beg for money.

"The moral support of every citizen of St. Joseph is needed," the earnest ad said. "United action is imperative. Immediate action is necessary. Attend the Mass Meeting and Help St. Joseph Grow."

Over two hundred businessmen and citizens showed up that evening in the Tabernacle. The mass meeting was sponsored by officers of the St. Joseph improvement company, fearing the deal for the *Eastland* would fall through. With thick dark hair and cellars for eyes, Hull told the group that they still needed some twenty thousand dollars to close the deal. "We are strictly up against it," he warned.

Captain Scott, billed as a steamship expert, took the floor. He explained that during the winter he had inspected the *Eastland* in detail. The captain made two vows that he would back up with "money, chalk or marbles." One, the speedy *Eastland* could cut a half hour each way off the St. Joseph–Chicago run. Two, it could carry five hundred passengers on average on the run for one hundred days during the excursion season.

"The name *Eastland* is a prestige in Chicago," Captain Scott said. "You must help yourself to get this steamer for St. Joseph."

Hull agreed, adding that the *Eastland* could actually carry two hundred thousand people a season, with a profit, he suggested, of nearly one hundred thousand dollars.

Hull asked Clarence Blake to make some remarks. Blake was co-owner of the Hotel Whitcomb with his father-in-law. The hotel was situated on the bluff at St. Joseph, with a commanding view of Lake Michigan, just above the E. A. Graham docks where the *Eastland* would park. The Hotel Whitcomb had mineral baths where the rheumatic and sick came to convalesce. Teddy Roosevelt, among other dignitaries, stayed there. The hotel had much to lose if the *Eastland* got away, from his point of view.

Blake, who had become friends with Walter Steele, simply said it wasn't time for talk, but for action. The chairman of the development board asked: "Who in this meeting will subscribe $1,000 in stock in the St. Joseph-Chicago Steamship Company?"

"Drake & Wallace will," immediately replied L. J. Drake.

"Murphy & Morrison," called out W. F. Murphy.

Peer pressure set in. More pledges.

The *St. Joseph Evening Herald* gave an additional push following the meeting. "The acquisition of the steamer is vital to St. Joseph's interests," it said, "and failure, when the goal is so near, only a few thousand dollars away, would be disastrous."

The fund-raiser paid off. The St. Joseph-Chicago Steamship Company had scraped together the final twenty thousand dollars, and by mid-June, Walter Steele was off to Cleveland to collect the *Eastland*. In Benton Harbor, heavy rain and unusually warm weather that summer meant baskets bursting with strawberries, cherries, melons, and peaches, the most productive acreage that season in all of Michigan.

Steele sent a telegram to Hull:

EASTLAND DEPARTS CLEVELAND.
IN ST. JOE IN 48 HRS.

The return to Lake Michigan, the original waters of the *Eastland*, was majestic, filled with pageantry. For two full days, sailors all up Lake Erie and down Lake Michigan ran to their railings to see it, the *Eastland*, tall, crisp, white, and that raucous calliope. After a seven-year absence, it was back.

As the *Eastland* passed Detroit on a Thursday afternoon that summer, dozens of passing ships in the harbor gave salutes. As it approached South Haven shortly after 10:00 a.m. on Friday, Captain Claude Ennes turned the eight-handle ship wheel on the bridge, steering the *Eastland* closer to shore, and Tony Lessing, the calliope manipulator, played the tune well known in that port town, the first home to the *Eastland*, "Goodbye, Everybody."

Some of its lyrics would prove prophetic:

> Good-bye, ev-'ry body!
> Good-bye ev-'ry thing!
> Farewell, golden summer,
> Farewell, lovely spring.
> Breaks my heart to think
> That I'm going goodbye!
> Goodbye!

§§§

About three hundred people were waiting on the wharf in St. Joseph as noon approached. It was foggy out in the harbor, and people squinted into the mist to be the first to see the splendid ship many of them had only read about.

There was much talk of the second-deck dance floor, thirty-six feet by eighty feet, larger than on any other ship. And that calliope up on top, between the smokestacks: What did it sound like?

Out of the haze, the *Eastland* glided toward St. Joseph. People on the docks could begin to make out dark lines, an enormous bow emerging from a cloud.

"Someone's Coming to Our House" blasted from the calliope, and every vessel in port whistled salutes. The *City of Benton Harbor*, of the Graham & Morton line, was the first to sound the welcome. The deep whistle of the *Eastland* responded to the hearty greeting. The calliope player then belted out "Home, Sweet Home." People cheered on the wharf as the ship pulled up to the E. A. Graham docks. And the calliope man switched to the nostalgic standby "Auld Lang Syne."

Once at the dock, the *Eastland* gave three blasts from its whistles, signaling that it was home. There was a symphony of shrieks and toots from factory whistles. The crowd waved hands in the air. The first man off the ship, touching foot on the docks, was a smiling Walter Steele.

CHAPTER TWENTY-FOUR

Broken Propellers

After such a welcome, the first few weeks then went very poorly. The ship was hard to handle, staggering like a drunkard. One week after the celebratory welcome, the *Eastland* was struggling to get through its piers at St. Joseph on the Monday afternoon return trip to Chicago. It took forty minutes to clear the channel. The *Eastland* kept striking the dock broadsides. Then it scraped along the wharf, gouging the colossal timbers of the pier.

Captain Ennes, who along with Chief Engineer Donaldson, agreed to come with the *Eastland* from Cleveland and serve out the 1914 season, blamed a "stiff norwester." But the *City of Benton Harbor* had no trouble that day.

It wouldn't have helped to throw water on the docks to make the damage look old; everyone knew what had happened. The sounds of the *Eastland*'s scraping and gashing its way out into the harbor drew many witnesses to the docks.

Captain Ennes reported daily to the St. Joseph-Chicago Steamship office at the dock. He spoke regularly there with Steele and Hull. Donaldson did too. Donaldson even overheard Steele and Hull one day talking about the *Eastland*'s reputation for being a "cranky," or difficult to handle, ship.

Ennes did not seem impressed with the new owners. Three weeks into the season, he packed his suitcase, got into his touring car, and drove back to Cleveland. Hull seemed to know Ennes was a short-timer and had already begun looking for a new captain.

Hull hired Harry Pedersen, a Norwegian-born captain of middling experience, who had immigrated to the United States in 1885. Though fifty-four, he still had blond hair. Oddly, Hull had asked his competitors at the Graham & Morton line whom they would recommend to pilot the *Eastland*. Pedersen, who had merely adjusted compasses for them, was a good choice, they offered.

On his first week out, in late June, the *Eastland* had some mysterious accident near the Chicago side of its run. The ship must have lost control and run into a bar or some underwater obstruction on the lake. The newspapers in Benton Harbor and St. Joseph, often carrying the minutiae of ship movements, did not have details beyond the fact there was an accident.

The only thing that is for certain is that the *Eastland* had somehow, remarkably, damaged both of its propeller shafts. And each propeller shaft was built to withstand considerable punishment. Each was rock-solid iron, ten inches thick.

The *Eastland*, crippled, arrived at the Chicago Shipbuilding Company's South Chicago shipyards for repair. Steamboat inspector William Nicholas ordered both propeller shafts replaced. It took two weeks, putting the *Eastland* out of commission and forcing the St. Joseph-Chicago Steamship Company to miss the July 4th weekend and the heart of the summer tourism season. It wasn't back in service until July 11.

There was, however, one good note that summer. Two weeks after the propeller mishap, the *Eastland* carried its largest crowd of the season, 1,395 people, to Michigan City, Indiana, from Chicago, on July 25, 1914. The charter business looked promising. The St. Joseph-Chicago Steamship Company was paid five hundred dollars to transport employees of the Western Electric Company to their company picnic and back.

All went off without a glitch, and Western Electric seemed happy; it began making plans to charter the *Eastland* for next year's picnic.

§§§

Steele and Hull had gotten a quick education in naval architecture and operating machinery. With the season over, and crushing repair bills, they were deeply in debt. Rival Graham & Morton, meantime, was financially thriving. It had five steamships, the *City of Chicago*, the *Soo City*, the *Holland*, the *City of Benton Harbor*, and the *City of Grand Rapids*.

When it became clear that Hull and Steele were going to succeed in bringing a steamer to St. Joseph, Graham & Morton put its shiniest new vessel, the *City of Grand Rapids*, onto the Benton Harbor–Chicago run to trounce the St. Joseph men.

Even the winter offered no respite. While the *Eastland* was moored at its off-season home at the docks in Benton Harbor, the ship's seacock froze and broke overnight in early February 1915, allowing water to gush into the breached hull. Company men discovered the ship one morning tipping on its port side, away from the dock, nearly sunk.

They pumped and pumped using gasoline engines, then steam ones, to keep the ship from being grounded in the channel. The leak was finally stopped, with a diver making repairs, and the *Eastland* was returned to an even keel. Steele, its largest investor, watched the mounting repair bills. He would soon start asking around about mechanical repairs to improve the *Eastland*'s handling.

CHAPTER TWENTY-FIVE

"To Be Nearer Home"

They exchanged vows at seven in the evening on Christmas Day, the bride's birthday. It was 1914, nearly a year to the day since they met. The ceremony was in the living room of Captain Reid's home in Grand Haven. Florence, who had a broad, ready smile, wore a fetching sailor suit of blue serge for a wedding gown. The attire was the idea of her groom, Joseph, who wore a black suit.

The wedding was small; only Reid and Erickson relatives and a few intimate friends were on hand. The next day a wedding announcement in the *Grand Haven Daily Tribune* appeared under the headline, QUIETLY MARRIED AT HOME LAST EVENING. It gushed about Florence: "To know her is to love her and admire her."

Yet Florence continued to struggle with her pleurisy that winter and ached to think of another long season away from her new husband. She asked Joseph about the possibility of working on another ship, one that didn't travel so far away.

By the end of February, Erickson met with his mentor, Chief Engineer Phillips, on his old ship, the *General Meade*. The two sat in his room on the familiar ship, wintering again in Grand Haven. He asked what ship Erickson would be on next season.

Erickson told him the Tomlinson line had offered him a job as chief engineer on the *Saxona*, a larger ship than the *Sultana*.

"I heard the *Eastland* is open," Phillips replied.

"Is that so?"

"Yes," answered Phillips. "I have a good notion to put in an application myself."

"Why don't you?" Erickson suggested.

Phillips couldn't say why, but he was hesitant to apply. "Well, you ought to try for her," he added.

Erickson said no, he wanted the larger ship with Tomlinson, and they dropped the matter.

That evening, Erickson went home and mentioned the *Eastland* job to Florence, who jumped at the mention. "I wish you would make an application," she pleaded. "It would be nice for you to be nearer home."

He thought over her request and then typed up a letter to the *Eastland* owners.

Grand Haven, Mich.
March 1, 1915

Mr. W.H. Hull,
St. Joe, Mich.

I wish to apply for the position of Chief Engineer on Steamer Eastland. The past season was employed as chief engineer of the steamer "Sultana" of the G.A. Tomlinson Fleet of Duluth, Minnesota, and I am engaged in the same company this season.

My reasons for a change is to be nearer home.

Hull wrote back, asking Erickson to detail his experience with twin-propeller and passenger steamers. Erickson replied.

Hull replied on March 15, asking Erickson to come to the office in St. Joseph for an interview. "The position must be filled by April 1st and will pay $150 per month for nine months." Erickson was disappointed with the salary. He wrote back:

As the position I now hold has better money in it for me than your offer, and if I made the change of steamers, it would be purely for the money that was in it, I cannot consider your offer.

I know you must have a good service, as your season is short and a delay of a day in the steamer's schedule means thousands to you and this means the engineer must be on the job night and day for upwards of 80 days. Realizing all that a good man must mean to this steamer, I cannot give my services for the terms you offer.

Thanking you for the consideration that you have given me. I do not think anything could be accomplished by meeting you, as I cannot consider your offer.

Hull asked Erickson to come to the offices for the interview. If he were satisfied with the meeting and his references, he'd raise the salary offer.

They met on Thursday, March 25, 1915. They discussed the steamers Erickson had worked on. When salary came up, Erickson said he had an offer to be chief engineer on the *Saxona*, at a salary of $175 monthly, and said he would not accept less to work on the *Eastland*. Hull said he would consider matching the salary, and then he asked Erickson if he wanted to see the *Eastland*.

The two went over to Benton Harbor and boarded the *Eastland*, which towered over the docks. Erickson had only seen it a few times ten years earlier when it was steaming in and out of South Haven.

He walked aboard and all over the ship and spent much time examining the engine room. "Lots of work . . . to be done," Erickson told him.

"I suppose so," Hull answered.

"Have any objection if I take my brother on oiling?" Erickson asked. Hull said fine, one of the assistant engineers last year had hired his brothers.

They shook hands. Erickson would be paid the $175 monthly and start April 1. He would fit out the *Eastland*, that is, get its machinery shipshape, until June 10. The sailing season was to start on the morning of Saturday, June 12.

CHAPTER TWENTY-SIX

May Day

It was an unusual visit, by Erickson's recollection:

The engineer had seen Walter Steele before, but typically in the company's headquarters office. Steele was in his early thirties, about Erickson's age, and a very snappy dresser. He had starched collars, cuff links, a nugget for a pinky ring. Steele was the secretary and treasurer of the St. Joseph-Chicago Steamship Company, Erickson came to learn, and its largest investor.

Erickson had been fitting out the *Eastland* more than a month, and he had made much progress. He had examined the tanks, pipelines, the engines, the pumps, the dynamos. He was intent on putting the *Eastland*, as he would later say, into "No. 1 A condition." After a decade in the United States, he still typically twisted idioms and had trouble with basic English grammar.

Steele boarded the ship to inspect the work that had been done. Erickson, covered in grease, greeted him. They went over the ship together. Erickson took his boss around the boilers, outside them, on top of them, through the engine room. The two walked or crawled through the whole place that May day.

Then, a surprise: The dandy showed deep knowledge of steamship mechanics. Steele asked him if it would be possible to install an additional seacock, even using the correct term. Yes, Erickson would recall replying, it was. They just needed to get the ship into dry dock: in other words, into a position to make repairs, out of the water.

Erickson told him it would take quite a while. A seacock, a hole in the shell of the hull, and underwater at that, is the kind of breach of integrity that shipbuilders installed with great caution. Holes, it was well known, sink ships.

Steele had another question. Could they place a valve in the center of the manifold—a division valve—so ballast tanks on each side of the ship could fill or empty independently, to speed up ship-trimming maneuvers?

Erickson considered the mechanics of the request. He told him he thought it could be done. They talked it over some more. When? Next fall, Steele said, after the coming summer season.

At that point, Erickson had never ridden on the *Eastland*. The only times he had ever been aboard were during his job interview back in March and in the past few weeks, preparing the ship for the coming season. The only time he had ever spent on the *Eastland*, it had been tied up to docks.

As to Steele's visit that May day, Erickson thought the whole conversation was unremarkable. But one thing stuck with him. Normally dapper, Steele was wearing, of all things, overalls.

CHAPTER TWENTY-SEVEN

A Spy Aboard

Raymond Gray and Albert Gray, two Chicago teenagers, stood before Judge Richard Tuthilland in June of 1915, accused of auto theft. The crime was new; autos were new. Their defense attorney didn't own an automobile, would never learn to drive one, in fact. In short order, Clarence Darrow got both the young joyriders off.

Peter Sissman, the socialist lawyer who once worked for Darrow, had persuaded his old boss to stick with law, after all. The two would get together again, and over coffee and cigarettes, map out plans for a new law firm.

Their offices would be on Ashland Avenue, well west of the humming Loop business district. Sissman opened a joint bank account, and using his savings, spent a couple hundred dollars to furnish the place with desks, chairs, and carpeting.

And now, two years into practice, their clientele was still meager. Sissman, less of a trial man, worked on contracts and divorces. Darrow took what he could. He represented a woman who mistook her husband for a burglar, she claimed, and shot him dead one night. Prosecutors pointed out that she had been receiving attention from another man, a jeweler who happened to work near her husband's hardware shop. The jury acquitted her. Darrow won another case, with an attorney charged with tampering with election ballots.

The man who once commanded nearly fifty thousand dollars for a case gladly agreed to represent Mildred Sperry, a woman charged with perjuring herself for her boss, an insurance agent charged with arson in a building fire. Darrow won an acquittal for her, though he conceded her guilt. She paid him $250.

"My prolonged absence from Chicago was enough in itself to destroy my business. I had to begin anew," Darrow would later reflect in his memoirs. "Neither then nor at any other time of my life did I go after business. I simply took it as it came, and the criminal courts and the jails are always crowded with the poor."

He confided in a letter to his former girlfriend Mary Field, who had since married another man, "I can only speak for a very small part of the poor and there seems to be no one to speak for the rest in court."

When Darrow returned to Chicago, having beaten the jury-bribing rap in Los Angeles two years earlier, he spoke at a banquet of two hundred lawyers at the Hotel Sherman. His words were high-minded. Yet no one in the room was buying it, judging by the distance they all kept from him.

"I know that all my life I have been fighting for the underdog," Darrow bellowed. "I know that all my life, whether in good repute or ill, whether free or confined, I shall continue to fight for the underdog."

"That I have always fought wisely, I do not know, nor do I care. I have fought. I have fought for the poor and the weak and the oppressed. I have fought for justice and liberty—and what is more than that—for charity for all men.

"During one of the darkest hours of my visit to 'The City of Angels,' I was riding to my rooms in a streetcar. There was an elderly lady near with her little granddaughter. The woman looked at me and asked: 'Are you Mr. Darrow?' I replied, 'That is my name.' She took up my hand and kissed it. I would rather have the memory of that woman's kiss on my hand than all of the gold you can pile up in the city of Chicago."

§§§

And the gold was piling up in Chicago, and many hands were grabbing for it. By year end, the 1915 crime tally would include: larceny, 5,935 cases; burglary, porch climbers and others, 1,538; contributing to the delinquency of children, 1,158; confidence games, 1,040; bigamy, 33. Fourteen cases were classified simply as "mayhem."

The year before, Fainting Bertha was caught shoplifting at Marshall Field's. A detective spotted the infamous thief, and a search of her fine dress revealed merchandise tucked stealthily in its folds.

The police force had doubled in the past decade, now standing at five thousand. A new mayor was in City Hall, who won by promising: "I will suppress crime, drive the crooks out of Chicago, and make the streets safe for men, women and children. I will protect women from insult in public places."

Mayor William Hale Thompson was broad-shouldered, a former football player, a youthful forty-six. He had a wide smile and used base humor.

Shortly into his term, he invited striking streetcar men and their bosses in to negotiate and, gracious and jovial, charmed them into settlement.

The last time the *Eastland* steamed into the Chicago River in 1907, the population was two million. In just eight years, Chicago was now bursting with a half-million people more. The fourth largest city on earth, this Chicago was seven times larger than the incarnation that burned to the ground in 1871. Thirty-seven whole states had fewer people than the city of Chicago.

The streets were host to an entertaining change in technology. On any given corner, one could smell fuel and horseflesh. Under Chicago's official street traffic rules for 1915, Article IV, "To turn, a signal shall be given by indicating with the whip, or hand, the direction in which the turn is to be made."

For the devout, there were 1,183 churches, and 7,006 saloons. Thompson dared to issue an edict no mayor had for more than forty years—the saloons shall be closed on Sunday. William Thompson would gain the nickname Big Bill all over Chicago, in no small part for his handling later that summer of an unimaginable disaster.

§§§

Erickson had finished the fitting out on the *Eastland*, getting it in "No. 1 A shape," as he put it. He and his brother and a handful of oilers and assistant engineers had tested, measured, and run every piece of machinery on the ship.

On Friday, June 11, he and Captain Pedersen took the *Eastland* out on Lake Michigan for a one-hour trial run. All was humming. They were ready for a busy 1915 season.

The first run was Saturday, June 12, at 2:00 p.m., from Chicago. There were only 146 passengers aboard. Shortly after the Chicago–St. Joseph roundtrips began, Pedersen seemed to have only one order for Erickson, which he issued repeatedly. "Keep her straight and trim her." Sometimes Pedersen, or first mate Del Fisher, would tell him to tilt the ship a bit so that the gangway was closer in line with the dock, to make it easier for passengers to get on and off. In time, Erickson and his men filled the tanks just-so, and the *Eastland* complied. Behind his back, the crew used a nickname for the diminutive Erickson: "Slim."

Their common Norwegian heritage aside, Erickson didn't seem to care for Pedersen. Erickson had worked with captains considerably more able. But Pedersen left him alone to his department, the engine room, so they stayed in their corners. The two most senior officers on the *Eastland* did not socialize, on board or off.

Not helping the atmosphere of trust, the company seemed to have planted a spy aboard. Ray Davis, the personal secretary to Steele, routinely began riding on the *Eastland* in the first two months of the season, occasionally checking in the engine room with Erickson, to the chief engineer's annoyance, asking if he was having any trouble keeping the ship steady. He was not, Erickson told him. Hull and Steele didn't seem to be riding the *Eastland* at all that second season.

The weather that summer turned out to be poor, rainy and colder than usual. Ticket sales slackened. Hull and Steele decided to let go of Captain Scott, their consultant. And Hull felt the *Eastland* was burning too much coal. It just wasn't running fast enough, an old refrain for *Eastland* management. Hull reached out to Donaldson, the former engineer in Cleveland, inviting him to St. Joseph to discuss how to burn less coal.

Donaldson's appearance on the *Eastland* immediately rankled Erickson. The *quality* of the coal is the problem, Erickson told Donaldson, not the engine room's handling of it. Erickson had apparently been harboring some ill feeling toward the amateur managers he was beholden to, as well as the passable captain.

The day Donaldson showed up, after only a month on the *Eastland*, Erickson had had it. He immediately sent a telegram to the St. Joseph-Chicago Steamship offices.

Mr. W.H. Hull
St. Joseph, MI

Please accept this as my resignation to take effect Monday, July 19th,
at St. Joseph.

Hull checked with Donaldson, who agreed, the poor quality of the coal the company was buying was the problem, not Erickson. Hull then spoke with Erickson at the offices, trying to appease him. Donaldson was there solely to consult on the coal problem, he told Erickson, not to do his job.

Erickson was pacified. He withdrew his resignation. He would stay on the *Eastland*. If staying proved a mistake, he could always quit again. No reason to worry until you need to—to cross that bridge till you get to it. In the old country, the Norwegian version of that proverb was: That day, that sorrow.

PART II:
WHAT IS HONEST NEVER SINKS

CHAPTER TWENTY-EIGHT

July 24, 1915

Pedersen flicked the ashes from his cigar.

He had just finished breakfast. The captain expected a foggy day and began to study his charts in his room aboard the *Eastland*. He wanted to acquaint himself with the course to Michigan City, Indiana, not a usual destination for the *Eastland*.

Pedersen had just passed Erickson, who was hurrying to his breakfast in the mess room. They had a full day in front of them. The busy summer season was half over. It was a Saturday, and the *Eastland* sat at the dock near the Clark Street Bridge, not their usual one on the Chicago River.

They were just about to board twenty-five hundred Western Electric workers who were on holiday. They would leave promptly at 7:30 that morning, on a two-hour cruise to their picnic grounds, forty miles away in Michigan City.

The *Eastland* needed to leave on time. After Michigan City, it had to get up to St. Joseph to pick up another load of passengers, then return to Chicago, then back to Michigan City to ferry the Western Electric picnickers back to Chicago. Then another two roundtrips, some four hundred miles of nearly back-to-back trips in the next day and a half.

Erickson sipped his coffee, unaware that the *Eastland* would not make any of those ports. Within three hours, he would be thrown into an underground jail cell with his watch stopped at 7:33, the exact moment he nearly drowned.

§§§

The day was gray, drizzly. Five ships were chartered for the Western Electric picnickers, and the *Eastland* was scheduled to leave first. Passengers were issued tickets good for any of the ships. Those eager to get to the picnic early headed straight for the *Eastland*.

By 6:30, five thousand people were massing near Water Street, just outside the *Eastland*'s dock. George Goyette, the foreman for Western Electric's woodworking department, was in line with his three sons, two of them toolmaking apprentices at the company.

His subordinate James Novotny, the cabinetmaker from Bohemia, was there with his wife and their daughter Mamie, nine. Their son, Willie, two years younger than Mamie, looked dapper in his new brown suit, knickerbockers, and black shoes.

Most of the women, in their twenties and thirties, crowded near the dock with long-sleeve embroidered linen dresses. Their hats brimmed with apples, sprays of lilac, shirrings of striped taffeta silk, poppies wound in wreathes, and black velvet bows. Some had brims tilted in grace, others in flirtation.

Men, lugging baggage and picnic baskets, wore derbies and straw hats, suits and ties. Boys in blouse suits and rompers held their mothers' hands. The girls wore dresses and bonnets or bows. They would all be funneled through a narrow set of stone steps between the street and the *Eastland*.

With two inspectors using handheld clickers to count the passengers, people began boarding across the *Eastland*'s white gangplank, four feet wide, eight feet long. They embarked quickly, about fifty a minute, polished shoes and boots clomping on the gangplank, which slowly began to dip downward, eventually a full foot.

Arthur MacDonald looked at the *Eastland* from his pilothouse. He was the engineer on the tugboat *Kenosha*, which was lashed to the bow of the *Eastland* and ready to tow it from the dock. Right out his window he could see that the *Eastland* was leaning curiously toward the dock, the starboard side. Thinking little of it, he went down to the mess room and ate his breakfast.

In the *Eastland* engine room, Erickson noticed that his inclinometer, a little metal arrow that swiveled as the ship tilted, was leaning toward the dockside. Unconcerned, he ordered his men to open up the valves on the river side, the port one, to correct the ship's slight starboard leaning. "Boys, steady her up a little," Erickson said.

In about three minutes, the *Eastland* was straightened up, and the gangplank was level for the parade of passengers boarding. All was back to normal. It was nearly seven in the morning, and the passengers herding aboard continuously had reached sixteen hundred.

The drizzle got heavier, and many people clopped down the stairwells to the lower decks, where Bradfield's Orchestra, a five-piece violin and mandolin band, strummed and plucked jaunty ragtime. People began to bop and hop on the immense dance floor to the string rhythms.

Stepping aboard, mothers began leading their children downstairs to the lower decks to keep dry. That nurturing instinct would prove most tragic.

The *Eastland* rolled. As his inclinometer began to tilt from center to the port side, Erickson started up the engines to warm them. It was a slight tilt, and he guessed that the passengers, whom he couldn't see down in his engine room, were congregating on the upper decks on the riverside. To correct for the tilting to port, he ordered his men to open the valves to the starboard side tanks. Perfectly routine.

The last of the passengers were boarding, and when the inspectors counted—*2,498, 2,499, 2,500*—that's it, they told the crowd, the *Eastland* is full. You'll need to proceed to two other nearby ships, the *Theodore Roosevelt* or the *Petoskey*. Move along now.

Some people begged to be let on, saying their family or friends were already aboard, but the inspectors wouldn't relent. The crew pulled up the gangplank, lodged it in a hallway, and drew a chain across the opening to block anyone from trying to board. That did not stop one Western Electric worker, E. W. Sladkey, who was in charge of the printing department, from hopping across the water and boarding illicitly.

Noticing that the tilt to the port side persisted, Davis, Steele's assistant, showed up in the engine room at 7:17, once again asking Erickson if he was having trouble straightening the ship. He reported to Davis that he had the valves to the No. 2 and 3 starboard side tanks open and that the ship should respond shortly.

Erickson told Davis to go ask the first mate if the ship was hanging up on the dock somehow. As a precaution, Erickson stopped the *Eastland*'s engines.

The ballast tanks kept filling, with a gushing sound Erickson knew well, and the *Eastland* began to straighten up quite noticeably. "I guess we got it," Erickson said to his men, his anxiety eased.

Reassured by the ship's recovery, Captain Pedersen, up in the pilothouse on the top deck, signaled a "Stand By" order, using an electric device called a Chadburn telegraph that rang the message into the engine room. Erickson acknowledged the standby command, meaning he knew the captain was now set to have the *Eastland* towed away from the dock. Then the engineers would take over propulsion.

The *Eastland* rolled again.

On the tug *Kenosha*, MacDonald came up from his twenty-minute breakfast. He was puzzled to see the *Eastland* now leaning the other way, toward the riverside. It was tilting about ten to fifteen degrees.

By 7:27, it was tipping an alarming twenty-five degrees. The engineers were flustered: Why wasn't the water ballast correcting this? What the hell? Growing desperate, Erickson dispatched his first assistant engineer to order the passengers on the top deck to the starboard side immediately, hoping that shifting the crowd there would help straighten the ship.

Harbormaster Adam Weckler had been watching the seesawing performance for about a half hour and wasn't alarmed until just that moment.

His duty was to raise the street bridges running along the Chicago River to allow ships to pass. The procedure that morning: the *Eastland* captain would blow a whistle, the signal that he was ready to proceed away from the dock and under the bridge. On hearing the whistle, harbor officials, by law, had to open it for the ship.

On the dance floor, on the promenade deck near the rear of the ship, the young men and women began to laugh and make a joke of the rolling ship. As it would tilt, they would slide on the waxy floor, giggling and shouting, "All together—hey!"

The lines at the stern, near where the passengers boarded, were released and the *Eastland*'s rounded back end began to ease out into the river.

It was then that MacDonald, in the tugboat, noticed a dreadful strain on the three forward lines still holding the *Eastland* by the nose to the dock. From his vantage point, so close to the *Eastland*'s pointed bow, he could see something almost no one else could: The bowlines, the only things that seemed to be preventing the *Eastland* from rolling over, were stiff, in miserable tension.

Just then, Harbormaster Weckler came running along the dock and shouted to the captain of the *Kenosha* tugboat: "Don't pull on her at all, cap. Don't pull on her at all. I am not going to give that fellow the bridge until he straightens up."

Then MacDonald saw something that he hadn't seen in all his thirty-one years. Six men on the top deck of the *Eastland* dashed to the dockside railing.

They had decided to make a break for it, and leapt overboard, grabbing a hold of one of the four-inch-thick Manila ropes lashed from the bow of the *Eastland* to the dock. Hands hooked on it, they began crossing the fat line, called a hawser, hand over hand, monkeylike, suspended above the river.

Inside the tilting ship, the mandolin players and violinists struggled to play, and began to dig their heels into the floor to keep from slipping.

The *Eastland* leaned farther.

In the engine room, a chute the black gang used to discharge ashes suddenly dipped under water. The river began to gush in. Some of the stokers and oilers hightailed it up steel ladders and fled with sooty faces.

On the tugboat, MacDonald was alarmed to see water starting to gush into the partly opened gangways, the square doorways used to load cargo and passengers. Before he could even shout a warning, one of the bowlines, pulling and pulling on a massive stake, lifted the timber piling right out of the dock. Then a second dock line snapped.

"Get off—the boat's turning over," shouted Mike Javanco, who was rolling his vegetable wagon across the Clark Street Bridge.

Struck now by the danger, Captain Pedersen yelled to a crewmember on the dock, "Open the doors, and take people off!"

A refrigerator tipped over on a lower deck and beer bottles crashed. Dishes slipped from their shelves and smashed. People sitting in chairs on the top deck didn't have time to rise, and they began flying into the air, still seated. A dozen passengers tried to leap toward the dock, but misjudging the distance, they hit the steel hull with a thud and careened into the river.

Children tumbled with grown-ups down the top deck, now diagonal, sprawling in a mess of milk bottles, lunch baskets, hats, and uncurling ship ropes.

The last line holding the *Eastland* to the dock had burst like a cracked whip. The six men hanging from it, trying to escape, ricocheted backward, arms and legs sprawling, flying back through the air, back toward the doomed ship.

§§§

The river, all twisting arms. Hundreds of men and women shrieked, as panama hats and parasols and picnic baskets and baby carriages bobbed about like corks.

Shouts and gurgles.

Men clawed at women, tearing dresses, then soul after soul disappeared into the murky, fearfully cold river. Ship bells clanged the alarm. Whistles shrieked. A tall man in an Uncle Sam costume flailed in the water.

Then it rained garbage. Workers at the warehouse companies along the river threw fruit crates, chicken crates, and all things wooden into the water, but most were swept away by the current. From the deck of the *Roosevelt*, the crew tossed fifty life preservers to those who were soaked, gasping and pleading in the water.

The cries were pitiful, from men and women, splashing, clinging to wreckage, life preservers, or chairs. A young woman was struggling to keep afloat by clutching one of the musicians' violins.

The sinking was within feet of the riverbanks, two blocks from City Hall, at one of the busiest intersections of Chicago's famed Loop. The "El" clanked along the Wells Street bridge nearby. Thunderstruck, legions of morning commuters looked on.

In an eerie symmetry, the letters EAST on the wheelhouse were just above the water, while the LAND ones were just underneath. The river's depth at that point, about nineteen feet, was exactly half the beam of the *Eastland*, meaning that the ship was laying on its side, half in the water, half out.

The fortunate passengers, those near the top of the ship and on the starboard side, grasped the dockside railing, then held on as the *Eastland* spun underneath of them. By crawling on top of the railing or onto the now-exposed side of the hull, previously underwater, many were saved. But it was slimy; some slipped off and began drowning.

George Olinger and his wife, Elizabeth, were on the starboard side and clung to a post as the ship capsized. Looking down, and fearful they would lose their grip, they could see the water gushing in below them, like waterfalls. "It rushed along by the stairs and spurted through cracks and portholes," George recalled. "Men and women were floundering around as the water rose, and screaming." He kissed his wife and, though he was no churchgoer, began to pray out loud.

Five girls were clinging to a beam from a musicians' stand hovering above the water in the hull.

On the *Kenosha*, bells jangling, MacDonald helped back the tugboat up until its stern rested against the *Eastland*, forming a bridge for passengers who made it to the high side. They simply walked deck to deck and then onto the dock. Some never touched water.

In the hull below, bedlam. Inside the *Eastland*, now sideways, the walls became the floor and ceiling, the floor and ceiling, the walls. In the madness, penned-in men and women began sloshing through the cold water, feeling their way in the dark for the stairways, the stair treads now vertical, useless.

Water gushed to their waists, then their shoulders, then their necks. Hundreds of terrified people entangled together at the grand staircase. Unable to maneuver the steps, most began to drown, clustered within the elegant curved railing and ornate spindles. A man named Brown, who worked in Western Electric's machine shop, made it past the stairs, with people clawing at him, shredding his pants and jacket.

Near the steps, trapped victims tore away cabin partitions, hoping for an escape route, only to scratch their fingers bloody when they reached the steel-plated wall of the hull.

Helen Thyer was pitched into the water with her husband and two children, Harry, seven, and Helen, eight. Her husband sank, and she struggled to tread water with a child in each arm. She lost strength in her left arm, and little Helen disappeared into the water.

William Raphael jumped in to save two women bobbing to the surface of the river outside his waterfront offices. A heavy man, his "face green with terror," Raphael recalled, paddled toward them and grabbed onto the women's dresses. Raphael yelled at him to let go and finally had to kick him in the face. He lost one of the women but made it to the riverbank with the other.

Julius Behnke and his wife were on the starboard side of the ship and raised their three-year-old little daughter, Martha, up through a porthole. A stranger took her. When they were pulled from the *Eastland* later, they were distraught because they couldn't find her. George Goyette grabbed a handkerchief and jammed it into his mouth to keep from swallowing the filthy water. He couldn't find one of his sons, Charles, an office boy at the phone company, who did not survive.

A young woman, Anna Goldnick, recalled seeing "men fight and tear the clothing as well as life belts and chairs from women."

Within moments, a graver peril dawned on the crew. Charles Dibbell, the *Eastland*'s radio officer, was standing at a sink to shave as the ship went over. His face was half-lathered when he realized: The boilers could blow up.

For several crucial moments, Joseph Erickson had stayed put in the engine room. When the climbing water reached his hands, his wristwatch stopped, at 7:33. With enormous poise, he had already ordered precautionary steps: shut both engines down, close portholes, pump the bilge from the engine room. He stayed at his post, working frantically in a world suddenly sideways, risking his life to save the ship and ensure that the two-hundred-ton boilers and main steam pipes didn't explode catastrophically.

It wasn't until the water reached his neck that he made his escape. At that point, he had secured the boilers, allowing water to be injected into them slowly, to gently reduce their temperature so that they wouldn't explode when the cold river water rushed in on the blazing boilerplates.

Seconds away from drowning in the dark hull, he reached up and grabbed a steering cable under the main deck and dragged himself above the waterline along an air pocket until he reached a porthole. Watchman Robert Brooks outside the overturned ship spotted Erickson through the round window.

Stretching his hand up, Erickson shouted to him, and the crewman pulled him through, tearing Erickson's pants as he squeezed through the porthole, only about fourteen inches wide.

One nearby fireboat, the *Graeme Stewart*, waited a crucial ten minutes before it approached the capsized *Eastland* to help people flailing in the water. The firemen aboard apparently feared an explosion.

Erickson was dazed. People were shouting and screaming and gurgling and drowning all around him.

After catching his breath on the starboard hull, now pointing skyward, Erickson hurried along the side of the *Eastland*, bending to peer into the portholes at his feet.

He spotted women and children in the capsized wreck, clinging to anything they could find above the water.

"Get some ropes," he shouted to the first mate. "People hanging on the benches down there."

Squeezing through one of the portholes, "Slim" slipped back into the half-sunk ship, ropes from the lifeboats over his shoulder. Erickson first rescued a little girl clinging to a bench. He put a rope around her, and the crew hauled her up. He saved four more, all women. After a few minutes, a fireman arrived with a ladder, to help rescue the remaining women.

§§§

The dragnet stretched far beyond Chicago. A little more than an hour after the sinking, Merwin Stone Thompson was driving from his home in Painesville, Ohio, toward Cleveland. Suddenly, at a rural intersection near Lake Erie, he hit the brakes. He faced a police blockade. The policemen ordered him out of his car.

"Are you Captain Merwin S. Thompson," one asked, "and were you formerly captain of the steamer *Eastland*?"

Thompson responded that he was, but hadn't been near the ship in three years.

Didn't matter, the officer replied. He was under orders to arrest anyone connected with the ship, and there was no escape: They had stationed police at all the other routes in the area to detain Thompson for questioning. The men stood in the cool morning, whipped by breezes off Lake Erie.

"Did you know," the policeman continued, "that the steamer *Eastland* capsized at 7:20 this morning in Chicago and that first reports indicate a possible loss of over one thousand lives?"

"I was master of that ship three years," the old captain said. He paused to consider his years at the helm, the crowds he had seen on its decks day after day. A thousand lives?

"I carried well over five hundred thousand people during that period, without one single claim," he continued. "It seems to me impossible."

§§§

In the Chicago River, in the current, the drowned, their arched backs hunched to the surface in dark suits and shimmering gowns, were swirling away in a hellish choreography.

Harbor police called for large fishing nets to be stretched fully across the river at the nearby Wells Street Bridge and farther south at Harrison Street, in the hope of catching some of them.

So many had drifted away that harbor authorities ordered the locks raised at the drainage canal port, some forty miles downriver, at Lockport, Illinois. They used the very apparatus that first engineered the miracle reversal of the river's flow all those years ago. They managed to slow the Chicago River from its normal eight-mile-an-hour current to a sluggish one-mile-an-hour, to contain the stream.

Fish nets that salvagers called "death nets" were being stretched bank to bank, and within minutes rowboats, motorboats, and tugboats glided along them, stopping periodically for crewmen to disentangle a body from the webbing and lift it aboard. Crowds looked on in horrified silence.

Making her way on a trolley car to the dock, Helen Repa was one of three Western Electric Company nurses scheduled to work the hospital tent at the company picnic planned for that day. Expecting to attend to the usual sprained ankles and heat exhaustion, she was on her way to the waterfront when a mounted policeman galloped up and stopped all the traffic, shouting, "Excursion boat upset—look out for the ambulance!"

She feared it was one of the ships the company had chartered for its picnic. So she ran to the front of the trolley, which the police had stopped at Lake Street, planning to hop off and make her way on foot the last few blocks down to the dock.

The trolley man tried to stop her, but she slipped past him and jumped off just as one of the ambulances came up. Clinging to the back of the ambulance, her white nurse uniform flapping, she reached the dock.

The air was clammy. The sun peeked through leaden clouds now and again.

Prostrate in the water, the upturned starboard side of the *Eastland* was still covered with the damp canvas sheets and the hastily spread sawdust and ash that gave police and rescuers a foothold on the slimy steel plates. The captain of the nearby *Missouri*, who saw survivors and rescuers slide off the ship and drop perilously in the water, shouted for ashes to be taken from the fireboxes of three nearby tugboats and spread for traction along the slick shell of the capsized ship.

The enormous curved hull, dark, resembled the side of a marooned whale. "They were already pulling them out from below when I got there," Nurse Repa recalled, "out of the water or through the portholes. People were being dragged out, wet, bleeding, and hysterical, by scores. Most of those from the decks and inside the boat were cut more or less severely, because chairs and benches had slid down on top of them when the boat went over."

A dozen tugboats had motored up near the *Eastland* some time ago to offer assistance, churning up the dirty water, stirring items for a day of play: cases of beer and soda, baby blue parasols, a baseball bat, oranges, picnic baskets crammed with sandwiches and pastries—all washed up against the pilothouse and the keel. The flailing, choking, and the splashing on the water was finally over.

CHAPTER TWENTY-NINE

Gone.

A slate sky. The tugs tilted under the weight of soaked corpses being lifted quickly from the murky water. "The bodies were laid out on the dock, on the bridges, some on the *Roosevelt*, others on the sidewalk," said Nurse Repa. "A crowd of willing but ignorant volunteers kept getting in the way, and made our attempts at resuscitation almost useless."

"Isn't there some building we can take these people?" she asked a policeman, her white uniform caked with mud and blood. "Some of them have a fighting chance if we can get them in out of the rain and away from this crowd!" Thinking there were enough doctors and rescuers on the scene at the river now, she hopped on another ambulance and headed for the nearby Iroquois Memorial Hospital, assuming it was overwhelmed and understaffed.

Among those at the river, some bystanders had had an impulse to jump into the chilly river and help, then thought the better of it. Standing at the north end of the Clark Street Bridge, Algernon Chandler Richey would have to live with his moment of decision right then, and for the rest of his life. Richey, a lawyer, considered himself a good swimmer, even a deft rescuer. But when he saw the mayhem in the water—a cluster of three or four survivors, desperate and drowning, grabbed hold and swamped one stronger swimmer trying to help—he decided he wouldn't "dare go into the water."

Another man, the one who was supposed to supervise the swimming races at the picnic and who was an expert swimmer himself, swam back and forth for more than half an hour rescuing others. Then, exhausted, he drowned.

The sinking just an hour old, the Iroquois Memorial Hospital and other area hospitals were overwhelmed with injured survivors, and ambulances were racing from the bridge to outlying hospitals. For blocks, the streets

were jammed, with thousands milling shoulder to shoulder, and cars thread-
ing through them. "When I got to the Iroquois Hospital," said Nurse Repa,
"more and more people were arriving every minute, dripping wet and shivering, and there were not enough blankets left."

People kept ambling in the doors, bewildered, disoriented: shrieking and
sobbing women, mothers calling for their babies, men hysterical and nause-
ated by the sights they had seen. A young woman, shaking and panicked,
resisted the attempts of nurses to treat her. "My sister," she screamed. "My
poor sister! You shan't do anything for me until you find her." Nearby stood
Josephine Behnke, hands folded, praying for her husband and her three-year-
old, Martha. "My husband! I left him in the water. My little girl! I thought
she was here. She is not. May God have mercy on their souls."

A stream of trucks and horse-drawn wagons made its way through
the crowds, bringing lung motors, tubes, and respiratory equipment. The
machines were switched on and rumbled and clanked in a ghostly symphony.
A doctor from the Red Cross injected the retrieved bodies, some with eyes
closed, some with eyes open, with strychnine, a stimulant. At one point, the
drug seemed to spark some life in one man, and the respirators were used to
try to pump the breath of life back into him.

Doctors started worrying about typhoid as they helped revive those who
had gulped in the filthy water. The whole river in that part of the city smelled
of steam, rust, death.

Sailors in white Dixie-cup caps stopped to wipe sweat with their square
kerchiefs, and they hurried stretchers from the ship to the doctors, who were
kneeling over victims laid under the worn awnings of the fruit-houses along
South Water Street. The crowds, seeing the black robes and white collars
of priests, allowed the clergymen to pass by. Inside the hull, Father John
O'Hearn splashed around to injured men and women to take their confes-
sions. Working on the side of the ship, Fathers D. J. Dunne and Herman
Wolff anointed the foreheads of victims, alive and dead, as they processed by
on stretchers.

Doctors with rolled sleeves and ties were quickly growing weary, checking each dire case carried to them, having spent an hour pressing their fingers
to the throats of the victims and then calling out one of two words.

The first: "Pulmotor." It was the name for a squeaking contraption,
recently developed to revive unconscious miners, which worked like a bellows

to force air into the lungs. When doctors spotted the twitch of life in one woman lying on the ground, arms flung far above her head, five firemen hunched over her, craning around one another, virtually holding their breath in anticipation. The doctors couldn't bring her back.

Besides "Pulmotor," there was only one other word the doctors would say: "Gone."

With a nod from one of the doctors, waiting stretcher-bearers would take the departed away. They would carry the body from the lung-motor area, across the bridge and into a nearby warehouse commandeered as a makeshift morgue. Some rescuers did not know how to use the Pulmotors, and the life-saving machines sat idle. Lying in crooked rows, women perished, waiting for a doctor. Men gurgled their last breaths.

Gone.

Gone.

Gone.

With seconds still meaning the difference between life or death, rescuers turned to an area both urgent and ghastly: the inside of the ship. Fourteen divers were dispatched to explore the depths of the *Eastland*. When three divers dropped shirtless into the steaming hull, ropes in hands, they developed a salvage procedure. They treaded water along a line until their feet kicked a passing body. Then they called to the men above, who snagged it and raised it with pike poles and grappling irons.

Other divers, equipped with ropes, diver-bell helmets, and snaking air hoses, hopped with a plunk into the water and quickly disappeared. They paddled and groped their way into the innermost recesses of the steel hull, through the scantlings and beams. They felt their way through the darkness. As quickly as a body was located, it was seized with grappling hooks.

Every other minute, an assistant, holding a rope in his fists and peering intently from the top of the ship into the dark depths, felt a tug. It was a signal to pull, and another victim, all deadweight and soaked clothing, was pulled up by four men who joined together, grunting as they tugged on the line. Body after body, stock-still.

Most victims, cold and already stiff, had clothing in shreds, their faces scratched, their fingers clenched. The rescuers suffered from the heat and steam of the hull, caused by the ship's boilers. They pulled and pulled and raised a man in a dapper dark suit, tie tied, slumped over at the waist where the lasso was fastened.

Women suffered added indignities. As bodies were lifted from the water, dresses sometimes shifted or rose up. As one young woman was pulled by her black-gartered legs upside-down from the muck, her ankle-length dress slipped fully down, revealing that she had no underpants on. In the rush to resuscitate, doctors tore open cotton dresses and chemises, leaving women with their bare breasts exposed.

§§§

Under the steel shell of the *Eastland*, rescuers could hear faint tapping. Men with tanks and blowtorches spread out along the hull, setting up equipment where they heard any panic below. The immense side of the ship, belly-up toward the thick, dark clouds, was so smooth and curved that some of the torch men had to be belayed by other workers with ropes to keep them from slipping off. Captain Pedersen, who'd struck his head when the ship went over, seemed to emerge from nowhere at one point. He saw men urgently beginning to fire up their blue-flame torches to burn holes in the three-eighth-inch steel-plated bottom of the overturned ship.

"Here, stop that!" the captain shouted.

"My orders are to save lives, not be careful of the boat," retorted one of the torch men.

J. H. Rista, another torch worker, was firing his flame into the hull when Pedersen rushed up to him and ordered him to stop. He shouted back at the captain: Go to hell!

When the crowds caught on that the captain was interfering, the angered rescuers advanced toward him, looking as though they were about to throw him into the river. "Drown him!" shouted a woman hysterically.

The police stepped in, circling Captain Pedersen and creating a ring of bodyguards around him. They led him away from the *Eastland*. As they moved along, a man managed to break through and slug the captain in the jaw, and the police clubbed the attacker down. With Pedersen and First Mate Delbert Fisher quickly interred aboard a nearby fireboat, the *Graeme Stewart*, the torch men returned to burning jagged, molten openings. Through them they spotted passengers clinging to life, those who had spent what they thought were their last moments screaming from air pockets and clanging on the hull with steel bars.

One of the rescued, George Olinger, recalled: "When they were cutting through with the acetylene torches, hot steel was blown all over us, and some of the women who had remained calm up to that point, began to shriek. Some of them were burned slightly, but I think all who had stayed above water after that first plunge were saved."

"As soon as we could get inside her," said Harry Miller, an *Eastland* deckhand, "me and my mate began fishing for bodies in the sunken half of her." They used long-handle pikes. "It was strange how many of them drowned hanging tight to some object below water. Some I hooked down at the bottom, others halfway up, others only two to three feet below water.

"I could tell by the pull it took to tear them loose that they had their hands gripped on a rail or table or some other fixed object below the water. I don't know how many I fished out."

One girl, about ten, was pulled from the hull. Three policemen lifted her lifeless arms above the lasso around her, and gingerly removed the rope. She was sitting cross-legged on the side of the ship, slumped forward, her long tresses dripping and touching the hull, a spot of mud on one glistening knee. One policeman held her shoulder so she wouldn't fall forward. Hers was a face in early bloom: her dress, lacy; her ears, delicate as china.

A news photographer, Jun Fujita, who was snapping pictures frantically at the disaster scene, turned his lens toward the little girl and took a photo that he felt would break hearts across the city when the newspaper came out the next morning.

He also saw a fireman, chubby, sweating, his uniform coat immodestly removed to reveal his T-shirt and suspenders. In his arms, a child slumped over, dress shoes still buckled. The child's head twisted back away from the fireman's thick arms, sickeningly. With his plump fingers, he grasped the slight body, in soaking, skintight play clothes. The old fireman, Leonard Olson, stared into the lens, bug-eyed, in shock, the entire frightful day in his face.

"I stayed until they began to take out the little children," said J. M. Crawford, captain of the *Puritan*. "I saw big, strong men leaning against the buildings, crying and sobbing."

As the day wore on, the awful toll mounted, one after another:
Gone. Gone.
Gone. Gone. Gone. Gone.
Gone. Gone. Gone. Gone. Gone.
Gone. Gone. Gone. Gone. Gone. Gone.

Gone. Gone. Gone. Gone. Gone.
Gone. Gone. Gone. Gone. Gone. Gone. Gone.
Gone. Gone. Gone. Gone. Gone. Gone. Gone. Gone.
Gone. Gone. Gone. Gone. Gone. Gone. Gone. Gone. Gone. Gone. Gone.
Gone. Gone. Gone. Gone. Gone. Gone. Gone. Gone. Gone. Gone. Gone.
Gone. Gone. Gone. Gone. Gone. Gone. Gone. Gone. Gone. Gone. Gone.
Gone. Gone. Gone. Gone. Gone. Gone. Gone. Gone. Gone. Gone. Gone.
Gone. Gone. Gone. Gone. Gone. Gone. Gone. Gone. Gone. Gone. Gone.
Gone. Gone. Gone. Gone. Gone. Gone. Gone. Gone. Gone. Gone. Gone.
Gone. Gone. Gone. Gone. Gone. Gone. Gone. Gone. Gone. Gone. Gone.
Gone. Gone. Gone. Gone. Gone. Gone. Gone. Gone. Gone. Gone. Gone.
Gone. Gone. Gone. Gone. Gone. Gone. Gone. Gone. Gone. Gone. Gone.
Gone. Gone. Gone. Gone. Gone. Gone. Gone. Gone. Gone. Gone. Gone.
Gone. Gone. Gone. Gone. Gone. Gone. Gone. Gone. Gone. Gone. Gone.
Gone. Gone. Gone. Gone. Gone. Gone. Gone. Gone. Gone. Gone. Gone.
Gone. Gone. Gone. Gone. Gone. Gone. Gone. Gone. Gone. Gone. Gone.
Gone. Gone. Gone. Gone. Gone. Gone. Gone. Gone. Gone. Gone. Gone.
Gone. Gone. Gone. Gone. Gone. Gone. Gone. Gone. Gone. Gone. Gone.
Gone. Gone. Gone. Gone. Gone. Gone. Gone. Gone. Gone. Gone. Gone.
Gone. Gone. Gone. Gone. Gone. Gone. Gone. Gone. Gone. Gone. Gone.
Gone. Gone. Gone. Gone. Gone. Gone. Gone. Gone. Gone. Gone. Gone.
Gone. Gone. Gone. Gone. Gone. Gone. Gone. Gone. Gone. Gone. Gone.
Gone. Gone. Gone. Gone. Gone. Gone. Gone. Gone. Gone. Gone. Gone.
Gone. Gone. Gone. Gone. Gone. Gone. Gone. Gone. Gone. Gone. Gone.
Gone. Gone. Gone. Gone. Gone. Gone. Gone. Gone. Gone. Gone. Gone.
Gone. Gone. Gone. Gone. Gone. Gone. Gone. Gone. Gone. Gone. Gone.
Gone. Gone. Gone. Gone. Gone. Gone. Gone. Gone. Gone. Gone. Gone.
Gone. Gone. Gone. Gone. Gone. Gone. Gone. Gone. Gone. Gone. Gone.
Gone. Gone. Gone. Gone. Gone. Gone. Gone. Gone. Gone. Gone. Gone.
Gone. Gone. Gone. Gone. Gone. Gone. Gone. Gone. Gone. Gone. Gone.
Gone. Gone. Gone. Gone. Gone. Gone. Gone. Gone. Gone. Gone. Gone.
Gone. Gone. Gone. Gone. Gone. Gone. Gone. Gone. Gone. Gone. Gone.
Gone. Gone. Gone. Gone. Gone. Gone. Gone. Gone. Gone. Gone. Gone.
Gone. Gone. Gone. Gone. Gone. Gone. Gone. Gone. Gone. Gone. Gone.

Gone. Gone. Gone. Gone. Gone. Gone. Gone. Gone. Gone. Gone. Gone.
Gone. Gone. Gone. Gone. Gone. Gone. Gone. Gone. Gone. Gone. Gone.
Gone. Gone. Gone. Gone. Gone. Gone. Gone. Gone. Gone. Gone. Gone.
Gone. Gone. Gone. Gone. Gone. Gone. Gone. Gone. Gone. Gone. Gone.
Gone. Gone. Gone. Gone. Gone. Gone. Gone. Gone. Gone. Gone. Gone.
Gone. Gone. Gone. Gone. Gone. Gone. Gone. Gone. Gone. Gone. Gone.
Gone. Gone. Gone. Gone. Gone. Gone. Gone. Gone. Gone. Gone. Gone.
Gone. Gone. Gone. Gone. Gone. Gone. Gone. Gone. Gone. Gone. Gone.
Gone. Gone. Gone. Gone. Gone. Gone. Gone. Gone. Gone. Gone. Gone.
Gone. Gone. Gone. Gone. Gone. Gone. Gone. Gone. Gone. Gone. Gone.
Gone. Gone. Gone. Gone. Gone. Gone. Gone. Gone. Gone. Gone. Gone.
Gone. Gone. Gone. Gone. Gone. Gone. Gone. Gone. Gone. Gone. Gone.
Gone. Gone. Gone. Gone. Gone. Gone. Gone. Gone. Gone. Gone. Gone.
Gone. Gone. Gone. Gone. Gone. Gone. Gone. Gone. Gone. Gone. Gone.
Gone. Gone. Gone. Gone. Gone. Gone. Gone. Gone. Gone. Gone. Gone.
Gone. Gone. Gone. Gone. Gone. Gone. Gone. Gone. Gone. Gone. Gone.
Gone. Gone. Gone. Gone. Gone. Gone. Gone. Gone. Gone. Gone. Gone.
Gone. Gone. Gone. Gone. Gone. Gone. Gone. Gone. Gone. Gone. Gone.
Gone. Gone. Gone. Gone. Gone. Gone. Gone. Gone. Gone. Gone. Gone.
Gone. Gone. Gone. Gone. Gone. Gone. Gone. Gone. Gone. Gone. Gone.
Gone. Gone. Gone. Gone. Gone. Gone. Gone. Gone. Gone. Gone. Gone.
Gone. Gone. Gone. Gone. Gone. Gone. Gone. Gone. Gone. Gone. Gone.
Gone. Gone. Gone. Gone. Gone. Gone. Gone. Gone. Gone. Gone. Gone.
Gone. Gone. Gone. Gone. Gone. Gone. Gone. Gone. Gone. Gone. Gone.
Gone. Gone. Gone. Gone. Gone. Gone. Gone. Gone. Gone. Gone. Gone.
Gone. Gone. Gone. Gone. Gone. Gone. Gone. Gone. Gone. Gone. Gone.
Gone. Gone. Gone. Gone. Gone. Gone. Gone. Gone.
Gone. Gone. Gone. Gone. Gone.
Gone. Gone. Gone. Gone. Gone.
Gone. Gone. Gone. Gone. Gone.
Gone. Gone. Gone. Gone. Gone.
Gone. Gone. Gone.
Gone. Gone.
Gone.
Gone.

CHAPTER THIRTY

A Luncheon

When news of the *Eastland* disaster reached St. Joseph, Walter Steele and his friend Clarence Blake, co-owner of the Whitcomb Hotel, boarded the first train to Chicago. But when they arrived, they did not head to the river, to the scene of the accident and the heartbreaking rescue operations.

Instead, they made their way through the crowds to the St. Joseph-Chicago Steamship Company offices, a few blocks away from the overturned *Eastland*. When they got there, two plainclothes policemen immediately arrested Steele.

With his captors looking on, Steele told his half-dozen office underlings to help out with the rescue work and care of the survivors. And then he told the police something remarkable: The young man had his own motorcar, right there in Chicago.

He wanted to drive to lunch with his father, Julius, who was waiting for him at the Chicago Athletic Association. The exclusive establishment, about a mile from the *Eastland* chaos, was one of the finest restaurants in the city. Its colonnaded façade, facing Lake Michigan, was modeled after a Venetian-Gothic castle, the Doge's Palace.

The policemen agreed to accompany Steele. When they arrived for their luncheon, the regular menu at the Chicago Athletic Club, as it was popularly known, had oysters including Blue Points, Rockaways, and Cotuits. Also Little Neck clams, fried, broiled, steamed, stewed in milk, scalloped, or à la Newburg. Live lobster could be ordered broiled, steamed (whole), à la Delmonico, à la Newburg, or à la Bordelaise.

There were stuffed deviled crabs. Frog Legs à la Wells. Filet Chateaubriand.

Among dessert offerings, Almond Soufflé Pudding, Méringue Glacé, Lady Fingers.

In all, 835 mouthwatering dishes.

CHAPTER THIRTY-ONE

The Human Frog

Among the underwater body hunters employed by afternoon was Charles R. E. Bowles, a volunteer diver. Only seventeen, he paddled through the inside of the ship, emerging with oil on his muscled arms, the whites of his sunken eyes in sharp relief to a face darkened with muck. The veteran divers, who marveled at his underwater daredevilry and stamina, began calling him the Human Frog.

He worked along with another diver, "Frenchy" Deneau, whose heroism and theatrics in the early morning hours inside the *Eastland* would turn to notoriety in a matter of weeks.

Among the bodies the divers found were those of two little girls, locked in a death embrace. Likewise, Charles Trogg, a middle-aged equipment assembler, and his wife, Katherine, were found dead in one another's arms.

Divers removed one dainty young woman. In her right hand was an unmailed love letter. The river water had begun spiriting some of the inked letters away.

"I left . . . for you the other . . . heard from you . . . are busy, dearest . . . shed tears some evenings . . . see Doc? . . . I hear it . . . beautiful Chicago trip . . . for . . . I understand he . . . I could only . . . while I care . . . life is Hell . . . Well again . . . O, well . . . I am . . . boat Saturday."

"Life was hell," said a policeman, reading the letter over the shoulder of the diver who found it. "The last minute of it."

Divers in a continuous stream went down into the hold and came up staggering under the weight of bodies they recovered. In mid-river, half a dozen men, hauling a rope with several sharp barbed hooks, were nearly dragged into the water. They sent a diver down to investigate what they had snagged. He found that they had the *Eastland*'s piano on their line.

Jack Billow, an *Eastland* deckhand who was inside the hull helping divers, had seen the piano at one point and heard a moan. He and his partner waded over to the piano and found a woman. "She was alive but the baby in her arms, obviously her child, had been pitifully crushed by the piano and was dead.

"The woman, in a daze, kept her child clutched tightly in her arms, and it took all of our persuasion to induce her to let us hold him." He tied a rope around the mother and tugged on it, signaling she should be raised to the deck. They took the dead boy up to the deck and turned him over to the firemen.

§§§

The half dozen tugboats, yachts, and fireboats nudged to the side of the *Eastland* became crude but workable walkways. And in the hour since the sinking, hundreds of survivors had already crossed deck to deck, amid the prattle of water, to safety. Some had stepped easily onto the deck of the *Siren*, a yacht brought to the stern of the *Eastland*. The elegant clipper bow of the *Siren* extended well over the *Eastland*'s hull, allowing easy footing for survivors. When women came off the boat dripping wet, men, who were standing by, took off their coats and hung them over their shoulders. The women pulled them tightly under their chins.

Gone. Gone.
Gone. Gone. Gone. Gone. Gone. Gone. Gone.
Gone. Gone. Gone. Gone. Gone.
Gone. Gone. Gone. Gone.
Gone. Gone.
Gone.
Gone.

§§§

The next passengers across the deck were carried. Over the side of the *Eastland*, across the deck of the tugboat *Kenosha*, along the narrow dock, and up the stairs to the street level, crept a continuous double line of stretcher-bearers, policemen in long blue coats and white hats.

In time, the stretcher work hit a rhythm, with bodies removed from the hull at the rate of two a minute, each one dressed in Sunday finest, heavy and dripping, nothing but deadweight, a torso with arms and legs hanging. Toddlers were arranged two to a stretcher.

One lifeless woman extracted from the hull was laid out on a stretcher with a blanket thrown over her. As the four policemen carried her up to the street, to an ambulance, someone on a bridge nearby shouted: "I saw that woman's arm move! She's alive! She's alive!" The policemen laid the stretcher on the dock, removed the blanket, and were stunned to see the woman, bound for the morgue, blink her eyes.

"My God, boys, she is alive!" shouted one of the policemen. "Where am I?" she asked wearily. "What, what happened?"

§§§

Keeping order on the streets fell to Hermann Schuettler, the first deputy of the Chicago police. Schuettler was one of the tallest, fiercest men on the force. He had his eye on the chief's job. He was still remembered for his arrest of an anarchist in Chicago nearly three decades earlier. With a revolver pointed at him, Schuettler, then a patrol sergeant, grabbed and disarmed the gunman by biting one of his fingers off.

Faced with the overturned *Eastland* and the unfolding mayhem at the river, Schuettler gave orders for five hundred men to report to police headquarters earlier that morning, then march in a blue-coated show of force into a two-block zone surrounding the wreck.

A flotilla of small boats—steamers, motorboats, and rowboats—bobbed around the one-block watery grave between Clark and LaSalle. The *Petoskey*, *Kenosha*, *Racine*, *Waukegan*, *Indiana*, *Rita McDonald*, and the *Alice Stafford* had all motored over to help. By noon, the fishing for corpses wore on, as thousands of onlookers packed rooftops, bridges, docks, and office windows. They peered through opera glasses and telescopes. They snapped photos with boxy cameras.

The police struggled with friends and relatives of the victims surging about the narrow landing, frantic to reach the capsized ship. Every time a new group was rescued from the water there was another rush on the Clark Street Bridge and docks. Deputy Schuettler's men controlled the surging mob with interlocked arms and with clubs, and several resistant men pushing forward were cracked over the head and taken away bloody.

So many people packed onto the immense Clark Street Bridge that the police had to clear it, fearing that it would buckle. Policemen shouted in many tongues. "I was told in English, broken German and blarneyed Irish that I could not get through," said Gretchen Krohn, a writer trying to reach the disaster scene.

On the exposed side of the *Eastland*, some nineteen feet above the river, a group of rescuers paused and removed their hats when two baby carriages, each with a dead child, were lifted from the hold. People on the street above turned their heads away as the stiff children were placed inside a truck.

A short time later, a tiny baby, a year old perhaps, was taken from the hold of the *Eastland*. The child smiled into the face of the fireman rescuing him, and the man held him up for the crowd to see. Cheers rang from the docks, bridges, and buildings. A physician examined the child and found only a slight scratch on his arm.

By this time, Rista, the salvager, had dragged forty passengers to safety out of one porthole. R. J. Moore, a varnish salesman, gasped in an air pocket for more than thirty minutes before firemen found him and pulled him out. "When I came out," he said, "I wandered away. My clothes were all torn, and I was dazed."

In a fortunate stroke, a new chapter of the Red Cross had just opened that year in Chicago, and John Jay O'Connor, its young director, not yet thirty, was still living in a hotel when he was alerted to the capsizing. He quickly penned out a relief action-plan on the wallpaper of his hotel room. He then ripped the wallpaper off and took it to his Red Cross office to give his staff orders. He organized firemen, police, and volunteer workers. All available doctors were summoned, along with around fifty Catholic priests.

The pulleys used to lift lassoed bodies creaked continuously over the hull, as they had been doing since the *Eastland* flipped over hours ago. The squeaks reverberated off the brick buildings. The rescue workers kept lugging stretchers along, their toes cold, their sopping socks squishing for hours.

By 2:00 p.m., Chicago coroner Peter Hoffman had begun selecting a jury to investigate. He had been coroner since 1904, after many years of working in the grocery and railroad businesses. Rain and sweat streaking his face, he stood on the north bank of the river and dictated names of people he wanted to serve. He had photographers snap pictures of the ship from every angle.

"We will get every fact bearing on this horrible affair," the coroner vowed. "Every man, woman and child who has any information will be heard at the inquests."

Dr. William A. Evans, former commissioner of health, was chosen as foreman, and the jury would shortly begin several hours of viewing the bodies of the victims. Chief of Police Charles Healey, inspecting the hull late in the afternoon, estimated that there were still three hundred bodies in the ship that rescuers couldn't get to.

More than forty crewmembers and eyewitnesses to the disaster would be listed for questioning at the state's attorney's office, which called in all of its stenographers, anticipating more than one thousand pages of testimony.

District Attorney Charles F. Clyne met with reporters at the river, telling them, "We will leave no stone unturned in fixing responsibility for this accident, which has taken so many lives."

§§§

The downtown hotels took in scores of survivors, having already furnished hundreds of wraps and blankets. Carson, Pirie, Scott and Company and other large stores sent wagons and trucks to the scene to assist in removing the dead and injured. Marshall Field & Company turned its grand store on State Street into a relief station, supplying clothes and other items to survivors. Store employees worked into the night making stretchers, which were used to carry the dead on Marshall Field trucks to morgues.

The body of Katharine Krebel, who lived only to twenty-five, was identified and her parents were notified to expect the remains delivered. But in the confusion the wrong corpse was put on the truck to the family's home in the Cicero neighborhood near Western Electric. A shock awaited them when they would later unwrap the blanketed body of a stranger.

Across the river, rescue officials designated the stately, brick Reid-Murdoch warehouse as a temporary morgue. It was on the north bank of the river, a stone's throw from the capsized *Eastland*. Reid-Murdoch's employees happened to be having their own company picnic that day, and a building caretaker got permission from the management to open the basement and first floor. The grocery warehouse quickly became a makeshift city hall; the police, the state's attorney, doctors, and the coroner's jury all took over the offices, turning it into a command post.

Each body, numbered and tagged, was brought to the cement basement, where a few embalmers were gowned and cutting. The police searched pockets and clothing for valuables. They inserted any articles they found into envelopes with numbers matching the tag on the corpse. Truckloads of stretchers, blankets, and emergency supplies kept arriving from the State Street department stores. The alleyway behind the Reid-Murdoch building quickly became congested with trucks and delivery wagons. The front façade of the building faced the Chicago River, looking directly onto the *Eastland* disaster scene in the water below.

Bodies were stored in nearly every room on the lower floors of the warehouse. By the afternoon, fifty embalmers were working on makeshift operating tables. The members of the coroner's jury shouldered their way through the crowds—the police, the friends and relatives hunting for their loved ones—to find bodies left on desks, tables, and floors. In the pockets of several men, rescuers found folded copies of the *July Jubilator*, the Western Electric employees' picnic newspaper. Its front page read:

WHAT, HO, READERS OF THE JUBILATOR. BE JUBILANT . . . IT WILL BE A WHALE OF A BIG SUCCESS.

The four-page newspaper was filled with cartoons of what might have happened at the fifth annual picnic of employees, the largest yet. It mentioned a great parade in Michigan City, Indiana, with prizes for the most novel and beautiful costumes in the parade. And the salvagers and police came to realize that this was why some of the women pulled from the ship had such gorgeous gowns and elegant attire.

Bowles, the Human Frog, kept diving and resurfacing, diving and resurfacing. He single-handedly brought forty bodies to the surface. When he refused to rest, he had to be forcibly removed by the police. As Bowles was led away, he resisted, saying, "Just let me rest a little and I will be back. . . . I want to go on with the work because I know where there are several bodies. There are three or four under a steel plate that fell in while the men were cutting out sections, and there is another—the body of a woman wedged under an icebox. I will be back tomorrow."

CHAPTER THIRTY-TWO

"Who Has Little Martha?"

Phones made by the doomed Western Electric factory hands were immediately useful. The Chicago Telephone Company installed a bank of free phones at a row of stores near the *Eastland's* dock, for fire companies, physicians, hospitals, and police to reach each other and coordinate efforts. There was a special hotline to the Western Electric information bureau, set up in a vacant store on North Clark Street, to notify victims' relatives. Telephone company officials had tried vainly to find the shop owner, and then broke the lock on the door, burst in, and took over the store, wiring up a dozen phones.

Margaret Condon, the head telephone operator at the Western Electric factory, returned to her switchboard early that afternoon, to help handle inquiries for the missing. She had planned to go to the picnic that day and had arrived at the *Eastland* dock just as the ship sank. She would stay at the switchboard with few breaks for thirty-four hours, saying she didn't trust anyone else with the delicate task of handling frantic relatives.

"Some of them are so distracted," she told a coworker, "that they can't even remember the name of the people they're trying to find. It's terrible to sit here and hear them crying for their dead."

West Side undertakers were charging double and even triple the normal price for coffins to bury victims, according to reports making it to city authorities. Western Electric officials and the state's attorney began investigating dozens of accounts of undertakers jacking up the prices of coffins. They believed the undertakers were taking advantage of the fact that Western Electric had agreed to foot the bills.

Though many showed up at the river to help, others sought to capitalize on the catastrophe. Detectives arrested a teenager whom they found in the hull of the *Eastland* picking through the pockets of the dead with one hand, a fistful of cash in the other. A janitor at a building on North LaSalle Street was carrying a sandwich board on his chest, advertising a "Gallery of Horrors." The poster read,

Here You Are!
Come See Them Take the Bodies
From The Eastland From
This Building, Sixth Floor. All For 10 Cents!

By afternoon, flags throughout the city drooped at half-staff. The doors of City Hall were draped in black mourning curtains. For the first time in Chicago history, Major League Baseball cancelled games amid sunshine.

Incredible stories of fate spread as the day wore on. When Edward G. Murphy and his family reached the dock that morning, he discovered that he had forgotten his tickets. He rushed back home for them, and as his wife and children waited for him on the dock, they watched in horror as their ship capsized.

Eastland passenger Joe Brozak was spared by a nail, which snagged his coat. Four of his companions drowned. "If it had not been for the nail, I would be on the bottom of the river, I suppose," he told a reporter.

The moment the ship flung over, Frederick Willard, a chemical engineer for Western Electric, impulsively grabbed the first thing in reach, a steel cable alongside a doorway, and he clung to it while ten people around him sank into the water. A little girl of ten, Libby Hruby, only survived because a stranger she never saw managed to push her up over the railing to safety.

Mrs. Behnke, the terrified woman at the Iroquois hospital, ended up finding her husband and then pleaded with the Chicago newspapers to run a story about her missing three-year-old, Martha. The *Chicago Daily Tribune* ran a short story whose headline made it sound more like a flyer for a lost kitty: Who Has Little Martha? Later in the day, the child would be returned home.

By evening, a stream of bodies being pulled from two great holes in the hull was running at a rate of one corpse every three minutes. As rescuers burned another hole in the steel plate around five o'clock, they found a boy, about ten years old, penned in, clinging to a stanchion just above the water. He had been treading between life and death since that morning. When the firemen lifted him out, he was too overcome and too weak to talk or stand. After a few moments, he got up and ran frantically from the ship, disappearing into the crowd.

Over gray hours, four, then five, then six hundred twisted, stiffened forms of men, women, young girls, and babies had been carried away in a mournful procession in unrelenting drizzle. On the docks, on the streets: winding paths of ashy footprints. Side by side, the black footprints blended with the drizzle and trickled in dark streaks back into the river. The night fell.

CHAPTER THIRTY-THREE

The Confession

Noon, the next day. July 25. In City Hall, Room 505, down the corridor from the mayor's office, Joseph Erickson sat face-to-face with Chicago's police chief, Charles Healey.

After only nine years, Healey had risen from the ranks of the mounted police to the top of the force, proving himself a particularly skillful interrogator. As the rescuers toiled through the dusk, removing the bodies of 844 unfortunates from the river and the *Eastland*'s hull, Healey was utterly convinced this was no act of God. Someone was certainly responsible, and the chief was determined to get answers.

Chief Healey was particularly interested in grilling Erickson. As the ship made its fatal plunge, Erickson was right there, he knew, in the engine room, furiously eyeing the gauges and turning the critical valve handles in the belly of the *Eastland*, the nerve center of the ship's stabilizing system. Healey had a strong hunch that Erickson held the key to the cause of the disaster.

The police chief took it slowly. Noting Erickson's thick Norwegian accent, the police chief began with the basics, testing the engineer's command of the language. "Mr. Erickson, I am the chief of police. You understand who I am. I just want to talk with you for a minute. Your name is what?"

The stenographer scrawled and five witnesses listened in.

"Joseph M. Erickson."

"How old are you, Erickson?"

"Thirty-two, the 28th of March last."

"Married man?"

"Yes, sir."

After a few more questions, the police chief asked what his responsibilities were on the *Eastland*. "My duty was to have charge of the machinery, see that it was in good, running order," Erickson answered.

A few more questions, on operations of the ship, any history of accidents, dangerous tipping, and exactly how many passengers were on each of the decks. Erickson offered that the assistant to the treasurer of the *Eastland*'s company had been coming on board more and more that sailing season—was even aboard when the ship sank—repeatedly asking him whether he could keep the *Eastland* properly upright. The man's name was Ray Davis, the assistant to Walter Steele.

Then Healey bored in with an inquiry that turned a bit technical. The discussion turned to how the *Eastland* mechanically maintained its stability. Erickson explained the water ballast system and how it was used to "trim" the ship.

Healey asked, "If the proper trimming had been put to her the minute she started to list, could this accident have been avoided?"

"Not unless there was two or more seacocks," Erickson answered.

"How many have you?"

"One."

"What are the requirements of those boats by the government, as to having that number . . . of seacocks?"

The law "does not state," Erickson answered, correctly.

Digging, Healey asked, "Have you ever advised having more seacocks?"

Erickson paused. He thought back to May, to the day that Steele, the company officer he'd just met, came aboard to discuss refinements to the ballast system, ways to make the *Eastland* operate more smoothly. In the dreary hours after the *Eastland*'s capsize, the Steele conversation, the one that seemed so unremarkable at the time, must have surfaced in Erickson's mind.

It was only then that something entirely different, entirely more heartless, might have dawned on Erickson: Steele didn't share that he knew there were troubling stability problems the first season they operated the *Eastland*, in 1914. He never shared such information with Erickson, but, in hindsight, that may have been why he solicited Erickson's opinion on mechanical ways to improve the ship's stability.

Steele asked his advice, but left Erickson in the dark.

Looking at the police chief, Erickson did not doubt it was best to be honest. It came naturally to him. And, as the Norwegian proverb put it: What is honest never sinks.

Erickson told the police chief about the discussion on board with Steele, the top investor in the *Eastland*'s company, how the two had discussed ways to repair the ship in mid-May, two months prior. They discussed plans for mechanical repairs to make it more stable once the current sailing season ended.

"What conclusion did you come to?" asked Healey.

"That it could be done next fall," Erickson said.

"Why in your judgment has not that same thing been done before?"

"I have no way of explaining it," Erickson said, having just joined the *Eastland* himself weeks earlier. "It might have been overlooked."

CHAPTER THIRTY-FOUR

No. 396

Emergency electric lights flared and flickered along the Chicago River. Workers for the Commonwealth Edison Company strung 125 electric tungsten lamps along the upper side of the *Eastland* and wound them through its interior. Ten spotlights were trained on the hull from the roof and tower of the Reid-Murdoch building, the temporary morgue. The spotlights broke the night, with bright flashes the size of manhole covers shimmering in a glassy row on the black water around the overturned ship.

The *Chicago Sunday Tribune* pressmen began setting pages for the morning edition. Under the headline BODIES AWAITING IDENTIFICATION, there was a list of 526 corpses. The listings reduced each life to the smallest of facts at hand.

No. 97–Woman, black hair, 40 years old, light lavender dress, white waist with green bow.

No. 98–Man, brown hair, black clothes with white sport shirt with polka-dot tie, belt with the initial 'B.'

No. 145–Girl, 8 years old, light hair, blue dress, white stockings and black slippers.

No. 168–Woman, 25 years old, brown hair and gold crowns on upper front of jaw.

No. 215–Boy 10 years old, blond hair, white sailor suit, with red trimming, black shoes.

No. 299–Woman, 18 years old, 5 feet, 1 inch tall, 120 pounds, no clothing.

No. 342–Woman, 22 years old, light brown hair, bracelet on left arm, initials L.F.K.

No. 359–Baby girl, 18 months old.

No. 398–One-year-old boy, no clothes.

Men with megaphones directed people on the street to a single, central morgue established in a former Civil War munitions building, the Second Regiment Armory, on Washington Boulevard, just west of the river. Bodies from the Reid-Murdoch warehouse had overwhelmed the space in no time and had to be moved. Then the other mass morgues were swamped.

The corpses were sprayed with fly-repellants or covered in netting. The city had simply never had so many people perish so quickly.

Inside the cavernous building, with bodies lined eighty-five to a row, each tagged and numbered, there was one job left for Red Cross workers. They moved swiftly. Relatives would be arriving soon to identify their dead. With tender fingers, the Red Cross women and men worked like morticians, composing the features on faces and trying to rearrange limbs to look less gruesome.

§§§

The first of the crowd amassed outside the brick Armory building were allowed in at 10:00 p.m. They stepped inside, handkerchiefs over their faces. So many bodies. They began to process through the rows of corpses, looking for their loved ones. Under blankets, the bodies were stiff, terror frozen on faces, fingers curled in a final clutch.

Eyes on the floor, most of the strolling onlookers peeked at the shoes. Only if those looked familiar would they pull the blanket back, to check the face.

The Red Cross set up a nursery outside, with volunteer babysitters to watch the babies who came in with family members. The inside of the armory, the nurses decided, was no place for children's eyes.

Several nurses attended to women and men inside the building who had collapsed in shock and grief. One man laid across the body of his wife, calling to her to speak to him. After a time, policemen tried to carry him away, but he broke from their grasp and rushed back to her.

An elderly woman dropped to her knees, keening over the body of her daughter.

Coroner Hoffman, overseeing the grim operation, grew angry at the crushing crowds that first night. He grabbed a policeman's megaphone and yelled: "Our work is being hindered by many curiosity seekers. All persons not relatives or friends of the dead will have to leave." The crowd thinned.

After a hellish two days at the Armory building, 707 bodies had been identified and removed. Fourteen unidentified bodies remained, one of which would consume the city.

No. 396—Boy, 11 years old, short; brown hair, black rubber sole shoes, brown suit.

Word spread all over Chicago of the unknown *Eastland* boy. How could he be left for days? Where was his family? The newspapers carried stories, hoping to identify him. They nicknamed him "the little feller."

In time, the authorities would learn that it was Willie Novotny, who was in fact seven. No one had survived to identify him. His whole family perished on the *Eastland:* his father, James, the Western Electric carpenter, his mother, and his older sister, Mamie. The four left their home on 25th Street the previous Saturday morning and never returned.

In all, twenty-two whole families were wiped out in the disaster, notably the Sindelar clan, who lost eight people on the ship.

All of Chicago was moved by the tale of the nameless little feller. And when Willie was finally identified, he became the face of all the *Eastland* victims. His funeral was a civic event. More than five thousand people attended, showing up at the *Skola Vojta Naprstek*, his Bohemian school.

Cars rode in a mile-and-a-half-long procession. Hundreds of schoolboys and girls were on hand. The four Novotny caskets were surrounded by elaborate flower arrangements. A Boy Scout bugled taps.

With thirteen thousand people arriving at the cemetery, Mayor Thompson spoke. "The hearts of all Chicagoans go out in grief to the sufferers from this calamity. The city mourns."

CHAPTER THIRTY-FIVE

"The Angel"

He lied, to begin with.

Walter Steele was the ninth witness called before the coroner's jury, the inquest run by Cook County coroner Peter Hoffman. Steele's stonewalling over more than an hour on the stand would infuriate the state's attorney. And Steele would lie demonstrably at least four times, on his duties for the company, his conversations with Hull—even whether or not he had ever ridden on the *Eastland*.

In a practice dating back to medieval England, a coroner's jury was convened to determine the cause of a fatal accident. Typically, the hearing named a single victim who stood in for all the deceased. *Eastland* passenger Kate Austin, a cook for Western Electric's Cable Shop restaurant, was chosen to stand in for all 844 of the dead. The juries, often convened right at the accident site, would quickly take testimony and evidence while events and memories were fresh, then weigh it, and then attempt to assign blame.

Over nearly a week, some two dozen witnesses would be called to the coroner's hearing, starting with several passengers who survived the disaster, then the Chicago harbormaster and his assistant, both on duty at the Clark Street Bridge when the *Eastland* capsized. Questions and answers would flow for days. The hearing would summon several *Eastland* crewmembers, including Erickson's brother, Peter. And the coroner would eagerly call Captain Pedersen and Engineer Erickson.

After hearing from the first few witnesses in the two days after the *Eastland*'s capsizing, it became evident to Hoffman early Monday evening that the level of technical detail was befuddling, and the jury would benefit from a break and an inspection of the *Eastland* itself.

"Let us take a walk down to the boat, and we can talk a lot more intelligently," said the coroner through his dark, walrus mustache.

When they returned from the horror at the dock at 8:00 p.m., they called Walter Steele to the stand. Coroner Hoffman had seen Erickson's testimony to Police Chief Healey that Steele had discussed ways to improve the *Eastland*'s stability.

The coroner began by giving Steele enough rope for his own gallows.

"Are you familiar with the steamboat business, Mr. Steele?"

"Not at all," Steele replied.

"Do you know anything about boat construction?"

"Nothing whatever."

"Or running of boats?"

"No, sir."

"What are your duties as secretary?" the coroner asked.

"Signing my name to blank checks."

"What?"

"Signing my name to blank checks," Steele repeated.

"Is that all the work you have to do?"

"That is everything I have to do."

Flustered, Hoffman switched his tack. Erickson had told the police that Ray Davis, Steele's assistant, had been on board the *Eastland* in recent weeks, asking questions about how stable the ship was. Hoffman seemingly wanted to connect Davis to Steele, to establish that Steele, contrary to his professed ignorance, had actually been taking steps to investigate the *Eastland*'s stability.

Noting that Steele had referred to Davis as his "secretary," Hoffman asked, "Does he do your work?"

"Why, he classes himself my assistant."

"And what do you call him, if he calls himself that?"

"I do not call him anything; I call him Mr. Davis."

Getting nowhere, Hoffman returned to the check writing and tried to get Steele to describe his duties with the company. Steele said that despite the fact he signed checks for payments, he did not know anything about any repairs or modifications made to the *Eastland* under his company's ownership.

He said he wouldn't know such things, as he wasn't an "acting officer." That language would become important in future litigation, when Steele would reverse his testimony and insist he was precisely that, an acting officer of the company.

"You think it a good business proposition to sign checks en bloc for someone else to fill in?" Hoffman asked.

"No, sir, it is not."

"Is that what you are doing?"

"That is what I am doing."

"You do not consider that good business tactics?" Hoffman asked.

"No, sir."

Hoffman pressed. He established that Steele had put thirty thousand dollars into the corporation, making him the largest investor in the *Eastland*.

"Did you know, at that time or since, that the *Eastland* was a boat that would list easily?"

"I have heard it, but never seen it list, I did not believe it." A little later in the hearing he admitted that he might have mentioned to Captain Pedersen that the ship was "cranky."

"As secretary of your corporation since this terrible loss of life, the turning over of the *Eastland*, have you made any investigation tending to place the blame for this tremendous loss of life, sadness and sorrow?"

"No, sir, I have not," Steele said.

"Has your company tried to make an investigation and place the blame?"

"As to that I don't know, I haven't heard from anyone of the company." Within minutes, however, he would admit that he had, on further recall, been over to the house of his business partner, Hull, just yesterday.

State's Attorney Maclay Hoyne seemed to want to pin down Davis's role: Was he a Steele spy as Erickson came to suspect after the accident, checking that season on the *Eastland*'s steadiness? Hoyne directed the line of questioning back to the check writing.

"What does Mr. Davis have to do with reference to those checks?" Hoyne asked.

Steele answered, "He might mail them."

"Now, are there any other duties that you are charged with that Mr. Davis gives you assistance in?"

"No, sir."

"So that so far as Mr. Davis assisted you, his sole duty was to mail checks when you sign them in blank, is that right?"

"Why, no," Steele said.

"This is a serious matter, Mr. Steele," Hoyne fired back. "I am not joking."

"I know, Mr. Hoyne. I am answering your questions just as plain as I know how," Steele said.

"I am trying to find out how your corporation is run," Hoyne retorted.

He asked a few more questions. Perhaps having gathered press accounts of how Steele was the first company officer to disembark from the *Eastland* when it arrived in St. Joseph in 1914, Hoyne wondered: "Have you ever ridden on the boat yourself?"

"Never," Steele said. A staunch denial. Also a lie, on the record.

"Was that matter discussed before your board of directors before you bought the boat, the matter of her safety?" Hoyne continued.

"No, the matter of profit."

Then, when Hoyne asked him about repairs that needed to be made to the *Eastland* after Steele's company bought the ship, he said there was nothing extraordinary, merely spring maintenance, for which he himself set a budget of only four thousand dollars. This completely contradicted his earlier assertions that he did nothing but sign blank checks and had no knowledge of the ship or its repairs or maintenance.

"We understood there were no repairs to be made other than the regular spring fit-out," Steele said.

"And did they mention what that would be, this item of cost?" Hoyne asked.

"I gave them a limit myself," Steele said.

"What did you give as the limit?"

"$4,000."

"Was there any objection to that as a limit by anybody?"

"No, sir, there was not," Steele replied.

The coroner asked, "Did you ever have a discussion with the officers of your company regarding the stability of the *Eastland*?"

"No, sir."

"Any complaints or any anxiety ever exhibited or reported by anyone as to her cause of listing very often and very easily?"

"No, sir."

"Nothing of that kind ever came up?"

"Why, I understood once Mr. Hull mentioned the boat was returning, and I understand that she listed a trifle up in South Haven, and I asked why she listed and he said on account of the shallow water." Steele was referring to the near-capsize of the *Eastland* outside South Haven in July of 1904. It had been in the newspapers in Chicago after it happened, and it had resurfaced in the headlines days after the *Eastland* disaster.

In further questioning, Steele admitted to meeting Erickson on the *Eastland* in May, just weeks earlier. He said that Hull had hired Erickson, and that at no time was his father-in-law, Inspector Reid, involved with the hiring. Steele then changed what he had said several moments earlier, testifying he had in fact ridden on the *Eastland* before.

"All right, you met Mr. Erickson on the boat," Hoyne continued. "Did you have anything to say to him about the [ballast] tanks?"

"No, sir."

How often, Hoyne wanted to know, did he meet Erickson and talk with him?

"I might have passed the time of day with him every time I went through the engine-room," Steele said.

"Ever talk to him about the condition of the boat?"

"No, sir, I did not," Steele said.

"About trimming the boat?"

"No, sir."

"Ever use the word stability or anything of that sort?"

"No, sir."

"From the time you acquired the *Eastland*, by purchase, is there any time any of the employees of the boat ever had a talk with you about the safety or security of passengers on the boat?"

Steele replied definitively. "Never anybody said anything."

Hoyne was incredulous.

"Then, as I understand, Mr. Steele," he said, "you say you simply put your money in the boat and never knew anything about the boat or the business or management of the corporation, or the boat or anything else, is that right?"

"Yes, sir," he said.

"You acted the part of angel?" Hoyne asked, meaning the leading investor in a private business deal.

"Yes, sir," Steele said. "I was the angel."

§§§

On the rooftop, several stories above the coroner's hearing room where Steele spoke, clothing sagged on laundry lines.

Shirts, rompers, pants, and dresses of the *Eastland* victims sopping with river water had been gathered by police and rescuers. To prepare for a vast lost-and-found for survivors, health-department workers dipped the clothing in disinfecting solutions and strung it all to dry across the roof of City Hall.

The next day, back in St. Joseph, Steele wrote letters to salvage companies, soliciting bids to resurrect the *Eastland*. He would mention to reporters in a few days that he hoped to make repairs to the *Eastland* and begin running it out of another port.

Steele also filled out the St. Joseph-Chicago Steamship Company's annual financial report for 1914, which had to be filed with the state of Michigan. In Steele's quite elegant writing, nearly calligraphy, he wrote that the company had $36.06 in cash on hand and $25,300.34 in debt.

CHAPTER THIRTY-SIX

Muzzling Erickson

In Chicago that same day, the coroner brought Joseph Erickson to the stand. Among other things, the investigators wanted to try to address Steele's denial that the two *Eastland* men had previously discussed ship stability.

After Erickson was sworn in, Hoffman notified him that any testimony he gave could be used against him in a criminal proceeding and that Erickson did not have to testify if he did not want to. Hoffman asked if he had a lawyer.

"I have no counsel," Erickson said. "I haven't seen any, and I haven't made any effort to see anyone. I will testify as near as I can remember every—all the fact, the truth."

"May I make a statement?" asked James Barbour, interrupting. He was the attorney for Walter Steele.

Only forty-seven, Barbour had had a brilliant career, having already brought two cases before the US Supreme Court. Bald and moonfaced, he was one of the leading lights in Chicago law. In 1905, Barbour had successfully defended the theater owners and others charged in the grisly Iroquois Theatre fire in Chicago.

"The Company wants the facts brought out, of course," Barbour said, "but the Company's interest may be entirely different than the individual's ... I should have to advise [the employees], if they want my advice, not to take the stand." Barbour similarly argued that Captain Pedersen, also not his client, should not appear before the coroner's jury.

Fired up, State's Attorney Hoyne looked at Erickson. "I am in the position of public prosecutor, who may be called upon to prosecute you in a criminal proceeding. Someone must be punished for what has happened here." He then mentioned that he had heard Erickson had already made a statement to the police chief, but that he had yet to read it. Given that, Hoyne suggested he not testify, to protect himself.

Erickson was clearly bewildered. "This is the first time I have been in court," he replied, "and I am not familiar with things."

The coroner asked Erickson if the statement he made to the police was "the truth, and the whole truth."

Barbour objected, suggesting that answering that would constitute testimony.

"Let it go at that, then," the coroner said, relenting. And he gave Barbour a warning: "He did so testify last evening, and if we wanted to use that, Mr. Barbour, we could use it just the same. I believe that statement should be used by this jury, anyway. If I can help them get it, I will do so."

Trying to squelch the damning testimony by Erickson before the police chief, Barbour replied, "I don't wish to make it a public record."

Coroner Hoffman was adamant. "It is a part of the investigation in this case," he said, "and they may want it for the purpose of getting information, and we can turn it over to them."

Five witnesses later, as the coroner's inquiry was winding down, Peter Erickson was called. He was only nineteen and, as merely an oiler, he knew very little about the technicalities of the ballast tanks and ship stability.

To many questions, he simply did not know the answers. As with other investigations that were to unfold, the zealous inquisitors knew little about marine matters, either, creating a pile of useless back-and-forth testimony littered with false starts, technical absurdities, and dead-end lines of inquiry.

The coroner, perhaps thinking the chief engineer's bumpkinly brother might spill something useful, at one point asked: "What was said between you and your brother regarding this matter: did he mention to you what you were to say if you were called upon to testify here?"

Peter Erickson thought about Joseph and replied immediately. "He told me to tell the truth."

CHAPTER THIRTY-SEVEN

"You Were Lucky in Cleveland"

The *Eastland* tragedy, from Chicago all the way to Washington, struck many as an indictment of big business. Carl Sandburg, who was a Chicago reporter for *The International Socialist Review* and was tinkering with verse in his spare time, railed against man's inhumanity to man, and the grinding of the working class in the gears of capitalism. "Men, women and children, trapped like rats in a cellar, are drowned," he wrote. "Grim, industrial feudalism stands with dripping and red hands behind the whole *Eastland* affair."

In President Woodrow Wilson's cabinet, William Redfield was the one immediately on the hot seat for the *Eastland* disaster. He was chief of the Department of Commerce, which ran the Steamboat Inspection Service. If a steamer capsized at its dock, killing hundreds, where were the inspectors? What inspector passed off on the safety of such a ship?

Redfield was an old-school industrialist, involved in manufacturing machinery and iron and steel products prior to being appointed secretary of commerce. In 1912, he authored a book titled *The New Industrial Day* with the implausible premise, in an era of violent labor relations, that scientific management procedures would produce greater harmony between employers and employees.

In the days following the disaster, the commerce secretary telegraphed Wilson, vacationing in New Hampshire, telling him that he would personally look into the matter. Redfield took a train to Chicago to preside over an investigation with the clandestine purpose, his critics claimed, of absolving his inspectors of any wrongdoing. In short order, he would hurry back to Washington, with several death threats, a trashing by Chicago's Mayor Thompson, and a derailed hearing.

The Redfield panel met in the federal building, which, like City Hall, was only a few blocks from the overturned *Eastland*, still laying on its side. As with the coroner's hearing, there were days of questions and answers, grandstanding, reprisals, flashbulbs, and a thicket of often-useless testimony.

They called early *Eastland* captains, the Customs Department men who counted the passengers boarding the ship, naval engineers, and inspectors. They plowed the same ground:

Was there nepotism between Reid and son-in-law Erickson?

What happened with the near-capsize in 1904 outside South Haven?

What about the five-thousand-dollar reward the *Eastland* owners offered in the Cleveland newspapers, the one to combat safety rumors?

The Redfield panel bore in on Nils Nelson, a supervising inspector in Cleveland, who oversaw the *Eastland* when it operated out on Lake Erie. Nelson said the water-ballast system wasn't the best but it worked. Asked what would be a better system, he ducked the question.

When Assistant State Attorney M. F. Sullivan rebuked him for not responding, Nelson replied, "From the very fact that we never had any accident there, I would say that the water system was alright to handle her."

"You were lucky in Cleveland," retorted Sullivan, "and we were not here."

Redfield, with his polka-dot ties and extravagant mutton-chop sideburns, made some bumbling missteps. The opening of the hearing was delayed fifteen minutes on one morning while he insensitively opened and read his personal mail.

He found a couple surprises. One letter writer vowed to "push the Secretary into the river" and was signed "Murderer." The other, signed "Republicans," advised Redfield to flee the city immediately before some crank killed him.

The Chicago papers began to carry parody caricatures of Redfield's "whitewashing" the whole *Eastland* tragedy. Editorials lambasted him. Chicago's mayor "Big Bill" Thompson publicly fumed that the Redfield investigation was a "farce," threatening to get on a train to protest to President Wilson himself.

Within a week, a federal judge in Chicago would effectively shut down the Redfield hearing, ruling that no one subpoenaed to appear before a federal grand jury looking into the *Eastland* disaster could testify elsewhere. That precluded all the officers and crew of the *Eastland*.

Scars from the Redfield debacle ran deep. Early on in the proceedings, Redfield summoned his two inspectors, Robert Reid and Charles Eckliff, from Grand Haven, Michigan. When they arrived in Chicago, overzealous city police immediately handcuffed them and brought them to the hearing. Redfield was incensed that officers of the United States were shackled, though no charges had been filed against them.

But the inspectors would be very grateful for those handcuffs when they had their day in court.

§§§

In his City Hall office, Maclay Hoyne, the Illinois state prosecutor, slammed down his phone. Police Chief Healey told him he had just turned over the revealing fifteen-page typewritten transcript from his interview with Erickson to federal investigators. State and federal prosecutors had fought each other for days to develop charges in the *Eastland* disaster. They each convened competing grand juries. And now the feds had custody of Erickson's signed statement, evidence so hot it burned through its thin pages.

The coroner's jury came to a verdict at 1:00 a.m. on Thursday, July 29, after twenty-five hours of hearings and questioning nearly two dozen witnesses. It recommended that six men be brought before a grand jury on the charge of manslaughter: Hull, Pedersen, and Erickson from the steamship company; Walter Greenebaum, who chartered the *Eastland* for Western Electric; and the two federal steamboat inspectors in whose district the *Eastland* operated, Robert Reid and Charles Eckliff.

Cocooned at his home in St. Joseph since the *Eastland* rolled over, Hull hired armed guards to resist any attempt to extradite him to Chicago to face charges.

His first visitor was George Arnold, a well-known shipping man from Mackinaw City, Michigan, who was nominally the president of the St. Joseph-Chicago Steamship Company. Arnold partnered with Steele and Hull to build a formidable legal team. Four days after the disaster, the two company executives met at Hull's home with Barbour, who was Steele's lawyer, and an even more high-powered attorney, Charles Edward Kremer.

The sixty-six-year-old Kremer, nicknamed "The Admiral," was one of the world's top experts on admiralty law and a lecturer at the University of Chicago. He had founded the Chicago Yacht Club in 1875 and routinely regaled audiences in his Irish brogue with salty old tales of the Great Lakes.

Behind guarded doors, the two executives and two lawyers discussed details of the tragedy, how to protect the company's interests amid the investigations, and the company's future. They also had to strategize over testifying: Hull had just been summoned before the grand jury in Chicago. Arnold would surely be called too.

After their meeting, Hull had Kremer issue a statement to the press. Kremer faulted improper water ballast for the accident and laid the blame squarely on Pedersen.

"The captain is an autocrat," Kremer's statement said. "He could throw the President of the United States off his boat if he tried to boss the job. I cannot imagine any reason in the world why the ship should not have been ballasted that day."

In hanging the ballast, of course, the owners also put the noose firmly around Joseph Erickson's neck.

CHAPTER THIRTY-EIGHT

The Charges

The man who closed the curtain on the Redfield hearing was Kenesaw Mountain Landis. The judge was named for Kennesaw Mountain, near Atlanta, where his father, a federal soldier in the Civil War, lost a leg.

Landis gained the national spotlight in 1907, two years after Theodore Roosevelt appointed him to the federal bench for the Northern District of Illinois, when he levied an eye-popping fine of $29.4 million on the large and unpopular Standard Oil Company. The judgment won the young judge wide acclaim, though higher courts set aside the ruling and the company never paid a penny.

Landis was fiery. He insisted the federal grand jury walk down to the *Eastland*, still overturned in the river. He seemed to want them to feel whatever pain, whatever violence, lingered there. They were photographed there, a group of twenty or so men standing in suits and hats, like some odd family reunion, on the side of the capsized ship.

The federal grand jury ran into repeated delays in the chaos after the sinking, and at one point, Landis became so impatient, so dad-gummit flustered, that he stepped from his bench, disrobed, and marched out of his courtroom. With a purposeful gait, punctuated by his swinging a small walking stick, he arrived moments later at the Clark Street Bridge to hover above the overturned *Eastland*.

Subpoenaed, Hull arrived in Chicago on Friday, July 30, to testify before the federal grand jury. His attorney, Kremer, refused to let him speak. "It is not because he has anything to conceal," Kremer told Landis. "But probably we can put it plainer than he can."

After hearing testimony, much of it first teased out in the coroner's inquest, the other grand jury, the state one, issued indictments for manslaughter against the company owners, including Steele, and criminal carelessness against Pedersen and Erickson.

"The instability of this vessel," the indictments read, "abundantly indicated by experience . . . could have easily been corrected by means of fixed ballast. That it was not corrected years ago we regard as indicating criminal carelessness."

The grand jury recommended moving inspections of ships from the Commerce Department to the Navy. It also said that ships going forward should be constructed so the ballast tanks could be simultaneously filled on one side and pumped out on the other, to make trimming maneuvers more responsive.

Bail was set at ten thousand dollars for the *Eastland* men. Steele had his handicapped brother, Blair, bring cash over to pay for his release, but the police refused to accept it. They might have been concerned Steele was a flight risk, that he might simply disappear if they released him. "I haven't done anything of a criminal nature," Steele told reporters, aggravated that he then had to find property or other assets to secure his release. "I am not worrying about myself, nor am I worrying about the $30,000 I put in the company."

He was released within two days, as was Captain Pedersen, who arranged for a saloon owner to cover his bail. Erickson, however, couldn't raise the cash. Behind bars and without a lawyer, he had no way to organize any compatriots with property or other assets to secure his release. He had neither the clout nor the assets of Hull or Steele. And it was clear from the company's actions; Erickson was on his own.

His wife, Florence, arrived from St. Joseph, and stayed with a girlfriend in the city. Born in Chicago and with friends still there, Florence undoubtedly began fund-raising for her husband's bail, but it would take some time.

It was not a good time for her to be stressed. Both her father, Inspector Reid, and her husband were facing the penitentiary, and she was carrying her first child.

§§§

The other *Eastland* crewmembers, imprisoned about a week, were released outright. Many had been living on the ship and, on being freed, were homeless. A few decided to write a letter to the *Chicago Tribune*, requesting help.

Maybe you know that the crew of the Eastland lost all their clothing and everything in the ill-fated ship. A couple of days ago we have been released from the several police stations in which we were held as witnesses.

As most of us were without hats, or coats or even shoes, we went to the relief committee and other places to get some clothing and every-where they told us they can't do nothing for the crew and that we should be thankful to have saved our lives.

Now, we ask you, what is the use, we saved our lives, if we are penniless, naked and unemployed? We don't ask thousands of dollars, we only ask some clothing and underwear . . .

SOME OF THE CREW OF THE DEATH SHIP EASTLAND

§§§

Two weeks after the sinking, several salvage ships, including the *Favorite*, worked the better portion of a day to raise the *Eastland* from the muck of the Chicago River. Finally righting the misbegotten ship, the salvagers were shocked when they got inside. A corpse was trapped in the wreckage. At forty-four years old, he had only managed a living of twelve dollars a week, as a Western Electric worker. He left a widow and eight children.

Gone.

§§§

A. B. Gibson, the national president of the Marine Engineers' Beneficial Association, Erickson's labor union, wrote a letter that August to all "Lake brethren."

"From newspaper accounts," he wrote, "it appears to me that the chief engineer and possibly the captain of the *Eastland* are to be made the goats of this disaster. If this is the case, it is certainly unfortunate that the real offenders cannot be reached."

He recommended a one-thousand-dollar defense fund be set up to help their brother, the chief engineer. The union immediately sent $150 toward Erickson's bail. Florence and others managed to scare up enough property to get her husband out of jail. Several Chicago homes and buildings were pledged to free Erickson, including an 1895 barn.

State and federal prosecutors in Chicago held a "harmony" meeting. They decided to let the federal grand jury proceed with the prosecution of the *Eastland* men. Fully in control, Judge Landis issued bench warrants for the arrest of the company owners and officers, the man who chartered the *Eastland*, and the two government inspectors. The charges were conspiracy to operate an unsafe ship and criminal negligence.

The conspiracy charge carried a fine of ten thousand dollars or two years imprisonment, or both. Under the carelessness charge, the maximum penalty was a fine of ten thousand dollars, or ten years in the penitentiary, or both.

Barbour and Kremer petitioned Judge Landis, telling him their clients would fight any extradition efforts to force them to Chicago to stand trial.

The federal charge of "conspiracy" was different than the manslaughter one recommended by the state. Within a few months, that would prove to be a tremendous boon for the *Eastland* men.

CHAPTER THIRTY-NINE

Fifteen Typed Pages

Clarence Darrow was busy that autumn. He was defending a lawyer charged with embezzling. He was also preparing a plea for a pardon for a confessed forger whose spectacular career bilked victims out of $1.6 million. At the same time, he was readying his defense of Frank Lloyd Wright, the architect whose fame was stretching far beyond Chicago. He had just been charged under the Mann Act for taking a sculptress across state lines and being indecent with her.

Reading a pamphlet or a book of poetry, Darrow would nibble on grapes or an apple in his rocking chair, when he wasn't at his heavy black desk, which a carpenters' union made to pay him for legal services.

Each time the door opened, he worried it would be Agnes Lindsay. She had been harassing him, coming to his office in recent weeks, complaining that Darrow had withheld settlement money from her. By early September, her protests had grown loud, spirited, and threatening. Darrow had had it. He called the police. They took her away.

One day, the figure in Darrow's doorway was slight, gaunt. The short man looked frightening.

He wasn't world-weary, like Darrow's other supplicants; he was traumatized. His cheeks were sunken. His eyes, dark sockets. He was sickly, skeletal.

He introduced himself as Joseph Erickson. He was the chief engineer of the *Eastland*, and he was in trouble.

§§§

War in Europe was bleeding into America. President Wilson was talking about "preparedness." Having amassed a fortune in the past decade, Henry Ford announced he would sail a Peace Ship to the continent, on a mission to help end hostilities. The auto baron began inviting along on his voyage peace-loving, Progressive celebrities, including Jane Addams and Darrow.

Darrow declined, releasing a measured statement to the press. "I cannot believe that it is either wise or right for us to interfere in this matter," he said. "Still I am hoping I am wrong and that good will come of it."

Privately, he had a more caustic response. In a letter to his old girlfriend, Mary Field, Darrow wrote, "I had an invitation to go on the Ford ship, but told some of my friends that I could make a D—n fool of myself without leaving Chicago."

And there was another reason. Darrow had a case to prepare for. He had asked for a one-thousand-dollar retainer to defend Erickson. The engineer told him he could pay it; his union brothers had started a defense fund. Everyone pitched in, with donations as little as $1.75. The thousand-dollar fee was one of the biggest retainers Darrow had booked since beating the bribery charges two years earlier, since returning to Chicago hoping to restart his career.

The newspapers would surely play up what promised to be a sensational trial. Coast to coast, the *New York Times, San Francisco Chronicle, Philadelphia Inquirer,* along with several Chicago city newspapers, had covered every step of the *Eastland* disaster: the accident; the sad parade of stretchers bearing corpses; the mass funerals; the hearings and investigations; and the unidentified dead boy, the Little Feller, No. 396.

There was one hole in all the coverage. That statement Erickson had given to the police chief had not been released to the public. It did not make any press accounts. It must have troubled Darrow as he began to prepare his defense. It was a bombshell. How to defend his client from that? He thumbed through a copy of the fifteen-page typewritten statement, making notes. The margins contained the words "Conversation with Steele," "Seacock," and "Listing."

At the bottom of page 14, the police chief asked Erickson precisely who within the company knew what would stop any stability issues on the *Eastland*. He replied, "Why, the general manager and the secretary, they all knew."

Next to that passage, in the pitiful penmanship that was signature-Darrow, were two words: Owners knew.

PART III:
TRIAL AND ERROR

CHAPTER FORTY

Running from the Law

Owners knew.

The federal prosecutors had very strong evidence. More than eight hundred deaths, a steamship capsized while still tied to its dock. No act of God. No iceberg. No torpedo.

Two chief engineers of the *Eastland* confessed to investigators in Chicago that the shipowners had discussed stability problems in 1914 and 1915. And one of those engineers, Erickson, told the police he had personally been asked by Steele, the largest shareholder among the owners, about modifying the *Eastland*'s mechanics to make it steadier in the water—a mere two months before the catastrophe.

There was a history of near-accidents on the *Eastland* going back a dozen years. Surely, the owners were negligent if they didn't bother to learn about them. Then, the stonewalling and outright lies. In front of the coroner's jury in Chicago, Steele—the self-proclaimed angel of the *Eastland*'s company— lied repeatedly.

As to the government's steamboat-inspection service, it simply didn't connect the dots as the *Eastland* moved from Lake Michigan to Lake Erie and then back. The inspectors themselves set off red flags, then failed to follow them up.

In the next ten days, the captain would weep on the stand, and the two sides would clash over everything, even whether the Chicago River technically existed anymore. Throughout, Clarence Darrow would shamble and drawl, slouch and cough, angling for moments to foil the prosecutors.

Now, seven months after the disaster, was the moment for justice. There was surely criminal misconduct with such a horrific number of wrongful deaths. The guilty would surely be exposed. Long penitentiary sentences were surely coming—unless the defense could somehow outduel the prosecutors.

§§§

It probably galled Darrow, the opening by prosecutors.

They filled two long tables, the teams for the defense and the prosecution, in the courtroom of Judge Clarence Sessions on Thursday morning, January 20, 1916. The federal court building was in downtown Grand Rapids, Michigan, a furniture-manufacturing town on the Grand River, the second largest locale in the state, after Detroit.

All but one of the men charged with criminal responsibility for the *Eastland* disaster lived in Michigan. Several of them petitioned the federal court in Grand Rapids to resist any prosecutorial efforts to return them to Chicago to answer the charges there. Michigan could extradite them, but first it required some assurance they were correctly indicted, not merely swooped up in some bloodthirsty quest for scapegoats.

The federal prosecutors under the law of the time would first have to make their case there in Grand Rapids. If they succeeded, the *Eastland* men would be ordered to stand full trial in Chicago. Both sides were set for a blistering fight in Michigan; between them, they had summoned seventy witnesses. And this was merely the dress rehearsal.

Sessions's jawline disappeared into his thick neck, adorned with a crisscross bow tie. He sat at his bench between two imposing Ionic columns, each eighteen feet tall, three feet around. Looking down, Sessions watched as the lawyers prepared to make opening statements.

The judge's father was a Presbyterian deacon, and Clarence Sessions, himself, grew up on his parents' farm. He married a preacher's daughter. President William Howard Taft had appointed him US district judge for western Michigan in 1911.

Opening for the prosecution was Myron Walker, who lived in Grand Rapids all his life, and went to the Fountain Street Baptist Church. Sessions, the federal judge there in Grand Rapids, a man about town himself, would see in Walker a familiar face among the rest of the prosecutors from big cities, Chicago and Washington.

It was exactly the kind of gesture Darrow used many times in the past. In previous cases on the road, Darrow frequently retained associate counsel from the community, someone familiar with the local laws, procedures, quirks, and judges. It was a way to bridge gaps. It said that Darrow was not an interloper, esteemed members of the jury, he was one of them.

And here the prosecution beat the defense to it. All the attorneys defending the *Eastland* men were influential high-dollar lawyers from Chicago, and one was a national expert on maritime law. But what could Darrow do? His reputation was battered at that time, and, anyway, it wasn't his case to lead, not yet.

For now, he had to coordinate with a team of six other lawyers. Several of the indicted men were ready to blame the others to absolve themselves, stirring a poisonous internecine well.

For them, Myron Walker was a bad start.

The six defendants sitting there, Walker began, were criminally negligent by allowing the *Eastland* to run on July 24, 1915, when they knew the ship was poorly constructed, dangerous, and improperly manned. Walker then put the *Eastland*'s liquid ballast machinery on trial, the one Jenks had installed in 1903 to hop the sandbar in South Haven.

Walker had just turned sixty-one and had been a lawyer for thirty-five years. Like Darrow, he was a social and industrial reformer. He was a member of the Consumers League of Michigan, an advocacy group founded in the reform spirit of Jane Addams to fight for fair labor laws and food-safety practices, among other things.

Walker, who had a high, bald forehead, a bushy mustache, and sunken cheeks, saw the *Eastland* case in the larger framework of consumer and worker protection. Prosecuting the *Eastland* men, for him, was about sending a message: Severe penalties await those responsible for industrial atrocity.

He bored in. The *Eastland* "was equipped with a water-ballast system which was inadequate and ineffectual to control the steamship." Among other flaws, Walker said, was the way the crucial water flowed into the bottom of the *Eastland*, the water used to counterbalance any unwanted tipping of the ship. A single seacock was inadequate, among other problems, he said, making the *Eastland* easy to mishandle.

"She was manned," he continued, "with an incompetent and untrained complement of officers and crew, who were incompetent to run and navigate said *Eastland* or operate her engines, ballast system or equipment." All of which, he said, made the *Eastland* "unsafe and unfit for navigation," especially carrying twenty-five hundred passengers.

These six, he concluded, "had knowledge of these facts and connived together still to send her upon this voyage in this unsafe and unseaworthy condition, thereby endangering the life of the passengers and causing loss of life."

He sat down.

James Barbour rose. The Chicago attorney would lead the defense on the first day. He was brief in his opening remarks.

He argued that the *Eastland* indictments did not jibe with the offenses as charged, and he asked, therefore, that the charges and the defendants be dismissed right then and there.

Sessions, who at fifty-seven had a great shock of gray hair above his black robe, noted the objection and denied the request.

The Red Cross Toll

The Red Cross immediately began tracking down the survivors of the *Eastland* victims and parceling out disaster-fund money according to the number of people who died, the loss of wage earners, the family's financial distress, and other factors.

In a final reckoning, the Red Cross listed each family's case by number and nationality; it boldfaced the relation and age of those who died on the *Eastland*.

No. 75. (German) **Mother, 21**; daughter, 6 months.
A young wife was drowned. She had been deserted by the husband a year before. When the child was born she had placed it in the care of her parents and had returned to work as soon as possible. The *Eastland* excursion was her first bit of pleasure since she had been deserted.

No. 393. (Irish) **Husband, 35; son, 4**; wife, 34; daughter, 9; daughter, 8.
The husband and little boy were drowned. He had been a Western Electric Company employee at twenty-three dollars a week. The wife's only "consolation" was that these two, between whom there had been an unusually strong tie, had gone to their death together. She planned to take boarders, as housework was all she could do.

No. 216. (German) **Daughter, 21,** mother, 56; son, 23.
A daughter, employed by the Western Electric Company, was drowned. She was the chief support of the widowed mother, and for that reason had been delaying her marriage. The son had but one leg and was able to earn but a small wage.

CHAPTER FORTY-ONE

A Toy Boat

Darrow and the defense team had several theories to work with. The press was filled with the musings of eyewitnesses, often faulty and contradictory. And several engineers, labor leaders, and naval experts had their own theories.

One: The *Eastland* tipped over because the crowd on the top deck rushed to the riverside when a boat with a movie-camera passed. Movies were fascinating, still fairly novel. A crowd would plausibly rush to see a movie man.

Two: The tugboat *Kenosha*, with its line attached to the *Eastland* to ferry it away from the dock, pulled the large steamer over. This was plausible as the *Eastland* did topple over that direction.

Three: The *Eastland* was top-heavy because of new maritime rules following the *Titanic* disaster three years prior where there were insufficient lifeboats for all those aboard. American ships were about to be required to carry more lifeboats and rafts. The *Eastland*, complying with the rules in advance, had been carrying a few extra lifeboats that July morning that made the ship tip over. Very enticing, blame the government.

Ultimately, none of these was deemed a worthwhile defense. Testimony at the coroner's hearing effectively tamped down the rumor that passengers rushed to one side on the top deck. A quick check of the facts brought out in the earlier inquiries showed the tugboat did not even have its engines running at the time it supposedly pulled the *Eastland* over. And the effect of the extra lifeboats that day was just too paltry, equivalent to the weight of one hundred or so passengers—they could not have sunk the gigantic ship.

The real problem was explaining the ship's bizarre behavior the morning of the disaster, when the *Eastland* tipped toward starboard for a time, then toward port, then quickly capsized. What made it seesaw? The prevailing theories couldn't explain this inarguable fact.

This is where Darrow used an old strategy: point the finger of blame at something else. If the prosecutors planned to blame the faulty structure and machinery of the ship, the defense would counter with a phantom excuse.

Their idea: The *Eastland* must have been sitting on some underwater obstruction, specifically, pilings driven into the riverbed. That would explain why it tipped one way, then the other. The *Eastland* was teetering on a wooden post or two sticking up just dangerously enough. The crew, owners, and inspectors weren't to blame for that, or the ship.

Instead, the City of Chicago would be culpable, for not keeping the river clear for navigation. And just as Darrow did in Los Angeles, when he reached for a model to demonstrate his alternate theory that a gas leak caused a building to explode, he planned to demonstrate his theory with a little model *Eastland*, as well. He would even employ divers to scour the bottom of the Chicago River for evidence of the deadly pilings to bring into court.

Engaging the judge with hours of testimony about the state of the river bottom could prove a very useful distraction. Darrow needed to bury the damning testimony Erickson had given about plans to repair the ship's ballast system, testimony all the more credible because Erickson himself could have been blamed, though probably unjustly, for not personally investigating the machinery's defects.

What also helped keep Erickson's bombshell testimony under wraps was that Steele had agreed to appear in court in Chicago, making him not a party to the extradition proceeding. In effect, Barbour did just what he did at the coroner's inquest. He kept Steele and Erickson, the whistleblower who told of their fateful discussion on the *Eastland* the previous May, from appearing at the same hearing.

In the extradition proceeding, technically called a removal proceeding, the defense got to present its side first. The first two days in Grand Rapids would be a reunion of old *Eastland* captains and chief engineers. Darrow and the defense team would call them one-by-one to the stand with two objectives. First, show the judge that while the *Eastland* may have had a reputation for being "cranky," or unstable, it just wasn't the case. Second, and more important, play down the near-capsize outside South Haven in 1904, the one that so eerily resembled the fatal horror in Chicago.

§§§

The first witness was Captain Dority, the captain on the *Eastland* from 1903 to 1907, a small part of a thirty-five-year career as a sailor.

Barbour switched conspicuously between two different pairs of horn-rim glasses, one for reading his notes, the other for looking into the eyes of witnesses. He asked Dority to explain what happened on July 17, 1904. The captain spoke matter-of-factly.

"As we passed out of the harbor at South Haven into Lake Michigan, the boat listed quite heavily to port and ran along that way for, oh, several minutes, perhaps 10 minutes, and all of a sudden without any apparent reason, listed much heavier to starboard, rolled the other way.

"I immediately checked the engines down and left the bridge. . . . The chief engineer . . . found that he had been unable to get his water ballast in the proper place, I think, after passing into Lake Michigan, but he was doing it as fast as he could.

"Perhaps in 15 or 20 minutes when he got his water ballast properly distributed, the boat was on even keel, and we proceeded on our trip to Chicago without any further trouble." It all took place, he testified, several miles out in Lake Michigan.

After speaking with the chief engineer, Dority explained, he went up on the upper deck, and tried to reassure the passengers all was safe. He told them, as he put it, "It would take us a good deal longer to right the steamer with people on top, and so some of them went below."

Asked about the angle of the list, he said the *Eastland* initially tipped to port about twelve to fifteen degrees, then flipped the other way, twenty degrees perhaps to starboard.

"Wasn't Captain Mansfield, the steamboat inspector in Chicago, aboard for that trip?" Barbour asked.

"Yes."

Captain Mansfield is dead now?

"He is," Dority replied.

CHAPTER FORTY-TWO

"I'm Trying to Forget."

Captain Mansfield, inspector of steamboat hulls in Chicago, died only three months after the *Eastland* sank. He was heart-stricken, perhaps with guilt. His death was a great advantage for the defense in Grand Rapids, as his testimony could have been damaging.

Mansfield was aboard when the *Eastland* tossed around in 1904; in a reprimand letter the next day he warned the shipowners to fix the ballast tanks or face losing their license. He then directly warned Captain Dority and Chief Engineer Eeles.

Eleven years later, Mansfield had to make two painful admissions to the Redfield Commission. No, he did not similarly warn the new captain and chief engineer when the *Eastland* returned to his jurisdiction in Chicago in 1914, though in hindsight he should have. And, yes, had a full investigation of the July 17, 1904, mishap been quickly conducted, the *Eastland* disaster of 1915 might never have happened, "no question about that in my mind," he said. "This accident never should have occurred."

The *Eastland* tragedy preyed on his mind, his wife said, and greatly harmed his health. "He told me over and over again that he would never recover from the shock of that morning," she said.

In between appearances before Redfield and other investigators, Mansfield began planting himself in his Steamboat Inspection Service office fourteen to fifteen hours a day. His assistants tried to persuade him to go home, but he refused. "I'm trying to forget," he would tell them.

On the night of October 6, 1915, his sixtieth birthday, the man whose career began in boyhood as a ship's cook apparently had a stroke and died in his bed.

§§§

The questions in Grand Rapids continued that first day, and Dority was on the stand all morning, most of it testifying about the July 1904 trip.

"There wasn't much attention paid to her water ballast. We didn't know the importance of it at that time, before that occasion," Dority said. But after that, he added, "we always had our water ballast in before leaving the dock with a crowd of people on board the vessel."

How could you get over the bar in South Haven, Barbour asked, with the ballast tanks filled? "By pulling over; the force of the engines would push her over the bar; push her through a foot and a half or two of mud and sand."

Overall, what did he think of the condition of the ship?

"A-1, first class." Dority elaborated: "She never listed dangerously. She is what we considered a cranky boat among sailors. I mean a boat that lists easily."

Not rolling?

"No sir," the captain said. "All boats will roll. She tilts. From my experience, I would say the steamer could not be loaded with 2,500 people anywhere, with perfect safety to the passengers, without some water ballast."

"In all your experience with the *Eastland*," Barbour concluded, "did you consider her at any time a dangerous or unseaworthy boat?"

"No, sir."

CHAPTER FORTY-THREE

The Shady Side

The defense had successfully downplayed the *Eastland*'s tipping incident out on Lake Michigan in 1904. On cross-examination, District Attorney Charles Clyne, the fat-jowled prosecutor, sought to undermine Captain Dority's characterization of the 1904 trip as merely a bit tipsy. Clyne asked: Was a fire hose turned on passengers, to make them retreat below?

"I remember that it was not, absolutely," the captain replied. The hose, however, could have been fired without his knowledge or orders, as Dority was on the bridge and elsewhere at different times.

Dority did acknowledge, though, that the ship could have been safer a couple of different ways. "With permanent ballast," he said, "I would have considered her a safer proposition." And later, "I presume if she had more than one seacock, she could have filled the tanks more rapidly, but it always seemed to me that one was sufficient."

Merwin Thompson, the *Eastland* captain the police chased down months earlier near Cleveland, took the stand on the second day of the trial. As the lanky captain took the stand, twenty-five fresh faces looked at him from the benches in the public seating area. Teacher Lou Wilson, a junior high school teacher in Grand Rapids, picked that morning to bring her eighth grade civil government class for a lesson in courts and justice.

The defense wanted to put its spin on those troubling newspaper advertisements in Cleveland in the summer of 1910, the ones promising a five-thousand-dollar reward to anyone who could prove the *Eastland* was unsafe. Didn't they suggest a systemic problem with safety?

Thompson indicated that there were rumors about the *Eastland*'s being treacherous, hurled about by competitors. In taking out the ads, the shipowners, he added, "wanted to try . . . and push it down permanently if they could."

Thompson, who ran the ship for three seasons, felt "she was undoubtedly a cranky boat, but she was a long ways from being an unseaworthy boat."

Next to take the stand was Captain Ennes, who ran the *Eastland* in Chicago its first few weeks in 1914. This time it was attorney Charles Kremer, "The Admiral," who would conduct the direct examination.

He was an expensive attorney, and it was Hull who hired him. Kremer agreed to come onto the case and also represent the inspectors, Reid and Eckliff. Kremer had an overweening air about him, Victorian really, down to the dated gray spats buckled around his ankles.

Kremer established Ennes's seasoning as a captain, licensed eighteen years, how they counted passengers at Cedar Point, passenger capacity, the dock at the amusement park, and on and on. Ennes called the *Eastland* "as good a sea vessel as I was ever aboard."

Kremer had a long history with the *Eastland*. He knew it from the blueprints up. As attorney for Pereue and Leighton, it was his effusive signature as witness on the original contract for Jenks to construct the *Eastland* back in 1902.

Since the prosecution was going to excoriate the *Eastland*'s ballast system, Kremer wanted to first get into Judge Sessions's ear just how effective it was.

First, the defense had to demystify it. They had a scale model *Eastland* built, with a removable bottom to show just what the ballast system looked like in miniature. Kremer called a particularly good witness, William Nack, who was chief engineer on the *Eastland* in 1906 and served for over eighteen years on five ships. After the accident, Nack had been hired by the Navy, which acquired the *Eastland* wreck, to reconstruct the ship, giving him further credibility.

To make it more visual, Kremer questioned Nack to establish some of the metrics of the system. The seacock was about six feet below the waterline, near the middle of the *Eastland*. It fed into a manifold, or a large tank, thirty-five feet long, that ran across the ship: nearly beam-width. There was a single wheel, about sixteen inches in diameter, that could be placed on top of the square stems of the manifold and the seacock, to open and close them.

Nack testified that the ballast system he saw the prior year was the exact same one he had seen on the *Eastland* in 1903 and 1904. This forestalled any argument that the ballast machinery had been changed in those twelve years.

The main ballast tanks were the two No. 3 tanks, each about sixty-four feet long, nineteen feet wide. About three feet deep, each accommodated two hundred tons of water. They took thirty to thirty-five minutes to fill, both sides.

But as a practice, Nack said, they didn't initially use the No. 3 tanks, fearing they would push the "ash chute" under the water: in other words, obstruct the discharge of ashes by the firemen from the boilers. Normally, the chute was above water, and the ashes would fly out into the air and settle onto the lake.

Down in the engine room, Nack explained, he could read the degree of list with an inclinometer, an eighteen-inch, arrow-shaped piece of steel, which tilted like a pendulum. It was pinned in the center of the ship in the engine room. It was still there when Erickson became engineer.

Kremer asked: When you saw it listing, what would you do?

"I would overcome it by counterbalancing the weight with water."

Kremer wanted to establish that the ballast system was ginger, sensitive, quite responsive.

On the bizarre behavior of July 17, 1904, Nack said, "This thing that happened, had to be found out. We had no idea and were unconscious of anything like a great list like that should ever happen to that boat. . . . After it did happen then we knew we had to overcome it by putting water in her."

Nack testified they could then nimbly maneuver the *Eastland* at will.

"If the passengers boarded the boat and went over to the shady side of the boat that naturally would list her to one side. Well, we put water on the opposite side. . . . We didn't put any water in the tanks until she showed she had been overbalanced or over-weighted either one side or the other."

Routinely, he added, they would pump the tanks out empty at the dock. This would prove to be a contentious point; the defense wanted to nail down its position early. "I never laid at the dock with any water in the tanks," Nack said. Having them empty meant he knew exactly where they stood.

He described odd metrics around rubbernecking crowd movements, revealing that large crowds could sway the whole ship as they roamed. He noticed that when another ship passed on one side, large crowds on the *Eastland* would move to that side and tilt it.

"Just as soon as I knew that we were by the other ship, which I could see through the porthole, I commenced pumping this water out because I figured that the people would go back on the side where they were before, and by the time they would get back I would have this water out."

He figured he could pump out about seven to eight tons of water a minute. "By knowing that," he said, "I knew just about how long I could wait before I could start this pumping and counterbalance the additional weight which would be exposed on the opposite side of the ship."

In 1906, he started experimenting, using the No. 3 tanks solo, before they started loading.

"She stood up," Nack testified.

This all suggested that a previous engineer ran the tanks precisely the same way Erickson did, with quite different results. It suggested that the disastrous outcome the previous summer resulted from something outside the crews' control.

Nack agreed the defense team's model, with the miniature ballast tanks and pipes, was an accurate representation.

Prosecutor Clyne wanted to discredit the notion that the ballast system, as designed and operated, was safe and effective.

Wouldn't it be a better design to come up with a way to fill the ballast tanks faster, Clyne asked, either by modifying the feed pipes or the manifold?

"It would," Nack replied.

And then Clyne wrung a significant admission from Nack. Over time, Nack said, he learned it was better to keep the huge No. 3 tanks filled as a precaution to prevent the sloshing of a partially filled tank that could aggravate a list. In other words, Nack learned how to eliminate the element of human error that necessarily came when an engineer had to fill a tank one moment, empty it the next, fill it again, and so on. He simply kept the largest tanks full.

A partly full tank presented danger, he explained. "The momentum and sudden stopping of this water would be the same," he said, "as if I hammered my fist on this table."

CHAPTER FORTY-FOUR

A Vanishing Gash

At the end of the second day, the defense called the old *Eastland* engineer, Grant Donaldson, whose testimony before the federal grand jury in Chicago pointed a finger of blame at the owners, Steele and Hull.

The swearing in of Donaldson wrested Darrow up from his adolescent slouch at the desk of the defense attorneys. Since Donaldson held the key to defending his client, Erickson, he was Darrow's man to question. The lawyer stepped toward the witness stand, the cuffs of his too-long trousers smothering his black shoes.

Darrow asked Donaldson if he kept the *Eastland*'s water tanks empty at the dock, before loading passengers. Yes, he did.

"Would you begin putting water in before the crowd came on?"

"No, sir, not generally."

"And when the boat began to list, then what would you do?"

"We would put some water in to counteract the list."

"When it was working right, would it respond?"

"Yes, sir."

"You considered that a safe way to operate the boat?"

"It proved so for me, yes, sir. I got the best results that way."

"That is all," Darrow said.

Joseph B. Fleming, Clyne's assistant, approached Donaldson. Young and fresh-faced, Fleming wanted to establish that Erickson, Donaldson's successor in the *Eastland*'s engine room, was incompetent. And Donaldson had suggested in the initial *Eastland* investigations that General Manager Hull, at least, thought so. On the stand in Grand Rapids, he would soon testify that Hull told him that Erickson "lacked system."

Fleming's questions showed that Donaldson had returned to St. Joseph, from Cleveland, at the request of Hull on July 18, 1915, roughly a week before the disaster. According to Donaldson, Hull complained that the *Eastland* wasn't running quickly enough and asked him if he knew why. Donaldson testified that Hull then offered him Erickson's job.

The testimony must have delighted Darrow, who was brought into the case to ensure that the management didn't roll over on Erickson. Darrow knew he could easily establish through letters of reference and Erickson's strong career in engine rooms that he was quite a good engineer. But now Hull could no longer try to blame the disaster on Erickson. To do so, he would have to explain his decision to leave a man he deemed incompetent in charge of the engine room.

The prosecutor wanted one other thing from Donaldson: admission that the owners of the *Eastland* knew they had an unstable ship. Steele and Hull swore in the initial Chicago investigations that they knew nothing about stability issues with the *Eastland*. And Fleming held in his hand a copy of Donaldson's previous testimony, showing just the opposite.

You testified before the grand jury, Fleming said, that the officers of the St. Joseph-Chicago Steamship Company knew about the boat's reputation as being "cranky." After a pause by Donaldson, Fleming then read that prior testimony back to him:

Donaldson: They had knowledge of that.
Q. How do you know?
Donaldson: I heard them speaking of it.

Objection, bellowed Darrow. Fleming, he said, did not read the previous testimony fully enough. "It should have gone back farther," Darrow said, "because it doesn't say what was being referred to, whether bad boat or cranky boat or what."

By objecting, Darrow hoped to cloud the issue or get it stricken from the record. The Donaldson testimony would damage a key assertion of the defense: that the owners were as surprised as anyone when the *Eastland* capsized, partly because it had no credible history of instability.

Fleming countered that Engineer Donaldson previously testified before the grand jury that the owners "had knowledge of her reputation before they bought it."

Fleming turned to Donaldson and said: "Let me ask you this question, to which you gave the following reply to the federal grand jury under oath:

Q. You are certain that they (meaning the officers of the boat) had full knowledge of the boat's listing; that they had full knowledge of the general reputation of the boat?
Donaldson: I think they had knowledge of her reputation before they bought it.

Looking Donaldson dead-on, Fleming demanded a single word answer to this question: Did you tell the truth before, when you said the owners knew they had bought a ship with a reputation for stability problems: yes or no?

Donaldson parsed: "That is, she was a cranky boat?"

"Her general reputation as a cranky boat," Fleming clarified.

"Yes, sir."

Fleming then turned to another piece of testimony damaging to the *Eastland* owners. He cited more of Donaldson's previous grand jury testimony:

Donaldson: They had knowledge of it . . .
Q. The fact of the matter is, you talked it over with all of them, Steele, Davis and Mr. Hull?
Donaldson: I suppose I did.

But before Fleming could ask his question, Darrow objected to the introduction of the old testimony, saying it was improper because it wasn't raised in order to impeach the witness, according to trial procedures, it didn't conflict with something the witness had previously said.

Because of Darrow's quick footwork the damning testimony teetered on a technicality.

Sessions thought for a moment, and then agreed: The testimony would be tossed out.

§§§

Darrow had effectively quashed the first testimony suggesting that the *Eastland* owners, Hull and Steele, particularly, had discussed stability issues before the disaster, something both had denied when questioned by investigators.

Joseph Erickson, an experienced seaman who told investigators the truth, was running the engine room when the
Eastland went over.

The Old Command, 1920

The *Eastland* painted all white. Note the open gangways perilously close to the water.

The *Eastland* at its home port
in South Haven, Michigan,
in its maiden season, 1903
Richard Appleyard Collection

Near the horizon, the *Eastland* races the *City of South Haven*,
leaving the pier in South Haven.
Richard Appleyard Collection

In July of 1909, Captain Merwin Thompson stands watch
on the *Eastland* bridge in Cleveland.

Moments after the calamity on the Chicago River, fortunate passengers walk
away unhurt. Note the man who saved himself by clinging to a propeller.
Chicago History Museum, DN-0064935

THE EASTLAND DISASTER.
CHICAGO. JULY. 24. 1915.

Rescue efforts fully underway. The stately Reid-Murdoch building across
the river will become a temporary morgue.
Chicago History Museum, ICHi-02033, Jun Fujita, photographer

The overturned *Eastland* at night. There are ghostly images
of guards atop the ship, created by the time-lapsed shot.

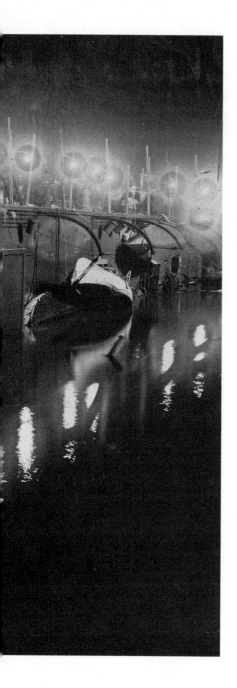

A Chicago fireman, the day's horror in his eyes, carries a child away from the ship.
Chicago History Museum, ICHi-02042, Jun Fujita, photographer

Salvagers remove a young girl's body from the *Eastland*.
Chicago History Museum, ICHi-30730, Jun Fujita, photographer

Walter Steele, the ship's largest investor, walks away from the sunken *Eastland*.
Chicago History Museum, DN-0065007

THE HAND TO BLAME

Days after the disaster, a newspaper cartoon correctly blamed "Greed" but mistakenly reversed, to starboard, the direction of the fatal plunge.
Chicago Herald/Author's Copy

The iconic lawyer Clarence Darrow in 1915
Library of Congress

The prosecutors were still hoping they would have a chance to question Erickson on what the owners knew, provided the defense put him on the stand.

Feeling flush with that victory, Barbour looked forward to questioning Henry Cordell. The defense was about to call its first witness to begin building its case that the *Eastland* was resting on a piling that was not visible above the water.

Cordell was a consulting engineer in Chicago. On his own volition, he went down to the accident site the day after the *Eastland* sank and saw a pronounced mark on the port side of the ship. This could greatly corroborate the theory that the *Eastland* was hung up on something below water.

"The paint of the boat was scratched off and there was a mark in the steel, running across the steel," Cordell explained.

Barbour asked, "About what size was it?"

"About three feet long . . . 18 inches wide," Cordell said.

Barbour handed him the defense team's model of the *Eastland* and asked him to point out where on the hull he had seen the scrape. It was nearly at the center of the little boat.

Clyne wasted no time, marching up to Cordell and handing him a photograph of the very side of the *Eastland* Cordell referred to. The defense and prosecution had many photos taken of all angles of the ship, once it was raised again.

Please show us, the prosecutor said, just where the mark is.

Cordell looked the photograph over and over, silent.

"What do you say?" asked Clyne.

"I can't see it on that," he replied.

"You say the mark doesn't appear in that photograph?"

There was no mark.

The Red Cross Toll

No. 446. (Bohemian) **Wife, 48; daughter, 21;** husband, 50; **son, 18;** daughter, 15; daughter, 12; daughter, 10.
The wife and the two eldest children were drowned. The son was a deaf mute and the father earned but nine dollars a week as a laborer, so the family depended largely on the wages of the daughter. They were making payments on the home and had no reserve fund to meet such a disaster. To add to the trouble, the husband, despondent over the loss of his wife and children, committed suicide.

No. 31. (Italian) **Son, 20;** husband, 46; wife, 35; daughter, 10.
The only son, an employee of the Western Electric Company, was killed. He had been the chief support of the family. In addition to his regular employment, he made photographs in the park on Sundays, and was in the habit of turning over all his money to his parents. The father earned very small wages as a day laborer.

No. 282. (Bohemian) Father, 60; **daughter, 18;** son, 11.
A daughter was drowned. Since the death of her mother, she had been the housekeeper for the father and cared for the eleven-year-old son. The father kept a small butter and egg store, but after the loss of his daughter planned to sell it at once. He said he could not go on without her.

CHAPTER FORTY-FIVE

A Vanishing River

By the time Sidney Jenks sat in the witness stand, he had been out of the shipbuilding business nine years, following the fire that destroyed the shipyards. The *Eastland* was the only passenger ship he had ever built. On his attorneys' advice he had refused to appear for either side until he was compelled to give testimony by Judge Sessions.

Prosecutor Fleming took Jenks back to the first conversation about the *Eastland* project with Captain Pereue, who came to Port Huron in summer of 1903. Fleming then asked a shrewd question: "In your conversations and negotiations, was anything ever said about the use of this boat as an excursion boat?"

"Not to my knowledge."

Fleming bore in. "When you designed it, did you ever contemplate its being used to transport 2,500 passengers?"

"We did not."

"Can you give me an idea now, if you had any at the time, how many people you expected the *Eastland* to carry?"

After an overruled objection by the defense, Jenks answered.

"We didn't expect the *Eastland* was going to carry more than 500 people."

It was a missile through the defense. The designer of the *Eastland* said he had anticipated the ship would carry perhaps five hundred passengers at most—nearly four hundred short of the total number who ended up drowning on it.

Jenks was cold as stone in the courtroom, at one point remarking, "Listing is not a detriment to the vessel. The only effect listing could probably have would be in scaring people."

Kremer cross-examined for the defense.

"Isn't it a fact that if loaded and properly handled, she can carry anything you put on?"

"Yes, sir," Jenks said, "I think that is right."

Kremer, suddenly confident, then slipped up by asking a follow-up question. "And isn't it further a fact that with her trimming tanks and her ballast tanks, she can overcome any list?"

"I don't think I am prepared to answer that."

Stunned, Kremer said, "You can't answer that?"

"I think not, sir."

Darrow came to Kremer's aid, approaching Jenks.

"If you thought you had designed a boat which was liable to tip over and drown a thousand people or more because it was operating as an excursion boat, you, of course, would have felt it your duty to say something about it, to warn somebody wouldn't you?"

"Why surely, if I had ever thought the vessel would tip over I would have done anything I could to prevent it."

Darrow asked if a ship built for the transportation of freight and five hundred passengers maximum might be seaworthy for that purpose yet totally unseaworthy for the transportation of fifteen hundred or two thousand, or twenty-five hundred people.

"That would all depend on her loading," Jenks said. "I couldn't answer that question. I think that is a mathematical problem as far as I'm concerned."

§§§

The defense needed to press the case for the underwater culprit. On Monday, January 24, the fourth day of the trial, it called Captain Walter Scott, a former Chicago harbormaster and the consultant to the St. Joseph-Chicago Steamship Company who recommended purchasing the *Eastland* in 1914. Hired by the company to do so, Scott also took soundings of the river bottom after the *Eastland* had been removed following the catastrophe.

The river depths were measured using a six-pound sounding lead and a line, a rope called a nine-thread ratline. He testified that he found a stone formation that at different points was at depths between eleven feet, nine inches, and twelve feet, nine inches. The stones might have hung up the *Eastland*, he added, which sank twelve to thirteen feet into the water. The defense now introduced another possible obstruction responsible for the disaster.

When the prosecution cross-examined Scott, things took a bizarre and contentious turn. Back in Chicago there was heavy winter flooding that week, and at one point city officials feared that the river would reverse itself, flowing in its original direction and reviving the old sewage-contamination issue. The health department issued warnings to city residents to boil their water.

The *Eastland* prosecutors, aware of the dangers back home in Chicago, apparently took that moment to assert that the federal courts were, indeed, the proper jurisdiction for the *Eastland* disaster. In its opening remarks, the defense had indicated that the jurisdiction was not in federal court, but properly in the state courts of Illinois, as the river was located in the state.

To make their case, the prosecutors would try to trick the former harbormaster for Chicago into agreeing that the Chicago River no longer actually existed. To do so, they would cite the historic reversal of the flow of the river.

After a few questions about Scott's duties as harbormaster, Fleming said, "Extending back a great length of time, in your early career as a mariner, I believe you stated that the Chicago River *as it was then known* flowed into the lake. And there was quite a perceptible current at times in the Chicago River at that time?"

"At times, yes sir," Scott replied.

"Now there is no current into Lake Michigan as existed formerly?"

"No, sir."

"And the facts are now that Lake Michigan comes in where the old bed of the Chicago River was?"

"Yes, sir."

After a couple similar questions, Fleming asked, "So that thing which was in fact known as the Chicago River has really passed away—and now, what is your answer?"

Scott finally saw where Fleming was headed. He was trapped; he didn't know what to say. With Fleming staring at him, Scott blurted out: "I have not said a word, I made no answer."

"Well, let me ask you," Fleming said, "do you say that the Chicago River is still there?"

"Yes, sir."

Fleming ended with this:

"Well, I say, captain, that which was formerly known as the Chicago River—where there was two streams united about at Franklin Street, and flowing on to the lake—does not exist any longer, that is true, is it not?"

"That is true, it does not exist," Scott finally affirmed.

The *Grand Rapids News* had a field day with the testimony, asking in a cheeky headline, DOES THE CHICAGO RIVER EXIST?

CHAPTER FORTY-SIX

Fool Killer

The vanishing Chicago River, through sleight of hand semantics, revealed desperation on the prosecution's side, and Darrow and the defense were ready to counter with concrete evidence.

They called a rough-looking character named William Deneau, an undersea diver. The twenty-five-year-old had more living on his face than other youths his age. In the melting pot that was Chicago, many men were known by nicknames indicating their ethnicity. Around the docks, Deneau was called "Frenchy."

Just before noon on August 25, 1915, Frenchy dove into the Chicago River at the dock where the *Eastland* wreck had been removed. He was in his bubble diving bell and breastplate, and he carried weights and air hoses. He began feeling his way around in the muck, he testified, when he found two submerged pilings. They had been placed there in construction of Chicago's underwater tunnels years before.

Frenchy was opportunistic. He had been paid ten dollars a day by the city of Chicago to dive around the submerged *Eastland* and help locate and remove bodies. And then after the ship was righted and hauled away, he worked for the *Eastland*'s owners for a well-paid thirty-five dollars a day to hunt for debris sticking up from the riverbed.

He took soundings for the whole area near the dock where the *Eastland* tipped. He worked underwater four to five hours, he testified.

Using a crosscut saw, he said he "sawed the pile off and took soundings on the top of the pile after it was sawed off."

Attorney John Black for the defense pointed to two wooden pillars that had been theatrically hauled into the room. "Are those the ones," Black asked, "the ones here in the courtroom?"

"Yes, sir," Frenchy said, "the same two."

The soundings he took, he stated, indicated that the *Eastland* would have had to have scraped at least one of them.

It all sounded a little too perfect, testimony too finely wrapped. When the prosecution questioned Frenchy, it emerged that another ship, the *Neptune*, had occupied the same berth as the *Eastland* after the wreck was moved—and before Frenchy cut the pilings. The hull of the *Neptune*, one of the largest ships on Lake Michigan, sank to a depth five feet deeper than the *Eastland*. The *Eastland* could never have touched the pilings the defense painted as the offenders in the disaster.

Within a month Frenchy would try to cash in again on his underwater antics. Advertisements in the Chicago newspapers trumpeted the latest find of "Captain" Deneau (though he was not a captain), the self-described "Hero of the *Eastland*, who recovered 250 bodies at the time of the *Eastland* disaster." The ads said Deneau had discovered the "Fool Killer" submarine and the "tragic and historic relic" would be on display at a hall on State Street in downtown Chicago, admission ten cents.

CHAPTER FORTY-SEVEN

Bubbles

The Frenchy-piling testimony was a mess. The defense had such a strong case going, and the prosecution was fumbling, stretching to prove a river didn't exist. And then the defense misfired badly with Frenchy.

Clearly in trouble, Darrow prepared to call a star witness who was credible, authoritative, and convincing. Joseph Lynn was the assistant harbormaster in Chicago and an eyewitness to the *Eastland*'s capsizing. Most important, he had already testified before the coroner's jury that he had seen some bubbles around the port side of the *Eastland* right after it sank. And given the way the *Eastland* pivoted out from its dock, he testified days after the disaster, he was convinced that the *Eastland* had been upset by scraping *something* on the river bottom.

Not only that, the testimony was not in his self-interest. He was an employee of the city, which had the most to lose if it was found that refuse on the river bottom caused the disaster. Lynn was precisely whom the defense needed right then. They could get back on track.

How surprised they would be, as Lynn was being sworn in, that he would completely unravel on the stand.

Darrow questioned Lynn about what he witnessed as the *Eastland* went over, its hanging on the port side and then falling over. Had he ever seen a ship do that before?

No, Lynn replied. He said he had seen ships tilt a bit as they approached the bank; it was what harbor officials called "smelling the bottom."

When Darrow asked him about his testimony the prior summer that he had seen bubbles, Lynn demurred.

"I neither can say positively in my own mind as to whether I ever made that remark or not; I am not positive. I don't remember saying that."

Judge Sessions stepped in. "Well, what do you say now as to whether you saw bubbles or not?"

Lynn said, "Well, I see them every day if I am along the river. I can't remember."

Adding injury to injury, Sessions then asked Lynn if he still believed the *Eastland* was on the bottom of the river, or some obstruction.

Lynn was unequivocal. "I don't believe she was on the bottom, or the piles." He thought for another second and added, "She was not on the bottom."

In further questioning, Lynn said he began to doubt what he thought he saw, the bubbles, shortly after he testified about them and after he took soundings around the wreck site. The nearest underwater pile he could find, roughly eight feet from the dock, was seventeen feet, seven inches below the water surface. The *Eastland*'s draft, meanwhile, was twelve to thirteen feet, he said.

The defense was collapsing, with only a handful of witnesses left to call. It was becoming clear that Erickson was going to have to save the defense. He was honest, credible, consistent. It was tempting to call him now, to get the momentum swinging back to the defense.

No, they decided, better to save him for later.

Darrow had something else in mind.

§§§

Inspector Reid took the stand and performed admirably. He said he allowed an increase in capacity for the *Eastland*, to twenty-five hundred passengers shortly before the accident, because he felt the ship had adequate lifeboats, and a working and dependable ballast system if the crew chose to use it. He also felt confident about the new capacity because he knew the *Eastland* had previously carried three thousand passengers safely. He had never heard of the ship's having a reputation for being "cranky" and had never seen it act perilously. Under questioning, he said he had nothing to do with the *Eastland*'s hiring of his son-in-law, Erickson, as chief engineer.

Clyne failed to undermine any of Reid's testimony, and in fact, allowed him to elicit sympathy at least twice from Sessions.

At one point, Clyne asked Reid if he recalled being questioned by the Redfield Commission. Reid turned the question to his advantage, arguing in dramatic fashion that he was unjustly pilloried.

"If I live to be 10,000 years old, I will never forget the experience I had over there, being dragged through the street handcuffed and other ways humiliated," Reid replied.

The federal government had nothing to do with that, Clyne responded. In fact, it was the US court that helped secure his release. Kremer on the defense team chimed in that it was the Cook County sheriff who handcuffed Reid, not the federal authorities.

Clearly annoyed, Sessions would later blurt out: "It doesn't make any difference who did it. Whoever did it, it was an outrage, that is the size of it."

And Sessions came to Reid's aid as Clyne questioned the inspector a little later. Reid told Clyne that he was satisfied "in my own mind" that if the *Eastland* could carry three thousand passengers in 1906, it could certainly carry twenty-five hundred in 1915.

Hostile, Clyne responded, "You mean you were satisfied in your own mind just by looking down on a boat and seeing that boat there, that you could then determine how much she could carry?"

Sessions jumped in: "He has not said that at all."

"I am asking the question," Clyne said to the judge.

"But he hasn't said it or anything like it," Sessions said.

"Nor tried to imply it," added Reid.

"Nor anything that intimated that," concluded Sessions.

CHAPTER FORTY-EIGHT

Another Toy Boat

A full week in, the defense was down to about six witnesses to call. When the prosecutors took their turn, they would swear in twelve witnesses. They were particularly eager to get at Erickson, given their zeal to blame the *Eastland*'s ballast system and management, but the defense was saving him.

Instead, the defense decided it was time to demonstrate their theory the *Eastland* was upended by something underwater. They called John Hutchinson, a mining engineer from Hillsboro, New Mexico. In Chicago at the time of the disaster, he became immediately curious about the erratic capsizing. He began experimenting with a model of the *Eastland* to determine the cause.

In the courtroom, Hutchinson produced a miniature tin ship, and with a tank of water he showed how the *Eastland* probably turned over from resting on the river bottom or an obstruction. Attorneys, newspapermen, and court marshals all gathered around the witness table. At first, Hutchinson had the tank filled with enough water to float the little *Eastland*. He began adding tiny weights on the port side of the ship and, with plenty of water underneath, the toy boat turned on its side, barely moving from the little dock as it tipped.

Then Hutchinson scooped out enough water that the toy boat was resting on the bottom of the tank. He reapplied the weights to the port side, and when it tipped the second time, the outer edge of the boat acted as an axis. And as it tipped it swung outward about half the beam of the boat, roughly mirroring the sweeping movement of the stern of the *Eastland* on July 24, 1915.

It was dramatic and, at least on a small stage, explained the *Eastland*'s position after it capsized. Barbour had the toy boat and tank marked as defense exhibits.

To try to impeach Hutchinson's testimony and demonstration, Prosecutor Clyne asked one question.

"Ever study marine engineering?"

"No," said Hutchinson.

CHAPTER FORTY-NINE

The Captain Trips Up

The remaining witnesses for the defense were all men there in court under indictment, two of the *Eastland* company's executive officers, Hull and Arnold, and the two top officers, Pedersen and Erickson.

The defense decided to call Pedersen first. He was cagey at the investigations in Chicago. And shortly after the disaster he publicly vowed not to let the management make him the scapegoat. Pedersen could be a loose cannon too, and the defense team couldn't afford for him to be the last witness, in case he surprised them with some blunder. They put him on the stand the seventh day of the hearing.

As Barbour questioned him, Pedersen, who was wearing a stylish white tie with a white shirt, established that he had been sailing for four decades. He was born in 1860 in Norway. And to suggest he was a learned man, he mentioned that he was born about three miles from the home of Henrik Ibsen, the renowned Norwegian playwright. Pedersen immigrated to the United States in 1885 and became the *Eastland*'s captain on June 26, 1914.

"Had you ever heard anything about the boat's being cranky before June 1914?" asked Barbour.

"No, sir."

After a few more questions about the performance of the *Eastland*, Barbour asked about the ballasting of the ship.

Pedersen denied knowing a thing about it, saying: The previous ship master "Ennes told me, 'The engineer takes care of trimming the boat . . .' He says, 'I don't know anything about the system' adding that the engine room men 'operate these tanks . . . and you better not interfere with it.'"

And Pedersen expressed confidence in the performance of the stabilizing machinery. "She listed a little bit once in a while, but the chief took it out of her quick," he said.

Barbour asked, "Other than arranging the list to straighten the boat out, did you direct the engineer as to how to regulate those tanks?" "No," the captain replied, "I could not do that because I didn't know anything about them. I am no engineer."

Barbour then wanted Pedersen to testify to Erickson's ability. The finger-pointing went all directions among the defendants and, of course, the company had left Erickson high and dry to find his own legal representation. Pedersen in that moment could easily burn Erickson.

Barbour asked the question tersely. "Erickson competent?"

"Yes, sir," the captain said. "He is a good man."

Pedersen was full of compliments for the *Eastland*, as well. "I will go back on her tomorrow if they fix her up; take her anywhere you want to," he said.

It was a full, long day of testimony, and Pedersen handled himself well. The captain faced a much harder time on the stand when the prosecutors got a hold of him the following Monday morning.

§§§

Walker, the local prosecutor in Grand Rapids, borrowed a trick Darrow had used himself before when questioning adversaries: dehumanize them. Walker approached the stand and looked at Pedersen, the man who was at the helm the day the *Eastland* fatally capsized.

"Witness," Walker began, "what other passenger steamer, if any, besides the *Eastland*, were you ever the master of?"

Pedersen listed a couple of private yachts and the steamships *Bay State* and the *Nortown*, but ended up admitting that the *Eastland* was the first passenger steamer he had ever piloted.

Then Walker asked what Pedersen knew about the water-ballast system. Had he been to the engine room to inspect it in any way once he stepped aboard his first large ship carrying passengers?

"Never was down there," Pedersen said.

Walker followed, "You paid no attention to this?"

"I was never down there; no, sir."

Walker pressed on other engine-room matters. No, Pedersen didn't know where the No. 3 tank was, or what its capacity was, or what it did.

"You knew," Walker asked, "the morning of the 24th of July when you were going to take on that load of passengers that [Erickson] was carrying his ballast tanks empty, did you not—carrying his water tanks empty?"

"I understand he started to give her water as soon as the passengers come aboard," Pedersen explained. He knew that Erickson, prior to the passengers' boarding, had pumped them out, as he had on the prior seventy-nine one-way trips of the season.

Walker had made little headway with Pedersen and so he moved to a different line of questioning, about a little barroom that was near the crews' quarters. After thirty or so minutes of questioning that seemed to suggest drunkenness by the crew, Sessions scolded him for wasting time.

Walker needed to get on solid footing. They finally had a shot at the commander of the *Eastland*, its captain, and all the prosecutor had managed to do was irritate the judge.

Tacking, Walker asked Pedersen what caused the disaster, in his opinion. "There is no question in my mind but that it was a piling turned the boat over," Pedersen replied.

Bull's-eye.

From the prosecution desk, he then picked up testimony Pedersen had given to the Illinois state's attorney on July 26, two days after the *Eastland*'s capsize. He read it:

Q. Is it possible for that boat to have been on the ground as she is there? Pedersen: No sir, I don't think so because she listed. She was listed in first and then listed out and that showed me, proved to me that she was free of the bottom.

Walker looked at the captain and asked, "Did you make that statement?"

Pedersen paused. For the couple hours he was on the stand, he was circumspect with his responses, slow to answer and cautious in his wording. News reporters would note in their stories the next day how nervous he was. The captain asked the court stenographer no fewer than a dozen times to read the question again before he would answer it, slowly.

"Did you make that statement?" Walker asked.

"I don't think so," Pedersen finally blurted. "I think that is mixed up because I have always been of the opinion when the boat listed in to the dock that she may have had a feeling somewhere, but as to listing out, I wouldn't say—I couldn't say to that."

It was a jarring discrepancy, but the prosecutors failed to follow up. Walker simply asked the captain if he told anyone he had changed his mind. He had not, he said. And Walker just moved on.

Under further questioning from Walker, Pedersen admitted he knew much more about the ballast than he did when testifying under direct examination by the defense. "Water counteracts the rolling of the ship and steadies the boat," Pedersen said. "The boat works faster than the water, and the water counteracts the work of the boat and steadies the boat."

Walker even pressed Pedersen into admitting that he occasionally asked Erickson "to list her out a little to one side for the convenience of passengers to pass on or off the boat."

After a couple hours of harsh interrogation, Pedersen slipped up. Walker asked him if the *Eastland* had been in the repair shop, or in dry dock, during the 1915 season. Evidently assuming Walker meant the 1914 season, Pedersen testified that the starboard shaft had been broken. He'd heard from the second mate that the *Eastland* might have struck something when they left Chicago one morning in June of 1914.

But having dug a tantalizing bit out about that mysterious accident, Walker then failed to follow up in any detail. If he had, he could have let into the record that this mishap cost the St. Joseph-Chicago Steamship Company two of the busiest weeks of the summer season and thousands of dollars in repairs and lost ticket revenue. It had left the company at year end with only $36.06 in cash.

The *Eastland* broke one ten-inch propeller shaft and damaged the other so severely that both had to be replaced, at the order of a federal steamboat inspector. If it had struck another ship or a harbor wall, it would have been in the newspapers, as there would have been witnesses and someone aggrieved. Had uncontrolled rolling the year before the *Eastland* disaster caused the severe damage?

Walker fouled the moment up. It was a rich vein to explore, to try to establish management's knowledge of the *Eastland*'s faulty machinery a full year before July 24, 1915. It might have been the precise trouble that prompted Steele to seek out ways to remedy the handling of the ship in the spring of 1915, to discuss modifying the ballast tanks with Erickson a couple months before the disaster. It could have been the key to everything.

CHAPTER FIFTY

The Captain Tears Up

When Barbour approached again to question the captain, his witness, he played the sympathy card. The defense team seemed impressed that Judge Sessions came to the defense of Inspector Reid, when he complained on the stand of being handcuffed and mistreated by the law-enforcement authorities in Chicago.

The defense would start a sustained campaign of arguing that the *Eastland* men had been treated unjustly in Chicago already. Could they possibly expect a fair trial if Sessions extradited them to the Second City, sent them back into that vengeful environment?

Knowing Pedersen faced several late-night interrogations in the days after the *Eastland* sank, Barbour asked him, "What time were you interrogated by the state's attorney and his assistant and the coroner? Do you remember how late?"

"Around 9 or 10 p.m."

"Were you under arrest at that time? Been in the police station?"

"We was taken there from the Hutchins Avenue Station."

"Have an attorney there?"

"No, sir."

Barbour established through questioning that Pedersen felt caught off guard by the capsize and had no time to do anything to rectify the situation. The attorney concluded, asking, "Was there a single thing that you could have done after you knew that something was wrong to prevent the accident?"

"No, sir. If the whole United States Navy had been in my place they could not have done anything."

§§§

Pedersen painted himself as a victim in his two days on the stand. At one point, he said he had struck his head when the *Eastland* went over and was at various times afterward "out of his head" and "staggering around." He claimed that he saved a drowning man by grabbing "hold of his breeches," and then four women pulled Pedersen and the other man to safety using a rope.

On the stand, Pedersen choked up. He said he got to the top of the *Eastland* and saw the scene of chaos and all the salvage efforts by his crew and others.

Rising in the witness stand, he became dramatic. "We were all working to save the people the best we knew how," he shouted, with tears streaming down.

The tears welling still in the captain's blue eyes, it was an opportune time in the trial to tamp down some controversy. Pedersen's own attorney, Barbour, knew the captain was vulnerable for having ordered the torch men to stop cutting into the hull when they were desperately trying to reach survivors. There were many witnesses to Pedersen's reprehensible behavior the morning of the disaster, when he showed greater concern for the company's property than the people dying inside of it.

Barbour chose this moment, when Pedersen displayed some compassion, to ask about that. "It was stated publicly that you objected to the people opening up the side of the boat. Will you tell us about that incident?"

"It appeared to me," Pedersen explained, composing himself, "that they were cutting down the coal bunker, and I says, 'I don't think you will find anything down there'—of course I knowed it was full of coal—but I says, 'Go ahead, go ahead, you can't tell.'

"I knew the inside of the boat better than those people," he added, but then he was quickly arrested and so, "I didn't get back to tell those fellows where I wanted them to cut."

The Red Cross Toll

No. 623. (Polish) **Daughter, 21;** husband, 46; wife, 42; son, 20; son, 18; son, 11; daughter, 7.

A daughter, who had been earning twelve dollars a week at the Western Electric Company plant, was drowned. The husband had been crippled with rheumatism for six months and was unable to work, and the only other wage earner was the eighteen-year-old boy, who brought in seven dollars a week. The daughter had postponed her marriage because her parents needed her wages. She and her fiancé had bought a bungalow on which they were making payments. They were drowned together.

No. 336. (Polish) Husband, 45; wife, 43; **daughter, 21**; daughter, 20; son, 19; daughter, 16; son, 14; daughter, 8; son-in-law, 21; daughter, 22.

A daughter, employed by the Western Electric Company, was drowned. She was working under an assumed name, because she had once resigned her position and under the rules of the company was not eligible to a position at that time. She was the chief reliance of the family, for she contributed about half the income. The husband, a street laborer, was in poor health and had been out of work for five months.

No. 679. (Bohemian) **Daughter, 24; son, 18; daughter, 16; son, 14;** husband, 65; wife, 41; daughter, 22; son, 12; sister; brother.

Two sons and two daughters in this one family were killed. The eldest had been an employee of the Western Electric Company. The second and third were also wage earners, while the fourteen-year-old boy was still in school. The husband was a shoemaker but not very efficient because his hands were crippled.

CHAPTER FIFTY-ONE

A Litany of No

The two ship executives facing extradition professed profound ignorance of nearly everything having to do with the *Eastland*. The questioning of Hull and Arnold, the No. 1 and 2 officers of the St. Joseph-Chicago Steamship Company, was the shortest, by far, of any other witnesses. Hull had two lawyers to defend him; Arnold, three.

To nearly every question his attorney, Kremer, asked, Hull, the vice president and most senior operating officer of the company, answered no.

"Any trouble with *Eastland* in 1915?"

"No trouble at all, except that she wouldn't steam properly."

The Admiral wisely steered clear of 1914, but couldn't avoid the near-accident in 1904 off South Haven. Know anything about it?

"The first time I heard that was in this courtroom," said Hull, looking through his cavern eyes.

"Did you hear anything about the *Eastland* being cranky or unstable or unseaworthy prior to the time you purchased her?"

"No, sir."

"Did you hear anything of that kind while you operated her?"

"No, sir."

"Did you see any evidences of that?"

"Never."

"In operating her?"

"No, sir. . . . She acted very well, indeed. I never saw her do anything out of the way at all, and I think I saw her leave the dock every day."

"Did you ever get any reports . . . that she was deficient in any respect?"

"No, indeed."

Was there any arrangement with the inspectors, or Erickson and Pedersen, you, Steele or anyone to increase the *Eastland*'s capacity to twenty-five hundred?

"No, sir."

"Did you have any conspiracy?"

"No, indeed."

"Now, Mr. Hull, what do you know about the ballast and trimming tanks on the *Eastland*?"

"I don't know anything about them; only I knew they were there."

Cross-examining, Fleming was ready to show that Hull was criminally ignorant of the ship's construction and operating history.

Harking back to the shocking testimony days earlier of *Eastland* architect Sidney Jenks, Fleming asked, "When did you first learn that this boat was constructed as a boat for the transportation of fruit by night from South Haven to Chicago?"

"In this courtroom," Hull said.

Fleming then asked a question tinged with suspicion. If you paid only $150,000 for the *Eastland* from a company that bought it for $275,000 a few years earlier, he wondered, why such a dramatic reduction in price?

"I was led to believe that they were forced to sell by the bank," Hull replied.

Fleming wanted to catch Hull in a lie. Moments earlier Hull had testified that he never learned about the *Eastland*'s near-capsize in 1904 until the past week, during testimony in Grand Rapids. This was remarkable, given that the Chicago hearings and newspapers were full of accounts of that previous mishap in the weeks after the *Eastland* fatally tipped in July 1915.

Again, Mr. Hull, Fleming asked, when did you first hear of that?

"I heard it in this courtroom for the first time."

Fleming asked, "Did you read the papers at the time of the disaster?"

Hull replied, "I certainly did not."

Fleming pressed: "Isn't it a fact it was published generally in all the local papers here along the coast of Lake Michigan as well as in the Chicago papers after the accident?"

Hull only offered, "It might have been."

Having cast doubt on Hull's honesty, he moved on to weightier matters, the innards of the controversial ballast machinery.

"Do you remember ever having talked with Davis, your private secretary there, with reference to the putting in of a 'double-action' in that boat?" He clarified, asking, had they talked about a stabilizing system that would be more responsive to the ship engineers, one that would allow water to be let in one side and pumped out the other simultaneously?

"No, sir."

"Did you ever talk it over with Steele?"

"No."

"Hasn't Steele mentioned that subject to you?"

"No, sir."

"Did you ever give any instructions at all with reference to the use of water ballast?"

"I didn't know anything about the water ballast, we never discussed it, never had any trouble with it, that I knew of."

"Haven't you heard of the general reputation on the lakes of this boat as a 'cranky' boat?"

"I have heard a lot of it here, but I never heard it before."

"You never heard it prior to your coming into this courtroom?"

"No, sir."

Hull's litany of denials came despite contrary testimony from a number of witnesses. For one thing, former chief engineer Grant Donaldson testified repeatedly that he had heard Steele and Hull discussing the cranky reputation of the *Eastland*. Donaldson also testified that the general manager offered Erickson's job to him. Hull denied that, as well, insisting he had no doubts about Erickson's competence as chief engineer.

George Arnold, who was sixty-nine and lived on Mackinac Island, at the north end of Lake Michigan, was nominally the president of the St. Joseph-Chicago Steamship Company, but had really been given that title for his role in helping start up the company in early 1914. He actually was not involved in any day-to-day decisions, invoices, ticket revenue, or hiring, as his testimony made clear. He proclaimed that he knew nothing about the water ballast system or the number of seacocks the ship had.

As to the July 1904 mishap, he said, "I think I saw something in the papers about that time," but it didn't make him doubt the ship's safety. Arnold also happened to be an executive of the company that owned the *Eastland* back in 1906, as well. Because of his money and maritime connections, he had interests in a host of ships over the years.

On cross-examination, Fleming fired a single question on the near-capsize in 1904, the answer to which might suggest appalling negligence.

"You knew of the South Haven incident," Fleming said. "Didn't you make any inquiry or any investigation as to what actually happened there?"

"Oh, yes, I saw it in the paper," Arnold admitted. "I did not."

The *Detroit Free Press* the next day had front-page photos of *Eastland* defendants Erickson, Pedersen, and Reid, all looking into the camera in their long winter coats and hats. It also ran a photo of Arnold, who raised his hand to shield his face. The caption reads, "President Arnold is shown, trying to dodge the snapshot."

It had been seven long days of testimony. The defense had some missteps, but the judge's caustic remarks to the prosecutors showed he was more favorably disposed to Darrow's side. To nail the case, Darrow was about to call Erickson, the last witness for the defense. During the investigations in Chicago, he had proven himself to be a man of integrity, forthright, knowledgeable, tempered.

Darrow walked back to the towering, luxurious Pantlind Hotel, a few blocks from the courthouse. He had been there throughout the trial.

He wrote a short letter to his son Paul, a businessman in Colorado, on hotel stationery. "Am still here on the Eastland Case. Will finish this week," he wrote. He discussed buying some shares of stock, and he closed, saying:

Will write again soon.
Hastily C.S.D.

§§§

It used to be called "Noah's Ark." As Grand Rapids grew, people found that the brick structure, the federal government building, had become too cramped. Then in 1906, Congress had earmarked a half-million dollars for harbor improvements in the Grand River, which runs crooked through the city like an *S*.

But a congressman from Grand Rapids, noting that riverboat traffic by then had become more nostalgia than industry, diverted those funds to build a new federal building to replace the old ark. There was talk of making the structure marble, but granite was selected as a more durable stone to stand up to the smoky waft of industry in the furniture manufacturing capital.

Still, for pizzazz, more than three railcar loads of Vermont marble were rolled in to construct the courthouse exterior. Fashioned in Florentine Renaissance style, the building had arched doorways, large pillars, and horizontal bands of stone called stringcourses. Pyramids crowned the windows. The doors were recessed.

The star of the dedication ceremony of the new court building, just seven years before the *Eastland* trial, was President Theodore Roosevelt's grown daughter, Alice, known as "Princess Alice" for her good looks and social shenanigans. During her short stay in Grand Rapids, she left an impression for, rumor had it, smoking large black cigars and being drunk at the train depot.

As the courthouse cornerstone was set in place on a February morning in 1909, Princess Alice said, "I dedicate thee to the use of mankind for all time."

§§§

The silence of winter. Erickson looked up as he crunched through the snow, approaching the solid bronze double-entrance doors. Once inside, he removed his hat and walked through the cavernous block-long public corridor on the first floor and curled along the wide spiral staircase up to the second floor.

The courtroom, more of a ballroom, two stories high, was likely imposing to Erickson. That morning as he stepped into it, he knew after facing questioning by Darrow, he would be grilled by prosecutors.

With an expectant wife and no way to pay the bills since the *Eastland* disaster, Erickson had taken an assembly job at the Story & Clark piano factory in Grand Haven. Unless he was cleared at the trial, he could never again work on a ship. And he wasn't ready to swallow the anchor.

CHAPTER FIFTY-TWO

"It Seemed Like a Century"

By this point, seven full days into the trial, more than fifty witnesses had been questioned: former captains, engineers, first mates, steamboat inspectors, divers, ticket collectors, the *Eastland* owners, passengers, harbormasters.

Every detail had been worked over to dizzying degree. The metrics of every corner of the *Eastland*. How the water-ballast machines worked, the size of their piping, the dimensions of the tanks. The engine-room layout. The tugboats. The diameters of the dock lines that tied up the ship. Dozens of water-depth measurements around the Chicago River and at the dock. The tree stumps. Hundreds of photos. The little *Eastland* models, one for the prosecution, a rival one for the defense.

By the time the defense called Erickson, its last witness, there were 1,061 typewritten pages of testimony already taken by court stenographers, a stack of paper six inches high. By having the other *Eastland* engineers and officers testify first, Darrow could dispense with having Erickson spell out the minutiae of how the ballast worked, the engine-room hierarchies, and so forth. That would distract from the soliloquy Darrow had set the stage for.

Instead, Darrow could use Erickson's time on the stand to build his client up as a seasoned veteran, a rising career man, a man of competence and authority. And because the defense deemed Erickson a man who oozed integrity, they knew that the last voice ringing in the judge's ear would be that of their upstanding engine-room officer.

Darrow cleared the way for Erickson to take center stage; the lawyer needed to establish that Erickson had no knowledge that the ship was fatally flawed even though he testified that a company officer, Steele, had asked him about ways to improve the *Eastland*'s stability two months before the disaster.

And he needed to show that his client did everything he could to save the ship.

Erickson had been truthful in the Chicago investigations the previous summer and his candor was going to haunt him in Grand Rapids, Darrow knew. He had to minimize the damage.

Called to testify first thing that morning, Erickson stepped to the witness stand, the polished Georgia pine floorboards creaking.

Sitting down next to the judge's bench, he looked out at the courtroom, whose ceilings and walls were simple white plaster with a festoon of flowers here, a garland of leaves there. Around the ceiling, crenellated trim. Along the four tall and narrow windows, ice branched.

Darrow approached the witness stand with letters in his freckled fingers. He had a casual, unassuming style on direct examination that allowed his client to unfurl all the critical information, to weave it right into the trial transcript.

Darrow began simply. "What is your name?"

"Joseph M. Erickson."

"Where is your home?"

After all Erickson had been through, nearly drowning in the disaster, his arrest, imprisonment, separation from his wife, loss of work, the tarring of his professional reputation, one would naturally feel alien in his new country.

"I was born in Norway," he said.

Seeing it was not the answer Darrow expected, he replied a different way. "My home? At present I am staying in Grand Haven, 605 Lake Avenue."

Darrow extracted his biography. Erickson was thirty-two years old, born in Christiania, Norway, moved to America a dozen years ago, married Christmas Day 1914, began sailing at fifteen years old, in Norway. He had seventeen to eighteen years' experience working in engine rooms on ships and had sailed ocean steamers in Norway, France, England, Germany, Sweden, Holland, and Belgium.

Got an "awful cold" on the trip over to America. After he recovered, he was on a steamer bound for Havana, Cuba, taking a load of sugar and mahogany to New York.

He worked six years on the government dredge ship, the *General Meade*. On April 2, 1913, he became licensed as a chief engineer of all tonnage vessels.

Those letters Darrow had in his hand, he began reading. Letters of commendation from captain after captain who had worked with the industrious, sober, honest, careful, hardworking young man. One even stipulated he had never heard Erickson utter an obscenity.

When he finished, Darrow turned to family matters. Darrow anticipated that the prosecution would press the *Eastland* engineer on his in-law relationship with steamship inspector Robert Reid, which the press had played up as case-closed evidence of some wrongdoing, some complicity. In a conspiracy case, the more the prosecution can show intimacy between suspected partners, the better. Darrow moved to dismiss the issue quickly.

"When did you become acquainted with Captain Reid?" he asked.

"The first time I saw Captain Reid was in the office when I took my first examination," Erickson replied.

"Well, you are married to his daughter, aren't you?"

"Yes."

"When did you become acquainted with her?"

"I became acquainted with her December 22, 1913, or about nine months after I had received my chief engineer's license."

Darrow reinforced that the licensing had nothing to do with Florence. "You already had your chief engineer's license before you knew her?"

"Yes, sir."

Darrow then established that Erickson knew his way around an engine room, was competent with water ballast. Yes, he had worked on four steamers with ballast tanks before the *Eastland*.

"Where were you in 1904, when she listed in South Haven?"

"I was on the Atlantic Coast," Erickson replied, adding that the first he heard of the 1904 incident was during the Chicago investigations last summer.

Darrow had a copy of Erickson's letter to Hull, applying for the chief engineer's job on March 1, 1915. He read it all the way to the last sentence, to reveal that Erickson was trying to be a good family man when he applied for the *Eastland* job. "My reasons for a change is to be nearer home," Darrow read.

Then Darrow asked if Erickson asked his father-in-law, Reid, for any help at all.

"No, sir."

What condition was the *Eastland* in after he "fitted it up" in the spring of 1915?

"She was in No. 1 A condition," Erickson replied.

Darrow knew a captain's supreme authority on a ship offered something of a shield for his client. "I will ask you in all your experience, 17 years, including the *Eastland*, who is the boss of the boat?"

"The captain is usually master of the steamer, always."

"Do you take orders from the captain?" Darrow asked.

"I have, in all boats I have been in, sir."

Later, Erickson spoke directly about Pedersen and how he issued orders to the engineer. "After starting out, the captain told me, I don't know how many times, but he says, 'Keep her straight, and trim her.' Either he or the mate would say 'list her' up or down to make it easier for passengers to get off and on the *Eastland*, depending on the height of the dock."

Then, addressing whether he was going to lose his engineer's spot to Donaldson, Erickson said he had heard rumors on the *Eastland* in mid-July to that effect, and so he wrote a letter of resignation. But then he and Hull met, and, as Erickson prepared to step off the *Eastland* for good, Hull implored him to stay. Hull explained why he called Donaldson, Erickson said, to help with the coal-burning issue, not to take Erickson's job. So Erickson rescinded the resignation, he said. Days later, the ship went over.

The morning of the disaster was to be his fortieth roundtrip; he knew a full load of passengers was scheduled for the trip, but never heard how many that meant.

As Darrow heard Erickson speak, inspiration struck. Darrow worked well on impulse. There was a way to draw Erickson out, to play on Sessions's evident pathos.

"Now I want to ask you a little more particularly about this engine room where you were," he began. Darrow shifted his questioning to portray Erickson's engine room as a dank, dark, loud, lifeless place, a dungeon. The attorney picked his words carefully, referring to it only as "that place" and "down there."

"Now to get down into that place . . . how did you get down there?"

"A ladder or stairway," Erickson said.

"A narrow stair?"

"Iron stairs or steel."

"About how far down is it?"

"About seven or eight feet; maybe nine, I never measured it."

"Any porthole?"

"No." No way to see out.

"Any place to get out excepting this stairway?"

"No."

"No other place?" Darrow reiterated.

"No, sir."

"Any light there excepting the electric lights when they are turned on?"

"No sir."

"And there is all this machinery and the water tanks?"

"Why, we had to attend to all of the machinery, dynamos, pumps."

Darrow then released Erickson to begin a powerful soliloquy. The engineer's account of the *Eastland* disaster from inside the engine room came from memory. Erickson relived that terrible morning precisely, without any notes, impressive in detail.

"At 7:10, she was on an even keel, as near as I can recall. She started to give a little port list, and I knew there wasn't very much water in No. 2 and No. 3 port, so we started the ballast pump and pumped out the No. 3. We had most of it.

"Then we didn't get her all the way up, or straightened, so when she was there for awhile, we opened the No. 2 and No. 3 starboard, the valves also, the seacock I had open. . . . Opened wide. . . . Water was running into those two tanks as fast as it could come."

After he instructed his assistant, Charles Silvernail, to get all the people to move to the starboard side, "I told him to tell the mate . . . then of course he would notify the captain . . .

"And she was listing more and more, and then I went over to the starboard side, past my room and past the fireman's and I called out to the passengers back there to get on the starboard side, and as I was calling out to the passengers, I saw the purser away back—his name is Monger—I called out as loud as I could to tell him to get the people on the starboard side.

"He looked over kind of, but he didn't seem to see me, so I went to him, and at the same time I was telling people to get on the starboard side, and I heard her—I felt her started to go—And she stopped an instant, maybe half a minute or more, and then I run into the engine room, and as I was coming in by the port dynamo, I got to the dynamo, and she went over.

"And as she did, she trembled like she was on a bump or something. The whole ship shocked. And I hung onto the railings, and it seemed like a century, water was coming in . . .

"And I couldn't see where it was coming from because I was so busy hanging onto the railing, and I worked my way up to the high side, but I don't know how long it took me, but I finally got up, and I stood on the railing, and I got right up to a porthole in the engine room on the starboard side, and I saw the water was nearly over the starboard engine. And I stuck my hand up, and I couldn't crawl up myself, I was so exhausted."

"How big is that porthole?" Darrow interrupted.

"Oh, about 12 to 14 inches in diameter, something like that. I saw a watchman named Brooks came by and he saw my hand, and I says, 'Pull me up.' And he pulled me up and when I come from these portholes, my clothes caught on these thumb screws or something and ripped my trousers.

"And I got up through, and I stood right on the side of the ship and rested for maybe a minute or two. He asked me if I was hurt. I don't know what I answered, and he went on.

"And I went over on the next deck, that is I got on my feet and got over to the next deck, and I looked down through the portholes and I could see people down there.

"And I saw the second mate . . . and told him to get some ropes and he went up and got some ropes from the life boats, and I went over on the promenade deck, and I seen people hanging on the benches down there. The benches were screwed right on the deck. I went down in there and the first one I took was a young girl hanging on the bench, and I worked her right up on the bench and by that time they got the lines down there. And I put a little line around her and pulled her up.

"And they lowered the line down to me three or four times, four or five times. There was lots of ladies down there and I fastened around their waist and they held on, and they pulled them up; and then the firemen came down over the side with a ladder and they took out all they could and all that was there.

"After I came up on the deck—or up on the side of the ship, I walked around and met the captain. . . . Later on, I walked up on the deck again and I could see the two local inspectors of Chicago, Mr. Mansfield and Mr. Nicholas, and we stood there talking, and they asked me what happened, etc., and I don't know how many questions I was asked, and what was said in general, but Mr. Nicholas saw me, I was shivering and freezing, and I was wet all the way through."

Judge Sessions had heard enough. He adjourned the court until nine the next morning.

CHAPTER FIFTY-THREE

"The Rich Stay in Hotels"

.

Darrow left the courthouse and walked several blocks to the Pantlind Hotel, whose lobby had one of the world's largest gold-leaf ceilings. He wore a light gray overcoat, while all the other lawyers wore black ones. He hurried along, needing to ready himself for a speech he was scheduled to give at seven that evening, at the Powers Theater. The five-story brick opera house could seat sixteen hundred. The lecture, advertised in all the papers in town, was sold out. The subject was crime and justice.

As he rejuvenated his legal career, Darrow was speaking about two to three times a week at that time, a regimen he would continue the rest of his life. Some of his favorite topics, his peeves, were impending rules to prohibit the sale of liquor, Sunday-closing laws, censorship, labor injunctions, segregation laws, the death penalty, and conspiracy laws, which he called punishing "the crime of thought."

Darrow was steeping his ideas about heredity and evolution; the latter would loom large in a case that would captivate the country within a decade. He had inherited his interest in science and philosophy from his father, and he had recently organized a discussion group called the Biology Club in Chicago that held a lecture series by eminent anthropologists, scientists, and philosophers.

§§§

The audience at the opera house included some of Darrow's defense partners, including Barbour. Standing in front of the towering theater drop curtain, Darrow held forth at the pulpit.

"There is no difference in people except degree. We are all criminals, more or less, and it is hard to classify us. Man is the product of heredity and environment. All life begins with a simple cell; all cells are alike and we cannot determine the future. Heredity fixes the character, and no training can substantially differ it, but the surroundings where he is placed determine what kind of man he is to be, whether a substantial citizen or a criminal. You cannot develop to be anything but what you were intended to be, but you can make a man better or worse than his natural heredity would make him.

"The Declaration of Independence says that all men are created equal, but that is not true. About the last thing nature does is create things equal, and in making our judgments all things should be taken into consideration. The law judges all alike, because there is no science of philosophy mixed with the judgments of courts, and the genius and the fool are sentenced alike."

Applause ripped through the opera house, as it would several other times that evening.

"Give every man a chance and there would be no jails or poorhouses.... If every man had the chance, which is his right, there would be no defectives or criminals. The whole theory of punishment is bad.

"We must get to the root of all evil and improve the conditions of every man. When we have got this thing right, all jails will be hospitals and we will pity those who are born poor, and will treat them as brothers instead of branding them as criminals, and then they will recover.

"The prisons are not only made by the poor, but filled by the poor. The rich stay in hotels.

"But there are some basic principles we ought to learn. First is that there are no property rights. More than nine-tenths of people go to jail for property crimes—stealing property and so on.

"On the other hand, a man may take all the oil in the earth; all the coal in the earth. A few railroads own all the anthracite coal in the United States. The Lord didn't put this coal on the earth for Morgan, nor the oil for Rockefeller. But they came along and took them.

"No man in the world is good enough to pass judgment upon his fellow-man, and I wish that every juror before declaring a man guilty would think whether or not he has ever done anything wrong.

"If they do, there won't be anybody to convict, much less any lawyers to prosecute. No person has the right to judge."

The Red Cross Toll

No. 736. (Polish) **Husband, 34; daughter, 4;** wife, 23; daughter, 2; daughter, 1. The husband, an employee of the Western Electric Company, was drowned, with the little girl. The wife was also on the boat but was rescued, apparently uninjured. Four months later, however, a child was born to her and lived but a few days.

No. 120. (Hungarian) **Man, 40.**
A man employed by the Western Electric Company was killed. The Red Cross, after difficult search, located his wife and three children in Austria and learned that he had been sending his earnings to them. The gift was sent to them through the State Department.

No. 74. (Polish) **Man, 30.**
A young man was killed. He was supposed to have been unmarried. His friends said that he had sent part of his earnings to his aged mother in Russia. The Red Cross, through the State Department, made inquiry as to the situation of this mother and had a letter saying that she was very old and quite needy. The letter said, further, that the decedent's wife and child "sent love." The Red Cross again appealed to the State Department for information. But before anything further could be heard of the wife and child, Russian and German armies had fought back and forth over the province a number of times and all trace of them was lost.

CHAPTER FIFTY-FOUR

A Wrong Irreparable

We are all criminals, more or less.

Perhaps his own words hung in his ears the next morning, for Darrow decided to press the case of empathy for Erickson. Before his address on crime and justice, Darrow focused on vividly portraying the dark underworld of Erickson's engine room. The engineer lived in a trap. If that didn't resonate as a prison for Judge Sessions, Darrow would open the morning's questioning by hammering home Erickson's actual time behind bars.

"Coming down to where you left off last night, you described the accident and said you were arrested," Darrow began.

Erickson corrected him; he had not yet testified about his arrest. "About 10:30 Mr. Schuettler [the No. 2 Chicago police official] came and placed us under arrest and we were taken to city hall and kept there—"

Assistant District Attorney Fleming saw where this was headed. "This is all incompetent," he interjected, questioning its relevance.

"Well," replied Darrow, "I will state to the court right now how I think it is competent. He made three or four statements. . . . I want to show the circumstances and conditions under which those were made."

"You may proceed," said Sessions.

Darrow wanted to drum up sympathy for Erickson's handling by the Chicago inquisitors and suggest that Erickson had been under duress when he answered their questions. He would thus attack the propriety of Erickson's previous testimony—notably the bombshell that Steele wanted to renovate the ballast machinery before the disaster.

It was a long shot. That testimony—true or not—could harm his client, and Darrow would have preferred to have it erased from the record.

Erickson continued that they had been arrested around 10:30 a.m. and taken to City Hall and kept there, and then he was placed in a basement cell at the Houston Avenue Police Station.

"The next day, July 25, I was taken to Chief Healey's office around noon. I was down there until about seven in the evening. . . . Every day, once or twice a day, we was taken to different courts and offices, from one place to another, at all hours.

"About the first of August, I think we was put in the County Jail. We were kept there until August 12, when I was released under bonds."

Darrow's client had been held in jail with no charges for nineteen days. And he wanted the judge to know it.

"You were under arrest all of the time up to August 12th then, and confined?"

"Yes, sir."

Erickson said he had been questioned by the state's attorney, the Chicago coroner, and the police chief.

"And what was your condition," Darrow asked, "during those first few days?"

"Nervous wreck."

"Did you have an attorney?"

"No, sir."

All of that laid out, Darrow dove into the controversial testimony, asking if he had had any conversation with the officers or owners of the *Eastland* about adding seacocks.

Erickson replied that in early or mid-May, he and Steele "went over the boat. He had his overalls on." Erickson's recollection of Steele's overalls bolstered his testimony; it was the kind of simple, concrete particular that makes accounts ring true.

He continued: "And he wanted to see what work was done, and I took him around the boilers, outside of the boilers, top of the boilers, engine room, etc.

"And I think he asked me if it would be possible to put another seacock in, and I thought it might be if we got her in dry dock some time. It would take quite a while. Also place a valve in the center, what is called a division valve, so that [the tanks] could operate independent, from each side. I said I thought it could be done."

Remarkably, Erickson never shrank from his account. He reaffirmed over and over, and now under oath in a federal courtroom, a discussion that could have incriminated him. His testimony had the fresh air of truth.

The talk was between him and Steele. Just two men. Had Erickson said nothing to the police, no one would have ever known. But he did not deny his earlier testimony, did not distort or downplay. Only an innocent man would behave that way.

"Was there anything said about doing it or when it could be done?" Darrow asked him.

"Nothing definite."

CHAPTER FIFTY-FIVE

The Missing Angel

The prosecutors were ready. They had their charts, their timetables, their stacks of previous testimony by Erickson.

This was their chance to retake the case. They would move swiftly.

Under cross-examination by Fleming, Erickson said he had spent about seventeen minutes trying to admit water into the starboard tanks to correct the port list.

"You could not feed all of those pipes leading from the starboard side by throwing the seacock open in its entirety, could you?" Fleming asked.

"No, sir."

"The inlet wasn't sufficient, was it—yes or no?"

Fleming had a rapid-fire, staccato questioning style that could unnerve a witness.

"It has been answered, and I object to it," Darrow said.

Erickson said, "I did answer that question."

"Well," Fleming said, "answer it again."

Darrow interjected, "Sufficiently large for what? If he is using this as a foundation that it should have been a bigger seacock, that is one thing; but if he is using it as not sufficiently large to supply them all at once . . ."

Sessions said, "Well, that is what he has been talking about. I think the witness understands the question."

"No, it is not large enough—not for five pipes, it is not large enough," Erickson reaffirmed.

Fleming had some damaging information, something a government diver found in the engine room, something that he had yet to divulge in the courtroom. "Isn't it a fact that it takes 20 revolutions to open that seacock?"

"It may take 12 or 14, I never counted them," Erickson said. He said his assistant, Fred Snow, personally unscrewed the seacock all the way open and he watched him the whole time to ensure it was fully opened.

"That seacock is sufficient in size, is it not, in your judgment, for the proper operation of a boat?"

It was a searing question. After seeing what he did the morning of July 24, 1915, the inability to control the ship, the hundreds of bodies carried out, Erickson could not help but come to a horrible conclusion.

"No sir, it is not."

"Haven't you made that statement on a number of occasions? Haven't you made a statement further than that—"

"Objection," said Barbour.

The testimony was heating up. The defense needed to douse it.

The oath Erickson took the previous summer was outside a court proceeding, Barbour said. Therefore it was "not free and voluntary and cannot be admissible against him."

It was a tense moment. If the judge tossed out the crucial testimony, it would be a huge victory for the defense.

Sessions thought for a time. And then he overruled the objection.

"In your appearance before the state's attorney of Cook County," a relieved Fleming continued, "wasn't this question put to you:

Q. The seacock in the boat wasn't large enough to let water in to right her up?
A. To right her up fast.
Q. That is what I mean; in other words, this boat as it was on that occasion didn't have seacock enough to let the water to right her up, no matter how you operated?
A. Yes, sir.

Erickson said, "I wouldn't deny it, no, sir."

"You remember," Fleming asked, "this question being asked of you later on:

Q. Did you have sufficient tanks on there to straighten her out?
A. I think we had, sir, if we had a larger seacock so we could run more water into her ballast tanks.

"I presume so," Erickson said. "Yes, sir."

"You recommended, have you not, to the management of the company that the boat be so changed as to permit these simultaneous operations?"

"I object to that," said Darrow. "Calls for a conclusion."

Over repeated objections, Fleming fought his way to Erickson's reaffirming that he and Steele had discussed the previous May, two months before the disaster, a way to pump out and fill the water tanks simultaneously. And adding another seacock. The modifications would make the ship more responsive, and it was a more modern method of construction than when the *Eastland* was built in 1903.

Steele, aware of the ship's history, may have known there was a grave danger to waiting on the repairs. But Erickson couldn't possibly have. Fleming tried to get Erickson to admit that he suggested the repairs to Steele, but Erickson insisted it wasn't true. Erickson had never sailed on the *Eastland* when the two met in May. Erickson had no idea how the ship handled.

"I didn't suggest it," Erickson said. "He asked my opinion, and I stated that I think it could be done. . . . At that time, she wasn't in operation. I didn't know what she would do. She was tied to the dock."

In your conversation with Steele, Fleming asked, the understanding was a double-action system was to be installed in the fall?

"No, it wasn't," Erickson replied. Fleming asked the question a little too precisely. Based on the way he was questioned the prior summer, Erickson said the work might have been done sometime later, perhaps winter, perhaps fall. In short, no, there was not a precise date chosen for the repairs.

"And when you made your statement before the mayor's office and the state's attorney's office, did you tell the facts?" Fleming said, asking Erickson basically if he were a liar.

Darrow objected; Fleming withdrew the question.

"You weren't under any compulsion to make any statement, were you?" Fleming asked.

"Why, it seemed that way," Erickson said. "They pressed me and they pressed me."

This was not what Fleming meant to draw out. Had Erickson really been coerced? Fleming moved to tamp this down quickly.

"When you appeared before the State's Attorney of Cook County, didn't he tell you it wasn't necessary to talk, and you said you would answer all the questions they put to you?"

"That I cannot recall, Mr. Fleming. I might have said it. There was a whole lot of excitement and strain I had gone through."

Fleming reaffirmed that Steele wanted to fix the *Eastland*'s tipsy behavior. "Did you make any other recommendation other than the talk you had with Mr. Steele with reference to the curing of the listing tendencies of that boat?"

"No, sir," Erickson said.

The prosecutors apparently figured they would have a shot at grilling Steele on this conversation when the full trial moved to Chicago. Having already agreed to appear in court there, he was not a party to the extradition action in Grand Rapids. The angel kept in the shadows.

§§§

Barbour asked permission to question Erickson, telling the judge he was "cross-examining," in order to defend his own client, Captain Pedersen.

Barbour wanted to try to undermine Erickson's testimony or credibility.

Sessions was unambiguous in his response. "No, there is only one side that can cross-examine."

"I thought that the captain was standing by himself, a defendant here," Barbour replied.

"No, there are only two sides to this matter."

At various points over eight days, the defense attorneys clearly tried to shift blame between their clients. The captain was the ultimate authority. The owners trusted that the inspectors wouldn't license an unsafe ship. The engineer wasn't competent. And on and on.

Sessions was saying that the federal court saw only two parties in the case, the alleged conspirators and the United States. The six men were all in the same boat, as it were, and would be found innocent or guilty as a group.

As the weight of that pronouncement settled in, Darrow had two more questions for Erickson.

"Had you ever experienced any difficulty because there was just one seacock?"

"No sir, at all times, she always responded when we give her the water." For Darrow, this would show that even if the *Eastland* was faulty in construction, Erickson had no way of knowing that. In effect, that he had been blindsided by the accident.

"Up to the time of this accident, had you ever heard that she was unsafe in any way?"

"No, sir," Erickson said. "I never heard; if I had, I never would have gone on her."

Darrow wisely did not ask Erickson what another defense attorney had asked the captain: Do you still view the *Eastland* as a safe and seaworthy vessel? Though Pedersen responded that he would sail the ship again, Erickson probably would not have gone on the *Eastland* ever again, having finally learned how deadly it could be.

Then the defense rested.

CHAPTER FIFTY-SIX

Striking Back

Finally getting its turn, the prosecution was set to dismantle the defense case. More than once the judge seemed favorable to Darrow and the others, seeming to sympathize with the harsh treatment of the *Eastland* men by the police. But prosecutors felt rather confident; after all, they did have something of a moral upper hand. They were there to bring justice to the *Eastland* victims, the twenty-two entire families that perished, the widows, widowers, and orphans whose spouses, daughters, sons, and parents died gasping, kicked bloody, swallowing water, eyes flaming.

All the prosecution had to do under federal law of the time was convince Judge Sessions that the *Eastland* men were probably guilty for somehow allowing that unimaginable mayhem, and he would be forced to dispatch them to Chicago for trial.

The defense had called most of the crucial witnesses for its side, leaving the prosecution with a bit of a ragtag group, including an underwater detective, whose testimony would send Darrow into a tailspin, and a world expert on naval architecture who would tear into the *Eastland* with a British accent and a blackboard.

If these indicted men were responsible, the prosecution could not let them slip away, avoiding justice in the city that had witnessed their crimes. Given such gravity, and their understanding of that gravity, it's puzzling how they could have blundered so badly with the choice of their first witness.

§§§

Robert M. Moyer was a typesetter who lived in Cleveland. He was on the *Eastland* on a July 1, 1912, trip from Cleveland to Cedar Point.

Walker, the local district attorney, questioned him. "Did you notice at any time of that trip anything unusual or peculiar?"

"I certainly did," Moyer said.

E. B. Cresap, one of *Eastland* owner George Arnold's three lawyers, interrupted. "We object. Now against whom is it being offered?"

Walker shot back, "It is offered against the boat itself."

"The boat is not on trial," Cresap replied.

Sessions stepped in. "What is your purpose to show?"

"The purpose," Walker said, "is to show that she listed dangerously so as to alarm the passengers and listed for a considerable period of time. Both to the port and starboard to a dangerous degree, and the captain's attention was called to it."

Sessions was skeptical. "Is this man a seaman?"

"No, your honor," replied Walker.

"Did he know anything about the construction of boats?"

"He does not."

Sessions grudgingly agreed to let him testify, but noted that at a regular trial, "it would be incompetent testimony."

Moyer testified that after they left the Cleveland harbor, the *Eastland* tipped about twenty-five degrees, scaring him, and then straightened up and then tipped about thirty degrees. He said he had to hold on to a post to keep from sliding. He saw chairs slide to the railing. People became seasick.

Moyer said that he became so frightened that he refused to take the *Eastland* on the return trip from the Cedar Point theme park, hopping on a streetcar back to Cleveland instead.

At the defense desk, Kremer listened in. Throughout the trial, he had been doodling in his notepad. He drew quite nice caricatures of Sessions, the opposing attorneys, the hounding newspapermen. Now he needed to sketch a witness as a fool.

In cross-examination, Kremer had little trouble discrediting Moyer. Kremer handed the typeset man a sheet of paper from his sketch pad and said, "Now, how much is 25 degrees? Just hold that paper and give us an idea."

Moyer held the paper and demonstrated ninety degrees and then leaned it nearly to the witness ledge. "I should say it was about this much."

Incredulous, Kremer said, "That's what you call listing 25 degrees?"

"Yes, sir, I would," Moyer said.

When Walker questioned Moyer again, he asked if he had seen what the wheelsman had done to overcome the tipping.

Kremer, the only real maritime expert among all the lawyers there, couldn't take it any longer. "I object to this because this man absolutely does not know a wheel from a wheelbarrow."

Sessions let Moyer continue. He said the helmsman turned the wheel opposite the list, as if to correct for it.

Kremer was indignant. "Do you know anything about steering a boat?"

Moyer said he knew the propellers were connected to the ship wheel.

The lawyers at the defense table burst out laughing. The judge did not even reprimand them. Rather, Sessions scolded the prosecutors for bringing a useless witness into his court.

"Men's liberty cannot be put in jeopardy by testimony of witnesses who are not competent to testify upon the subject," he told them. "I simply express the hope that we are not going to be led into a bewildering number of witnesses to testify in this manner."

The prosecution, at its moment in the limelight, flubbed its very first witness. They would persist in bringing landlubbers to the stand, nonetheless, to establish a history of troubling stability for the *Eastland*. Some were passengers aboard during the July 1915 disaster, a couple were on the Cleveland 1912 trip, and two were on the controversial July 17, 1904, postal employees' trip.

John H. Harrington, a postman in Chicago, could still recall his encounter with the *Eastland* nearly twelve years earlier. "It listed first to port quite dangerously, and then she came back and listed to starboard.... I urged a few not to put on life preservers, as it would perhaps create a panic. But they told me the water was rushing in down below and I had better get one myself."

The prosecution wanted to cement that passengers were panicked. The list was so severe, the postman said, that the crew ordered passengers to go belowdecks to help straighten it out. When they resisted, the crew turned on the passengers.

"My recollection is that the [fire] hose was turned on them and their dresses or shirt waists became wet. My recollection is that the hose was used from the bow of the boat."

Prosecutors called several witnesses to prove that the *Eastland* dangerously tipped more than other ships over the years. Arthur D. MacDonald, the engineer on the tugboat *Kenosha*, towed the *Eastland* in Chicago four to five times. "I have noticed she has an awful tendency to list," he testified. "It don't take very much to list her."

Charles Davis started as a coal passer on the *Eastland* just days before the disaster. He noticed the ship's tendency to tilt because it was harder for him and the crew to dispense ashes out the discharge chute in the boiler room. "If the boat was listing, I noticed, because when we tried to shoot these ashes out what we call the 'gun' the water backed down in the fire hole. If she straightened out, we would shoot them into the lake."

After a slow start, the prosecution called H. B. Vehstedt, a naval architect for the city of Chicago, sixteen years on the job. He would stun the defense with his testimony.

He and his staff took soundings of the water at the dock where the ship sank, immediately after the shipwreck was removed. It was before Darrow sent his diver down to cut the two pilings for the defense. Vehstedt's team had found the pilings too and measured their distance to the water surface. He calculated, in painstaking detail, and revealed in blueprints and charts, that with an *Eastland* packed with 2,570 passengers and crew, coal bunkers and ballast tanks loaded—heavy as it could possibly be—the bottom of the *Eastland* would still float three feet above the underwater pillars.

The ship was so massive that the addition of all 2,570 people, equal to 175 tons, would push the *Eastland* down in the water a mere eight inches.

Darrow was unable to discredit the man or his testimony at cross, further hurting the defense theory of an underwater culprit.

Fleming asked the naval architect in conclusion, "Is it possible for the lowest portion of that boat to get near that pile?"

"No," he responded.

CHAPTER FIFTY-SEVEN

The Diving Detective

The prosecution was on a roll, and the next two witnesses were about to alarm the defense even more. Hinton Graves Clabaugh was division superintendent of the Justice Department's Bureau of Investigation, the "BI" in what would later become the FBI. He had previously run the New York City division. He had worked for the Justice Department for six years and had been in Chicago for eighteen months. Before that, he was a confidential investigator for the US Senate.

The attorney general in Washington named Clabaugh the point man in investigating the *Eastland* disaster on Monday, July 26, the capsizing not yet two days old. Special Agent Clabaugh figured there were answers in the hull of the ship, and he wanted to investigate there before anyone else. On Saturday morning, July 31, a week after the tragedy, the Justice investigator sent a diver he had hired, Harry Halverson, down into the ship for the whole day to examine the engine room, its seacock and valves.

Clabaugh wondered whether any of the pipes were obstructed, if all the valves had been properly opened. He had specific instructions for Halverson on how to handle the seacock. He told him to start to close it and to keep a careful count of how many revolutions it took before it was shut tight.

The diver followed the instructions, came back up to the surface and reported the number. Clabaugh then sent him back down, instructed him to open it wide up and count the number of turns that took.

The prosecutors did not ask what the findings were; they would save that for the next witness. On cross-examination, the defense dared not ask him what he found.

Halverson stepped into the witness box. A Chicago marine diver for about seven years, he worked for the Great Lakes Dredging and Dock

Company. Questioned by Clyne, Halverson affirmed that he had been sent to the engine room by the Justice Department to examine the machinery under specific instructions. He made a mark on the valve of the seacock, indicating a starting place. Each time he turned the wheel and it passed that mark, he counted one revolution.

"It took about eight turns to close it, sir," Halverson said. At the defense desk, Darrow took note of the answer.

Halverson said he resurfaced and reported that finding to his boss, Clabaugh. He then returned to open it wide, as instructed. Fleming asked how many turns that took. "It took about 19—no about 20 to 21 turns to open it wide, sir," Halverson said.

It was a thunderbolt. If he was right, that showed that the seacock valve was not open wide, that the critical in-flow of water might have been limited at the time of the disaster, a major engine-room mistake.

Since this testimony directly implicated the engine room—Erickson—Darrow rose from his customary slouch, hands on his paunch, and approached Halverson. How to discredit the testimony? Erickson had already testified that he instructed his immediate assistant, Snow, to open the seacock and further swore that he watched him to ensure it was opened widely.

"How big is the wheel?" Darrow began.

"About 12 to 14 inches in diameter."

"Where did you get the wheel to turn it?"

"That was on there, sir."

Darrow asked: "Fastened?"

"Fastened to the stem, yes, sir."

An idea came to Darrow. "What kind of light did you have down there?"

"Didn't have no light, sir."

"You went there in the dark and turned this around, turned the wheel around?"

"Yes, sir."

"Tell me again, I would like to get it so I can understand it, how you marked it?"

"I take a string and tie around the hub of the wheel, sir, which I mark it to the thing on the side there where the stem goes through, which I hold my hand and turn it around, follow it around, I come back to the same hub again, sir, keep on counting that way."

"You tied a string on and turned it, and when you got around to the string again, you knew you had gone around once, is that it?" Darrow asked. Yes.

Then, offering some bait, he asked, "How many times did you turn it around?"

"Eight turns, sir," Halverson said, taking the bait.

"Well, a while ago you said 'about eight,' didn't you?"

"Well, about eight, yes, sir."

"Did you see any difference between 'about eight' and 'eight'?"

"Well, sir, I guess not, sir."

"Well, which is it 'eight,' or 'about eight'?"

"As far as I can—"

"That's it," Darrow pressed, "you are not exactly certain. Is that it?"

Clyne interjected on behalf of his witness. "No, no—he doesn't say that, Mr. Darrow."

"Well, you are not exactly certain as to how many turns you made, is that it?" Darrow had introduced doubt about the diver's methods, how he worked in the dark and how he counted. By the time Darrow sat back down, the damaging testimony had fizzled.

The prosecutors quickly switched the subject. Earlier the defense had suggested that among the obstructions that might have capsized the *Eastland* was a pile of cement, refuse of some kind, on the river bottom.

Questioned by Prosecutor Clyne, Halverson said he did indeed find some cement and even brought a foot-long chunk of it to the surface to show Clabaugh. Clyne asked him what condition the cement was in.

"Well, sir, it was pretty clean," the diver said. "If it had been laying on the bottom of the river any length of time it ought to be slimy," implying that someone had dumped the cement there recently, someone who would benefit from a sudden pile of riprap in that exact spot. The testimony was a veiled indictment of the defense, the prosecutors' accusing their rival lawyers of some late-night dumping in the river.

§§§

The prosecutorial momentum continued. When testimony came out previously that the *Neptune* and other ships larger than the *Eastland* comfortably sat at the dock where the *Eastland* turned over, the defense argued that the level of the Chicago River could fluctuate several feet day-to-day and that it was probably low the morning of the disaster.

The prosecution prepared to refute that. Colonel W. V. Judson, an officer with the US Army Corps of Engineers in Chicago, called to the stand, reported that his men made periodic readings of the river at hourly intervals. The Chicago River was one-tenth of a foot lower than normal at seven in the morning, just before the *Eastland* turned over. It rose three-tenths of a foot by noon. And by 6:00 p.m., it was down two-tenths of a foot from normal. The river had been virtually flat all day.

The Army colonel mentioned at one point that his men had to go on into the river shortly after the *Eastland* was removed. They had to haul away one of the iron smokestacks that broke away and sat on the riverbed fifteen feet below the surface of the river.

Sessions perked up. A lightbulb went on for him. He jumped in, asking what was the boundary for federal jurisdiction of the river. Judson said that federal officials control the river beginning twenty feet out from the docks.

"Your work is all done outside of the 20-foot line?" the judge asked.

"Outside the 20-foot line, so that the United States would not be responsible for the undermining of docks," Judson replied.

"Who does the other work, the city?"

"Well, the city or the dock owner," he replied.

Sessions adjourned the court until the next morning, the last day of testimony. Neither side knew it, but Sessions had just signaled what would become the crux of the case in his mind.

CHAPTER FIFTY-EIGHT

A Moment of Honor

The prosecution had two strong witnesses left, the Chicago harbormaster and a professor from the University of Michigan, a world-renowned scholar on naval architecture. In the case of the harbormaster, the strongest testimony would come when Barbour tried to trip him up—and it backfired.

Adam F. Weckler had been on the job as Chicago harbormaster exactly one month when the disaster struck. He arrived at his post at the Clark Street Bridge at 7:10 that morning.

He and his assistant, Captain Lynn, were in charge of opening up the bridges to let large ships pass. Normally, once all the passengers were aboard, and a captain felt his ship and crew were ready to proceed, he would order a single blast from a whistle and the harbor officials would open the bridge.

When Weckler saw the *Eastland* topsy-turvy at its dock, he testified, he spoke to his assistant. "I says to Captain Lynn, 'Don't turn any bridge over until the boat is trimmed.' I called up to Captain Pedersen, who was on the starboard side of the bridge and told him to trim his boat. He answered back, raising his hand, and said they were trimming all the time. I says, 'We won't give you the bridge until the boat is righted and trimmed.'"

Rather than focusing on Weckler's significant testimony, the prosecutors decided to pound away on the *Eastland*'s reputation. "I don't know as I have ever seen the *Eastland* on an even keel," Weckler said. "Whenever I have seen her, she has always been listed. The general reputation among marine men and river men is that the *Eastland* is a very cranky and unseaworthy boat." This testimony is troubling but perhaps not for the reason the prosecution brought it out. If Weckler thought the *Eastland* was not seaworthy, didn't he have an obligation to act somehow?

Weckler joined a chorus of previous eyewitnesses who swore they saw the *Neptune* at the Clark Street Bridge dock the morning after the *Eastland* wreck was removed. The *Neptune* was immense, one hundred feet longer than the *Eastland*. Its draft was much deeper as well, eighteen feet versus thirteen feet. It was pretty easy to remember the *Neptune*. Aside from being colossal, it had a nautical name, and everyone had learned as schoolchildren that it was the last planet in the solar system.

Weckler attacked the *Eastland*'s ballast system. "One seacock would not be sufficient in my mind for the filling of her tanks, to fill them rapidly enough to correct any list which might take place on the boat.... She should have a water supply enough in order to correct any list within a period of a half minute to a minute, that is my general opinion of passenger boats from what I have seen."

How? "That's normally accomplished by larger [seacock] openings and a 'double-operation,' that is, the ability to take water out of one tank and put it in another simultaneously."

Barbour approached to cross-examine. He hoped to trip up the harbormaster, to show that his assertion that he planned to refuse to allow the *Eastland* to proceed in his harbor was nothing but bluster.

"You can refuse to turn a bridge for an unsafe boat, can you not?" said moonfaced Barbour, knowing the answer full well.

"I cannot, no sir. The bridge is an obstacle to navigation, and when a boat blows the whistle, the United States law requires me to open that bridge."

Feeling the trap had snapped, Barbour didn't even follow up with a question. "Well, then," he stated, "you couldn't have held the bridge on the *Eastland* that morning as you said you were going to."

"I could, yes," Weckler fired back. "I felt moral responsibility."

The Chicago harbormaster testified that he was prepared to break federal law, to face punishment for doing so, because he thought it was immoral to allow the tilting *Eastland* out that morning.

Barbour decided to question his integrity.

"Have you felt all the time that the city of Chicago might be in some degree responsible for this disaster if it should be proved that the boat, the *Eastland*, was on the ground, and because of being on the ground, turned over?"

Clyne objected for the prosecution; this line of questioning to impeach the witness was improper and had no foundation.

Sessions allowed the question.

Barbour restated his query: "If it is found here from the testimony that the boat was unseaworthy and turned over because it was in an unseaworthy condition, that would exonerate the city, would it not?"

Clyne objected again, and this time Sessions relented.

Still, Barbour had made his point. Maybe Weckler cared more about protecting the city than about justice.

CHAPTER FIFTY-NINE

A Miscalculation

The defense had saved its best witness, Erickson, for last. Likewise, the last man to take the stand for the prosecution was the government's star witness. Herbert Charles Sadler was an egghead with perfectly round glasses.

The university professor came to some fame in the marine world following the *Titanic* disaster. President Wilson chose him to represent the United States at the International Conference for Safety of Life at Sea, convened in London in 1913, a year after the infamous sinking. The conference would end up recommending new rules requiring, among other things, that every ship have lifeboat or life raft space for each person aboard.

Sadler took his doctorate at the University of Glasgow and worked briefly in shipbuilding in Scotland. The University of Michigan reached across the Atlantic to recruit him, at only age twenty-eight, to establish a program in naval architecture and marine engineering in Ann Arbor. While there, he had a novel model-testing tank built and experimented to determine the safest and most economical form for vessels carrying freight on the Great Lakes.

Only forty-four when he appeared in Grand Rapids, he was brilliant, one of the world's leading experts on ship design. But the morning Sadler took the stand, Darrow would overshadow the star witness with a single question.

The government hired Sadler to compare the condition of the *Eastland* with its original blueprints, noting the removal of staterooms and any other changes. He boarded the wreck shortly after the *Eastland* toppled and then later when it was raised and hauled away.

Sadler described a calculation he devised for the deadly capsize. He used highly technical language, terms like neutral equilibrium and metacentric height, which along with a British accent, clearly threw both the judge and the attorneys. It didn't help much that the professor used a blackboard and chalk to present his findings.

He assumed how the twenty-five hundred passengers fully loaded were distributed, three hundred on the top deck, then eleven hundred on each of the next two decks, and none on the main, or lowest, deck. Aside from the tonnage of passengers, he estimated the tons of coal the ship had, the sixty-five tons of water in its ballast tanks, and then he calculated that with a list of only fifteen degrees, which he called "not excessive," the *Eastland* would capsize.

Over an objection from the defense, Sadler was asked what changes, if any, he would make in order to make it a safe, seaworthy ship.

He began by noting, "It is a very different set of conditions, carrying 2,500 people, as compared to carrying 400 or 500 in staterooms where they are not likely to move around that quickly."

Thinking further, he added, "Personally, I would have recommended permanent ballast. . . . If you were designing a new vessel, you probably wouldn't design her where her stability depended solely on water ballast."

Why permanent ballast?

"Because it is foolproof," he said, adding that it would remove any chance of mistakes by the captain or the engineer. Sadler said he thought the *Eastland* would have been stable with half the number of passengers it carried the fateful morning, 1,250, and no water ballast.

Prosecutor Clyne asked, "Do you consider the form of ballast she had in a safe or unsafe form?"

"I object," Barbour said. He was thinking back to South Haven, the sandbar. "There is one element that is not in that question, and that is the shallowness of the water in the harbor that it was designed for it to run into."

"That doesn't make any difference," Sessions said stiffly. "You may answer."

"I think it is unsafe," Sadler replied. "I think that a scheme where the ballast could be handled quickly or transferred quickly from one side to the other is preferable," he later added.

Sessions perked up and intervened with what would end up being ten minutes of questions for the professor. Hearing Sadler out, Sessions reached some conclusions. "The question," the judge said, "gets down to this: taking into consideration the design and construction of the boat, in your judgment was she a safe or an unsafe boat to be used in the passenger trade and to carry 2,500 people?"

"I think she was unsafe without permanent ballast," Sadler said.

Sessions then asked: "Suppose she had no water in her tanks at all, what would you say? Suppose the water ballast was not used at all."

"Then she would be unsafe," Sadler said. At the defense table, Darrow was getting restless.

Sessions continued. "If I understand you rightly, if her tanks No. 2 and No. 3 were filled and kept filled, she would carry 2,500 people in safety?"

"Yes."

"So the element of danger," Sessions asked, "is in the filling and emptying of the tanks?"

"Exactly."

Darrow was edgy. It was all damning testimony for the defense; the ship was unsteady in construction and dangerously dependent on a hair trigger of a ballast system. In short, it was an accident waiting to happen. More troubling, the testimony wasn't just being presented by the prosecution, it was being drawn out by Sessions, the judge.

Normally unflappable, Darrow wanted to interrupt, to discredit Professor Sadler somehow. But Professor Sadler had more knowledge of naval science than everyone else in the courtroom combined. Darrow could hardly object to the judge's line of inquiry. He had to do something.

Unable to hold his tongue any longer, and still seated at the defense table, Darrow fired off a question.

"Doctor, I ask you what you assume was the amount of coal in the bins?"

"Sixty tons," he replied.

"*Sixty* tons of coal?" Darrow repeated, incredulously. His answer was way off the mark. Erickson, who personally ordered the coal, previously testified that there were 110 tons of coal the morning the *Eastland* capsized, as it was scheduled to do four trips in a row with little time to refuel. Sadler was not present when Erickson was on the stand.

"Suppose there were a hundred there," Darrow said.

"A hundred tons of coal?" Sadler asked, peering at Darrow through his rounded glasses.

Clyne stepped in to help his man. "Just a minute, to interrupt, they couldn't get that much into the boat, we will show that."

"We will show it was there," Darrow snapped back.

"I think gentlemen," said Sessions, separating the sparring lawyers, "you had better wait and examine the witness when the time comes. I confess to have been at fault myself in interrupting the examination, which I ought not to have done."

Within minutes, Darrow stepped to the witness stand to cross-examine Sadler, his Napoleonic lock down his forehead, his unkempt hair bristling at the back of his dark suit coat.

"If there were 120 tons of coal, it would change your estimate as to the number of passengers that could be safely carried and the stability," Darrow asked, "would it not?"

"Yes," Sadler said.

Sadler may well have had good reason to believe the *Eastland* was unsafe, may well have been right, but his calculations about the morning of the disaster undermined his authority in explaining it. It was a masterful moment for Darrow, who pointed out how Sadler had seriously miscalculated one of the main metrics for his capsize scenario, the tonnage of coal, which was off by about half.

Sadler was also demonstrably wrong about the distribution of passengers. Salvagers found most of the bodies of the victims on the main deck, many trapped at the very bottom of the ship, where Sadler assumed there were no passengers at all. The precise location of passengers was critically important. The only other element he considered was the weight of water in the ballast tanks. Since the ship sank, the tanks probably took on much more water. How much was anybody's guess.

But two of the three quantities in his equation, he got wrong. Sadler's errors threw into question his entire forensic analysis of the fatal accident. His education, his high profile, his erudite British tone—all were shaken when Darrow outnumbered him.

CHAPTER SIXTY

At Sea

Before closing arguments, Sessions brought some real trouble for the prosecution. He was bothered by a couple of territorial matters and wanted them addressed in closing arguments.

"I would ask that counsel give particular attention to two questions of law in making their arguments," he said. First, he wondered if the statute under one of the indictments applied to vessels on Lake Michigan. Second, was a steamer voyaging on Lake Michigan being, according to the relevant law, "sent to sea in the coastwise trade"?

Friday morning the prosecutors went first, turning the closing argument over to the same man who led the opening one, District Attorney Walker. He wanted to impress upon Judge Sessions that there was a larger purpose to the trial beyond punishment, one of warning and prevention.

"The government does not seek vengeance for the deaths of the 800 victims of the *Eastland* disaster alone," Walker said, "but rather does it desire the removal of these defendants to a court of trial in order that the result may be a warning and some means provided for the prevention of a repetition of the accident insofar as human agencies and human laws can prevent it."

Sessions asked at length about what he called the "puzzling feature" of the law under which the indictments were brought. How to interpret the words "sent to sea"—did that apply to all navigable waters or to the high seas alone? Walker replied that the term was meant broadly, and he declared that the word "coastwise" applied to ships on both the Great Lakes and the high seas.

His partners then tried to set a very low bar for Sessions. Clyne followed Walker, saying if even one count was found correct, it was the duty of the court to extradite the defendants. His assistant, Fleming, further appealed to

Sessions not to halt their effort for justice, reminding the court that they had no recourse for appeal in the event of an adverse ruling.

The court adjourned after four hours, and Fleming made an extraordinary claim to the clutch of newsmen there. He said that the government had not presented its complete case against the *Eastland* men. "It is only natural that the prosecution withhold the most important part of its evidence," he told them. "We believe, however, that we have offered sufficient proof for purposes of this hearing."

§§§

The next morning, Clyne closed the government's side. "The two inspectors hopelessly failed to perform their duties according to the laws of the country," he said, in summing up. "The officers of the owning company knew of the boat's condition and the nature of the service it was first intended for. The captain and the engineer were inexperienced in the operation of vessels of its class. The proofs submitted by the government show conclusively a crime was committed and they point to the six defendants here.

"The *Eastland* was inherently defective and when sent out on Lake Michigan with 2,500 persons aboard a chance was being taken with death," he said, carefully molding his words to the contours of the maritime-safety law the men were charged with violating.

Clyne argued that it was within the power of the two steamboat inspectors to deny a license if they determined the ballast tanks were unsafe. "These men knew that the *Eastland* was being used as an excursion boat, and it was their duty to see that the lives of the people traveling upon it were protected," the prosecutor said. He went into considerable detail about why the ship's ballast system was faulty. And he pointed out that it was the duty of the inspectors to ensure that the *Eastland* had a sufficient number of seacocks to fill the ballast tanks.

Then Kremer, the maritime law expert, began closing arguments for the defense. Each of the defense attorneys would hammer away at whether the indictments were brought under the proper laws, sensing Sessions's doubts on this point.

"The officers and crew had nothing to do with the sending of this ship to sea," Kremer began.

"*Send* does not mean *take*."

"The statute does not contemplate including the two federal inspectors. It is also doubtful if it touches the officers of the company."

The defense attorneys appeared one by one, reiterating that the federal court had no jurisdiction over the case since the ship was tied to its dock in the Chicago River. If any offense were committed, they told Sessions, it was up to the courts in Cook County, Illinois, to get to the bottom of it.

They contended that no conspiracy was proven, that they had proven the ship was seaworthy, and that the soundings of the Chicago River taken for the government and submitted at the trial were fraudulent.

"We do know," Barbour said, "that there are two piles in the river and all imaginable refuse and obstructions. A boat on the bottom will roll. The evidence shows that the boat was seaworthy, that the defense has established its case, that this boat tipped over as a result of outside agencies, and not by any fault of its owners or experienced navigators."

CHAPTER SIXTY-ONE

A Secret Singing

Darrow stood up to seal the case with his trademark poignant appeal for justice. He had ninety minutes to close. He would pace the floor in his droopy trousers, his watch fob arched in front of his buttoned vest and his oversized coat. He would pluck at his suspenders.

He would alternately attack the prosecutors, express sympathy for the *Eastland* victims, sound a note for forbearance in light of so massive a tragedy, and absolve Erickson and the other men of criminal wrongdoing.

He would drum the word "Chicago" again and again for effect, as if it were hell itself, a pit of certain punishment.

"To return these six defendants to Chicago," he began, in his booming evangelist voice, "it must be shown there is probable cause to believe there was willful, malicious and gross carelessness on the parts of these defendants, which the government has failed to show.

"It is not a question as to whether a mistake was made. We all make mistakes, and possibly mistakes were made by these defendants.

"But I submit, if you please, that if any mistakes were made, they were not willful and malicious for there is not one of these six men here whose liberty has been placed in jeopardy, who would not have given everything he possessed, if by doing so, this great disaster could have been averted."

With the gallery filled hip-to-hip with spectators draped on his every word, Darrow proceeded to walk through many elements of the indictments, the ship, and each man's individual case.

"The law under which the charge of conspiracy is brought specifies the 'sending to sea' of ships. This cannot apply to Erickson and Pedersen. They were 'taking' a ship to sea. The accident occurred in the jurisdiction of Cook County, Illinois, one mile from the lake. The boat was not on a voyage but tied to a dock. Four of the defendants were not aboard the vessel. This statute was meant to prevent the sending of inherently unseaworthy boats to sea by owners."

As for the *Eastland* men, he proclaimed their complete innocence.

"There is no evidence here to show that Erickson did not do his duty. But assuming that he did not, then he could be individually returned to Chicago to answer a charge of manslaughter; but the fact that he failed to do his duty could in no way hold these other respondents. His failure to do his duty, or the failure of the captain, or members of the crew to do their duty, would not make the *Eastland* an unseaworthy boat, even though she might capsize when improperly handled."

"It is laughable to assume that Engineer Erickson would have entered into such a conspiracy, or that he could be held under this statute, when he is the man the statute was designed to protect.

"His place was in the very bottom of the ship. His life was endangered more than any other life on the ship.

"There he was down in the engine room without hardly an avenue of escape, yet he is here in court charged with conspiracy to send an unseaworthy ship, thereby endangering his own life."

Darrow said the two inspectors were blameless because they were merely doing work the government assigned to them and they did it according to the rules provided. The owners, meanwhile, could not be blamed for following the regular practice of hiring men to operate their ship and depending on their human judgment.

"It would be a travesty on the law to send these men away from their homes on the evidence produced here to face trial for offenses their connection with which has not been even remotely proved," Darrow said.

He ridiculed the prosecutors. "The government has said it had more up its sleeve to prove their guilt," he noted, calling their probable bluff.

"If that is so, the sleeve should have been shaken in this court in all fairness to these men."

He built his argument incrementally, cumulatively, like a coral reef.

"This awful calamity directly or indirectly touched over 10,000 homes in Chicago; the whole city was aroused and the newspapers flamed with it for weeks. Yet these defendants are asked to go back in to the midst of people mad with passions and take a chance on their lives and liberty.

"The feeling aroused by the disaster, just or unjust, permeates the whole community and is bound to affect the courts and juries. Human feelings and passions are strong in a case like this, and those accused should be given every safeguard the courts can provide."

Darrow also emphatically declared that the government had not proved a specific charge worthy of winning extradition.

"These defendants have a right to protect themselves," he said. "When they refuse to leave Michigan, their home, they are not only acting within their rights, but as prudent men. The feeling over in Chicago as a result of this terrible tragedy is at a high pitch."

Tempering his tone, he added, "I live in Chicago myself, and I am casting no reflection on the people of the city. It is only human to feel that way, but that is the reason these men object to facing a jury in Chicago.

"This case is an unusual one," he said, in conclusion. "There is hardly a home in Chicago and Cook County in which this disaster did not take sorrow. And if these men are forced to return there for trial it would be the same as placing them on trial before a jury of men whose wives were lost in the accident."

His final words resonant in the room, Darrow shambled back to his chair, and sat down.

§§§

Sessions told the full courtroom that he would move as swiftly as he could to reach his decision. He also permitted, for now, the six defendants to return to their homes, saying they would be notified by the US marshal to appear in court when he had reached his verdict. Attorneys on both sides told reporters they were confident of a victory.

Sessions retired to his sparse chambers, lined with shelves filled with books. Disrobing, he sat at his desk, a glass inkwell at the ready. At his disposal were the boat models and hundreds of exhibits: soundings, charts, photographs, a topographic model of the riverbed, blueprints, tree stumps, affidavits, inspector reports, correspondence of the St. Joseph-Chicago Steamship Company.

The ten-day trial transcript alone ran 1,549 pages, ten inches tall, the same size as the *Eastland*'s single seacock.

CHAPTER SIXTY-TWO

"An Impossible Crime"

It would take him twelve days to render his decision. He had in his hands the fate of the men accused of a stunning industrial atrocity, over eight hundred wrongful deaths, a city traumatized. Here was an opportunity to remind the Republic that the nation's courts were the great equalizer, that the rights and lives of hardworking people paid twelve dollars a week could not be trumped by negligent men of wealth, armed with the best legal defense money could buy.

To the twentieth century, an era in which machines were to grind millions of people into perishables, his ruling was a prologue:

"The magnitude and far-reaching effects of the catastrophe naturally . . . aroused intensely bitter feeling against all persons connected with the ownership, operation and navigation of the boat," Judge Sessions began. "Federal and state authorities vied with each other in their efforts to investigate the affair and to prosecute all persons thought to be responsible."

"A large part of the testimony upon this hearing has been directed to the question of whether the *Eastland* rested upon the bottom or upon some obstruction in the bottom of [the] Chicago River at the time she overturned. This question of fact cannot be determined in this proceeding but must be left to the decision of a jury at the trial."

In fact, the evidence presented abundantly proved the *Eastland* must have been floating free of any obstructions at the time of the disaster.

"The undisputed evidence shows," the judge continued, "that at the time of the accident the steamer *Eastland* was securely tied to a dock in [the] Chicago River at least one-half mile from Lake Michigan." Therefore, he wrote, "the crime charged . . . against these defendants in this indictment was not committed 'upon the high seas,'" or, in other words, outside the jurisdiction of Illinois.

He belittled the prosecutors' hocus-pocus with the Chicago River. "By no fiction of law or fact can [the] Chicago River be regarded as Lake Michigan or one of the high seas. . . . It necessarily follows that none of the defendants could possibly be found guilty under this indictment if held for trial."

The ruling repeatedly mirrored Clarence Darrow's closing argument.

"Engineer Erickson's . . . station was in the engine room, deep in her hold and in the place of greatest danger," Sessions wrote. "In view of these conditions, it is difficult to see how he can be justly accused of the crime charged here against him."

Moreover, the judge asked, did the defendants know the *Eastland* was unseaworthy? "It is alleged in the indictment that the vessel was unseaworthy in that she was top-heavy and 'cranky' and in that her water-ballast system and apparatus were defective and insufficient both in construction and in operation. Aside from the fact that the vessel capsized and the testimony of one witness [Dr. Sadler] whose theories are shown to be incorrect by actual experience and indisputable facts, there is no satisfactory evidence to sustain these allegations."

Ignoring the testimony that Erickson had been asked by Steele how to modify the ballast tanks two months before the disaster, Sessions continued, "there is nothing to indicate that the defendants knew or ought to have known" that the *Eastland* was so dangerously unseaworthy it jeopardized lives.

He then cited the twelve-year record of operating and carrying hundreds of thousands of people, and the fact that the *Eastland*'s licensed passenger capacity early on ranged from twenty-eight hundred to thirty-three hundred without accident or loss of life. "Her water-ballast system and apparatus had not been changed since she was built, and, unless defective in original design and construction, was in perfect working condition."

The judge was particularly critical of the conspiracy charge. By this time it became clear to the prosecutors that that allegation, penned by the fervid Judge Landis himself, was a grave mistake. "A wicked combination is the essence of the crime," Sessions wrote. "An agreement to be criminally negligent can scarcely be imagined. A combination of these defendants to destroy human life is both unbelievable and unthinkable. A conspiracy to commit an impossible crime is itself an impossibility.

"After the event, it is always easy to say that someone must have been careless or the trouble would not have occurred. Broad and far-reaching as the law of conspiracy is, it is neither comprehensive nor potent enough to transform, without proof, apparently innocent conduct into criminal misconduct.

"The dead cannot be restored to life. The sorrows of the living cannot be lessened by claiming other victims. The majesty of the law cannot be upheld and vindicated by forcing men from their homes to stand trial among strangers upon accusations which there is barely a scintilla of proof to sustain."

Sessions thereby denied the petition to force the *Eastland* men back to Chicago to face charges for the disaster.

All—they had all beaten the criminal charges.

§§§

Inside the Story & Clark piano factory in Grand Haven later that afternoon, men with rolled sleeves, suspenders, collars, and greasy aprons toiled at their worktables, filled with glues, wood stains, and tools. Pianos were taking shape amid the clatter echoing inside the brick walls. Pipes and rafters ran exposed along the ceiling.

The news, that he was exonerated, reached Joseph Erickson there. He collapsed in his soiled apron and had to be taken home.

The Red Cross Toll

No. 357. (Polish) **Sister, 18**; brother, 10; brother, 8; brother, 6; aunt, 29.
The only wage earner of four orphans, an employee of the Western Electric Company, was drowned. An aunt had been living with them to do the house-keeping, and she earned about nine dollars a week by needlework.

No. 279. (Polish) **Daughter, 21; daughter, 17;** husband; wife; son, 13; daughter, 11; daughter, 6; daughter, 4.
Two daughters, the principal wage earners of a large family, were drowned. The husband was a carpenter, in ill health and not always able to work even when there was work to be had. The wife was subject to frequent attacks of insanity by reason of a streetcar accident in which she had been injured four years previous to the disaster.

No. 51. (German) **Daughter, 23;** husband; wife; daughter, 25; daughter, 20; daughter, 19; son, 14; daughter, 8; niece, 20.
One daughter was killed and another injured. Both had been employed by the Western Electric Company. The injured daughter was unable to work for several weeks, and the mother had to be taken to a hospital because of the shock. The family did not wish any aid until the final settlement.

Epilogue: That Day, That Sorrow

With his exoneration, Erickson was able to leave the piano factory for good and return to the sailing life. Licensed as a chief engineer, he had no trouble finding work and was soon running engine rooms of freight ships that took him out to Lake Erie, hauling salt, coal, and other cargo.

Two months following the trial, Florence bore their first baby, a boy, whose name was a combination of the two men prominent in her life, her father and husband, Robert Erickson.

Sadly, perhaps because of the strain Florence endured with both her father and husband facing penitentiary time for the *Eastland*, the child lived only three months. They buried him a month shy of the anniversary of the *Eastland* disaster, in June of 1916, at the Lake Forest Cemetery in Grand Haven. On his tombstone, there is one word above his name and brief dates on earth. It says, "Baby." In her mourning, Florence would write such a touching letter to Clarence Darrow that he would promise to keep it forever.

She also began a victory garden in the yard of her parents' home in Grand Haven. During World War I, civilians were encouraged to plant fruit and vegetables at home to help boost food supplies. It was pushed as a matter of national defense.

Florence quickly conceived again, and it was when she was four months' pregnant with their second child that Erickson wrote to her in the twilight while in port in Buffalo, New York, in July of 1917.

Dear Florence,

I was Happy to receive your letters and papers at Detroit, and to know that you are well, or as well as can be under the conditions.

I would be more than glad to see you in your gardens, and to help you pick strawberries. You know my weakness for "shortcake"—don't think you would have any to can if I was around.

The potatoes, tomatoes and beans . . . will be a saving in two ways, for the country to help feed Uncle Sam's Men and the Allies, and also for the Household, so I am proud of you to do "your bit" in such a big way.

I am so glad that you are contented and Happy, which is of such great importance and will help you and the baby much . . .

When the opportunity offers itself, I will do my best to get into the Naval Reserve and be glad to serve my Country on Uncle Sam's ships . . .

So goodbye with lots of love and kisses,

Joe

Within months, he would become Lieutenant Joseph Erickson, senior assistant engineer on the US Army Transport Service ship *Beaufort*, running US soldiers to France and other European countries. As usual, he wrote to his mother in Norway.

Nov. 19, 1917
Hoboken, NJ

Dear mom:

Was very pleased to get a few lines from you and to know that you are well, also that you don't have to worry now, I am on this side of the "pond." Sad to say, there is loads of mothers worrying now, and I think there will be many more before this awful war is over . . . .

Aren't you glad, Mother, that you haven't any more Sons helping "Uncle Sam"?

. . . I am well, and like my work and the ship very much. We expect to lie here till the later part of this month. I will be very glad to see you and the others, and give my best to all.

With love from Joseph

With his exemplary work on the *Beaufort*, Erickson was promoted to chief engineer and later the same position on another Army transport ship, the *Peerless*. His trips running soldiers across the Atlantic were made when the seas were infested with German submarines. Under constant threat by prowling U-boats, he endured some narrow escapes in his noisy engine rooms. While he was away at the war, Florence bore their second baby, a girl they named Frances.

§§§

After their release by Judge Sessions, Erickson and the other Michigan men were afraid to return to Chicago, as their state indictments for manslaughter and criminal carelessness remained open and state prosecutors had vowed to try them if they ever set foot in Illinois.

But the reality was, the federal case was so botched that another trial would be difficult at best. The notion of double jeopardy, or a prohibition on being tried twice for the same crime, remained murky then at the state-court level, and it would be hard to convict any one or two men if the others couldn't be compelled to appear in Chicago.

At the same time, Chicago's law enforcers were being overwhelmed with a new crime spree. By early 1918, five hundred rifles were distributed to Chicago patrolmen and new automobile squads were formed to combat gangs of gunmen and armed robbers who had been terrorizing the city. A man named Al Capone would soon move to Chicago and organize one of the nation's most notorious criminal networks.

The manslaughter charges against Steele and Hull and the other *Eastland* company executives were dropped in the fall of 1918. There is one intriguing summons in the Cook County Criminal Court records, indicating that Captain Pedersen was called to trial in Chicago at ten one Friday morning in October of 1918. But the state's criminal carelessness charge against him was later dismissed, two days after Erickson's was.

Judge Sessions's absolution of the men in 1916 would be the last word on attempts to pin criminal responsibility for the *Eastland* disaster.

After two years of service, Erickson began having severe chest pains and was sent home to Grand Haven on sick leave in December of 1918. Doctors began treating him for heart disease, and by spring they had given up hope, though they never informed him how dire his situation was. All the while, Erickson, sickly for years, spoke of returning to the front, and to his ship.

On Wednesday, April 3, 1919, shortly after six in the evening, Erickson's heart gave out. Not yet thirty-five, he was buried at the Lake Forest Cemetery in Grand Haven in a plot right next to his baby boy.

Two years before his death, he reflected on his ill health in a letter he had written to Florence, while he was away on a freight ship on Lake Erie. His words mirrored Clarence Darrow's ideas on nature, heredity, and survival of the fittest.

"Perhaps nature has not been as kind to me as to others," Erickson wrote, "but I am not complaining at my lot, as I am not responsible for being brought into this world, nor the work of nature . . ."

§§§

Captain John Pereue sold off all his shipping interests in 1904 and moved to South Carolina, where he invested in the lumber business. In 1929, he and his wife moved back to South Haven, into the family home they had lived in for forty-four years, down the street from the one-legged lighthouse keeper's house, on Michigan Avenue. At age eighty-six, Pereue died there in 1931. The house, with delicate, curling trim woodwork, still stands.

Four years after the *Eastland* ruling, Judge Clarence William Sessions made national headlines in one of the most famous political cases of its time. The trial involved allegations of illegal expenditures to elect a US senator from Michigan. Instructing jurors in the same courtroom where the *Eastland* case played out, Judge Sessions told them, "Nowhere are men more equal than at the bar of justice." The senator and sixteen others were found guilty and sentenced to two years in a federal penitentiary. But, on appeal, the US Supreme Court set the verdicts aside. After gardening in retirement on his six-acre country estate near Grand Rapids, Sessions died in April 1931 at age seventy-two.

William Cox Redfield kept his appointment as commerce secretary until November of 1919. He then became a financial investor and later president of the Brooklyn National Bank. In retirement, he amassed a large collection of rare coins. In June 1932, he died just shy of his seventy-fourth birthday, in bed at home in Brooklyn, New York, of a cerebral hemorrhage.

William Harvey Hull became a banker in St. Joseph, Michigan, after the *Eastland* sank, and he sang tenor for various church choirs the rest of his life. He died of a heart ailment in September of 1933. His will, written on E. A. Graham Docks stationery in January of 1906, left all his earthly possessions, which would end up being one thousand dollars and no real estate, to his wife, May Graham Hull. His obituary did not mention the *Eastland*.

§§§

Shortly after the *Eastland*'s sinking, Judge Landis appointed commissioners to adjudicate claims by the survivors of the *Eastland*, who were seeking some compensation from the insurers of the ship. The case would wind through the courts torturously for an incredible two decades. Time would not be kind to the survivors.

Walter Steele, facing criminal charges in the days after the *Eastland* sank, swore to investigators that he was not an active officer of the St. Joseph-Chicago Steamship Company. But he flip-flopped in the civil litigation, saying he was exactly that, a position more advantageous in the battle over compensation.

Pedersen again perjured himself, this time saying he had a standing order to keep the *Eastland*'s ballast tanks full when the ship was at dock— reversing his testimony from the criminal case. Worse, new testimony erroneously blamed Erickson, claiming he had filled the port tanks of the *Eastland*, causing the ship to capsize on its port side.

All the evidence in the criminal trial made it perfectly clear that this was not the case; Erickson had unquestionably been filling the proper tanks, on the starboard side, which would only help prevent a capsize to port. But the defunct ship company and its insurers found it tempting and convenient to blame the *Eastland* disaster on Erickson, as he was dead and unable to correct their account and defend himself.

Taking advantage of Erickson's demise, the old officers of the St. Joseph-Chicago Steamship Company won the case, meaning the *Eastland* survivors suffered a further injustice, losing their chance to receive ten thousand dollars each for a wrongful death.

The Supreme Court then refused, without comment, to review the case in 1936, ending any hope of recompense for the suffering of the *Eastland* victims' families.

§§§

Clarence Seward Darrow would go on to become the best-known attorney in America, largely because of two cases he took inside a decade of the *Eastland* one. With a passionate rebuke of the death penalty in his closing argument, Darrow would save two young University of Chicago law students, Nathan Leopold and Richard Loeb, from hanging in 1924, after they admitted kidnapping and killing a Chicago teenager in an attempt to commit "the perfect crime." The Leopold and Loeb case was one of several that would be called the Trial of the Century.

The next year, Darrow would defend a Tennessee high school teacher, John T. Scopes, accused of breaking state law by teaching the theory of human evolution. The court proceedings, which became a media circus in 1925, came to be nicknamed the Scopes "Monkey Trial." The case helped cement Darrow's reputation as a legal legend and wily rhetorician. Decades later, it continued to stir culture, as a 1955 play and a 1960 movie, *Inherit the Wind*.

Darrow would shrink from the *Eastland* case the rest of his life, not mentioning it in his memoirs, titled *The Story of My Life*, published in 1932. The marine engineers' union paid him more than one thousand dollars for his work on Erickson's behalf. With the funds, he and Sissman were immediately able to move their offices into the Loop business district, on swank Dearborn Street, where they would remain for years.

Whatever victory Darrow may have enjoyed in exonerating Erickson, he perhaps felt guilty that he helped all the other *Eastland* men escape punishment in the wrongful death of 844 men, women, and children.

On the back cover of a notebook, he once wrote, "World is made up of two classes; one who pretend to be decent, and those who do not."

After he died in 1938, Darrow's remains were cremated. His ashes were dropped into a lagoon in his beloved Jackson Park in Chicago, outside the apartment he had resided in for decades.

Nearly twenty-four years to the day after the *Eastland* disaster, Captain Harry Pedersen died in July 1939 of kidney disease in Cook County Hospital in Chicago. After the *Eastland*, he retired to his farm near Millburg, Michigan, where he continued adjusting compasses for shipping companies.

In November of 1944, Judge Kenesaw Mountain Landis died from heart troubles at age seventy-eight in Chicago, after a storied, twenty-four-year career as the first commissioner of Major League Baseball. Five years after the *Eastland* indictments, he would issue an order banning eight players for the Chicago White Sox from professional baseball for life. He ruled that the eight had forfeited their right to play, despite their having been acquitted of accepting bribes to "throw" the 1919 World Series, in what came to be called the Black Sox Scandal.

After living in a Chicago hotel for twenty-seven years, Judge Landis had moved to the suburbs just before his death, working so hard on his own victory garden that he overtaxed his heart.

The *Eastland*, itself, was reborn as the Gunboat *Wilmette*. The Navy, which acquired the wreck for thirty-four thousand dollars, reduced the height by about half and added four, four-inch guns, among other modifications. It was then used to train Naval Reserve men on Lake Michigan. The ship's bow was removed in late 1918 to allow the *Wilmette* to get through locks headed east, as the Navy prepared the *Wilmette* to join active forces in the Atlantic in World War I. The war ended, though, before the *Wilmette* was deployed.

In its early days, the *Wilmette* was dispatched on one particularly unusual mission. It had orders to destroy a U-boat captured from Germany and brought out to the Great Lakes as war booty for temporary exhibition. The German submarine, called *UC-97*, was towed out about twenty miles east of the Navy base at Fort Sheridan, on the Lake Michigan shoreline north of Chicago, on a Tuesday morning in June 1921. The *Wilmette*, sites set, fired thirteen shells. In a puff of smoke, the submarine sank, leaving only bubbles, an oil slick, and assorted shards of wreckage. The *Wilmette* never did see combat, and after three decades with the Navy, it was finally cut up for scrap metal in 1947.

Shortly after the Navy acquired the *Eastland* and shrank it down to the *Wilmette*, naval engineers said it was no longer necessary to carry any water in the ship's ballast tanks, as the vessel was amply stable without it. The crew, nervous about the ship's stability, had other ideas. At an inspection on the Chicago River in 1923, the Navy found that the *Wilmette*'s ballast tanks were so religiously kept full of water by anxious crews that the tanks had become corroded, rusted red.

After completing the *Eastland*, his only passenger ship, builder Sidney Grant Jenks left shipbuilding after his family closed the shipyard following the fire in 1906. He got involved in building automobile engines in Michigan, and moved later to New Jersey. He was a district officer of the Emergency Fleet Corporation during World War I and then worked as a manager at the New York Shipbuilding Company. He died at age ninety-three in December 1965. His obituary did not mention the *Eastland*.

After charges were dropped against Walter Clarke Steele, he continued to run the farm outside St. Joseph, and by the 1930s he was working for Theisen-Clemens, a large distributor of automobile fuel and oil in town there. He and his wife would occasionally winter in Florida, where they would eventually move. In the 1960s, Steele was a painting contractor in the Sunshine State. Several years after he had had a stroke, Steele died in Tampa in January of 1967. His remains were cremated.

§§§

Years after removing her widow's veil, Florence Erickson would remarry and move first to Indiana and then out west to the Seattle area. She regularly returned to Michigan for Reid family reunions into the 1970s, where she showed up white-haired and smiling.

Over the decades, she kept a few mementos of her brief but passionate marriage to Joseph Erickson, including some letters he wrote to her in his cabin while sailing on the Great Lakes, and a head-and-shoulders photo of him, handsome in his Army Transport Service uniform and white hat.

There was one special letter she kept from that time, as well. It was from Clarence Darrow. She had written to him shortly after the trial ended in Grand Rapids. She thanked him for exonerating her husband.

She told Darrow that she had just lost her firstborn child, Robert, possibly from the stress of the *Eastland* tragedy. She also wrote that she and Joseph decided to make a touching vow to Darrow, and, on reading that, Darrow wrote to thank her.

The letter, on Darrow & Sissman office stationery and dated October 3, 1916, was scratched in black pen in Darrow's pitiful handwriting.

My Dear Mrs. Erickson,

It was a very nice letter you wrote me and I shall always keep it. I am so pleased that Mr. Erickson came to me and that I was able to help him. He is a fine fellow and it was too bad that he should have ever been indicted. I am sorry about the baby and would be proud if there was another if you and Mr. Erickson thought I was grand enough to give it my name. If either of you are ever here, be sure and call on me.

With best wishes always,
Clarence Darrow

Whatever remorse Florence may have harbored for encouraging her newlywed husband to take the job on the *Eastland* all those years ago, she kept to herself. Relatives cannot recall her speaking about the disaster.

Florence lived to be eighty-eight and died near Port Orchard, Washington, on a Friday in 1978. She had her ashes spread to sea.

Acknowledgments

Jim Hornfischer, my literary agent and a fine author in his own right, was this book's first champion and worked diligently to find it a nice home. Editor Jon Sternfeld, instantly spellbound by the story, helped me keep my footing on the page. Project editor Lauren Brancato magically orchestrated text and images throughout.

I am also grateful to three student journalists in Virginia, where I was briefly a college instructor. Anne Elder and Lindley Estes helped organize my research files. Charlotte Rodina proved invaluable in helping tame the volumes of material about Clarence Darrow. Straight A work, students.

Carla Bailey, interlibrary-loan wizard at my old college, chased down several rare books, including brittle century-old marine-engineer texts.

The more I learned, the more I began to sense that the heart of this tale resided in *Eastland* engineer Joseph Erickson. I had to know more. After fruitlessly searching census records, and taking out classified ads in Michigan newspapers, I finally found some of his distant relatives, who kindly shared revealing family correspondence.

Special thanks to early readers, Edward McCarthy, an attorney and my uncle, who commented on legal issues, and Matthew McCarthy, my son, who read with an historical eye.

When this all started so long ago my son and my daughter Sadie endured many trips to museums and libraries across the Midwest, quietly doing their homework, reading *Goosebumps* and *Baby-sitter's Club* books, ever patient as I gathered *Eastland* records. Daughters Eastin and Gabrielle were also supportive when they later arrived. I am indebted to Carlisle, my heavenly brother, who taught me empathy.

I have to thank the numerous Cracker Barrel waitresses throughout Illinois and Michigan, who fueled me for years with smiles, poached eggs, and iced tea.

My wife, Marci, deserves special praise for allowing ten milk-carton crates of *Eastland* documents, photos, and research papers to inhabit our home for the past decade. The cartons always crowded the car, wherever we vacationed. Marci is a true pilgrim. And *can* she pack for a trip.

MM
South Haven, Michigan

WORKS CITED

Abbott, Karen. *Sin in the Second City: Madams, Ministers, Playboys, and the Battle for America's Soul.* New York: Random House, 2007.

Adams, Stephen B., and Orville R. Butler. *Manufacturing the Future: A History of Western Electric.* Cambridge: Cambridge University Press, 1999.

Altgeld, John Peter. *Live Questions: Including Our Penal Machinery and Its Victims.* Chicago: Donohue and Henneberry, 1890.

American Lumbermen: The Personal History and Public and Business Achievements of . . . Eminent Lumbermen of the United States. Chicago: American Lumberman, 1905.

The American Marine Engineer, the Journal of the Marine Engineers' Beneficial Association, 1907–1919.

Annual Reports of the War Department: Report of the Chief of US Engineers, US Army. Washington, DC: US Government Printing Office, 1904.

Anthony, Mabel. *I Remember When.* South Haven, MI: Baars Printing, 1979.

Appleyard, Richard B. *Images of the Past.* S.l.: S.n., 1984.

"Application for Social Security Card." Letter from Walter Clarke Steele. July 30, 1937.

Application of Jacob Miller to become Surety for Harry Pedersen, August 14, 1915, August 12, 1915, Criminal Court of Cook County, Chicago.

Application of James Barbour to become Surety for Walter C. Steele, August 12, 1915, Criminal Court of Cook County, Chicago.

Application of Steven J. Clark to become Surety for Joseph M. Erickson, August 12, 1915, Criminal Court of Cook County, Chicago.

Asala, Joanne. *Norwegian Proverbs.* Iowa City, IA: Penfield Press, 1994.

Benton Harbor: The Metropolis of the Michigan Fruit Belt. S.l.: M.W. Alger, 1915.

Bicknell, Ernest. "The Eastland Disaster: An Incredible Tragedy in the Heart of Chicago." *American Red Cross Magazine* 10 (1915): 305–9.

Billow, Jack. "The Tragedy of the Eastland." *Inland Seas: Quarterly Journal of the Great Lakes Historical Society* 16 (1960): 190–95.

Blegen, Theodore Christian. *Norwegian Migration to America: The American Transition.* Northfield, MN: Norwegian-American Historical Association, 1940.

Bosley, Edward R. *Greene & Greene.* London: Phaidon, 2000.

Bowen, Dana Thomas. *Lore of the Lakes, Told in Story and Picture.* Daytona Beach, FL: D.T. Bowen, 1940.

Brockmann, R. John. *Twisted Rails, Sunken Ships: The Rhetoric of Nineteenth Century Steamboat and Railroad Accident Investigation Reports, 1833–1879.* Amityville, NY: Baywood Pub., 2005.

Brown, John Kennedy. *Limbs on the Levee: Steamboat Explosions and the Origins of Federal Public Welfare Regulation, 1817–1852.* Middlebourne, WV: International Steamboat Society, 1989.

Casson, Herbert Newton. *The History of the Telephone.* Chicago: A. C. McClurg & Co., 1910.

Cemetery Records. April 6, 1919. Joseph M. Erickson Tombstone, Block 41, Lot 8, Grave 2, Lake Forest Cemetery, Grand Haven, MI.

———. June 20, 1916. Robert Erickson Tombstone, Block 41, Lot 8, Grave 1, Lake Forest Cemetery, Grand Haven, MI.

Certificate of Death. Joseph Erickson. April 3, 1919. Ottawa County, MI, State of Michigan, Grand Haven, MI.

———. *Walter C. Steele.* January 20, 1967. Tampa, Florida.

Chicago Daily News Almanac and Year-Book. 1916.

Chicago (Ill.). Bureau of Statistics. *The Chicago City Manual.* Chicago: Bureau of Statistics and Municipal Library, 1915.

Chicago Stories: The Eastland *Disaster.* Produced by Harvey Moshman. By Chuck Coppola. Chicago: WTTW, 2001.

Chicago Vice Commission. *The Social Evil in Chicago. A Study of Existing Conditions with Recommendations by the Vice Commission of Chicago.* Chicago, 1911.

City of Chicago. *Report and Handbook of the Department of Health of the City of Chicago for Years 1911–1918.* By John D. Robertson, M.D.

The City of Grand Rapids and Kent County, Mich., up to Date, Containing Biographical Sketches of Prominent and Representative Citizens. Logansport, IN: Bowen & Co., 1900.

Clarence Darrow to Florence Erickson. October 3, 1916. Author's copy.

——— to Mary Field. December 6, 1915. Mary Field Parton–Clarence Darrow Papers, Box 1, Folder 6, Newberry Library, Chicago.

———. July 4, 1913. Clarence Darrow Papers, 1894–1941; Collection of the Manuscripts Division, Library of Congress, Washington, DC.

———. November 28, 1912. Clarence Darrow Papers, 1894–1941; Collection of the Manuscripts Division, Library of Congress, Washington, DC.

——— to Mary Field Parton. February 1, 1915. Mary Field Parton–Clarence Darrow Papers, Box 1, Folder 6, Newberry Library, Chicago.

——— to Paul Darrow. January 31, 1916. University of Minnesota, Clarence Darrow Digital Collection, Minneapolis, MN.

Cowan, Geoffrey. *The People v. Clarence Darrow: The Bribery Trial of America's Greatest Lawyer.* New York: Times Books, 1993.

Crandall, Allen. *The Man from Kinsman.* Sterling, CO: Published by the Author, 1933.

Darrow, Clarence. *Notebook Cover, Clarence Darrow Papers, Manuscripts Division, Library of Congress, Box 3.* Washington, DC.

———, and Leon Mathis Despres. *Crime & Criminals: Address to the Prisoners in the Cook County Jail & Other Writings on Crime & Punishment.* Chicago: Charles H. Kerr, 2000.

———. *The Story of My Life.* New York: C. Scribner's Sons, 1932.

"The Dead." *Western Electric News,* August 1915, 9–15.

Decision of Justice Sessions in Case of Steamship "Eastland," Letter from the Secretary of Commerce Transmitting Transcript of the Decision of Justice Sessions of the District Court of the United States for the Western District of Michigan, Southern Division, in Case Relating to Steamship "Eastland," H.R. Rep. No. 814 (1916).

Dowling, Edward J., Rev. "Tragedy at Clark Street Bridge." *Steamboat Bill: Journal of the Steamship Historical Society of America* 94 (1965): 43–49.

Draft Registration Card, Joseph Mallings Erickson. September 17, 1918. World War I, Division 1, County of Ottawa, State of Michigan

Dutton, Fred W., and William Donohue Ellis. *Life on the Great Lakes: A Wheelsman's Story.* Detroit: Wayne State University Press, 1991.

Eastland Disaster Photos. Maritime Disasters, Chicago History Museum, Chicago.

Eastland Disaster Relief, American Red Cross, 1915–1918, after the Capsizing of the Steamer "Eastland" in the Chicago River, July 24, 1915 to Completion of Relief Work. Final Report, Eastland Disaster Relief Committee, Chicago Chapter, American Red Cross, 1918. Hereafter, "The Red Cross Report." Chicago, 1918.

"Engineer's Log." Joseph Erickson to US Local Inspectors. July 25, 1915. National Archives, Record Group 41, Bureau of Marine Inspection and Navigation, Steamboat Inspection Service, Numerical Correspondence, 1905–1923, No. 71330, Box 546, Washington, DC.

Erickson, Joseph. *Petition for Naturalization.* October 10, 1908. Circuit Court of Ottawa County, Michigan.

"Erickson Recommendation." D. A. McDonald to County Clerk Ottawa County, Grand Haven, MI. September 25, 1908.

Ewing, Wallace K., and David H. Seibold. *Grand Haven Area: 1860–1960.* Chicago: Arcadia, 2002.

"The Experiences of a Hawthorne Nurse." *Western Electric News* IV (August 1915): 19–20.

The Farm Journal Illustrated Rural Directory of Berrien County Michigan. Philadelphia: W. Atkinson, 1917.

Farrell, John A. *Clarence Darrow: Attorney for the Damned.* New York: Doubleday, 2011.

Feinberg, Matilda. "A Lawyer's Dream Shattered." *Chicago Bar Record*, May 1962, 396–98.

Francis, David. "The Eastland Navigation Co., 1907–1914." *Inland Seas* Fall (1978): 182–89.

———. "The Eastland Navigation Co., 1907-1914." *Inland Seas* Summer (1978): 96–100.

Francis, David W., and Diane DeMali Francis. *Cedar Point: The Queen of American Watering Places.* Canton, OH: Daring Books, 1988.

Ginger, Ray. "Clarence Seward Darrow, 1857–1938." *Antioch Review*, 1953, 52–66.

Gjerset, Knut. *Norwegian Sailors in American Water: A Study in the History of Maritime Activity on the Eastern Seaboard.* Northfield, MN: Norwegian-American Historical Association, 1933.

———. *Norwegian Sailors on the Great Lakes; a Study in the History of American Inland Transportation.* Northfield, MN: Norwegian-American Historical Association, 1928.

Hallet, Richard Matthews. *The Rolling World.* Boston: Houghton Mifflin Company, 1938.

Hannah Erickson to Florence Erickson. September 11, 1919.

Hansen, Harry, and Harry Timmins. *The Chicago.* New York: Farrar & Rinehart, 1942.

Havighurst, Walter, and John O'Hara Cosgrave. *The Long Ships Passing, the Story of the Great Lakes.* New York: Macmillan, 1942.

"Hawthorne's Automobile Fleet." *Western Electric News* IV (August 1915): 17.

"Herbert C. Sadler Obituary." *Transactions: The Society of Naval Architects and Marine Engineers* 56 (1948): 591–92.

Hill, Libby. *The Chicago River: A Natural and Unnatural History.* Chicago: Lake Claremont Press, 2000.

Hilton, George W. *Eastland: Legacy of the Titanic.* Stanford, CA: Stanford University Press, 1996.

Hilton, George Woodman. *Lake Michigan Passenger Steamers.* Stanford, CA: Stanford University Press, 2002.

Hough, William, and Jean Gilbert, writers. "Good-Bye Everybody." Recorded 1911.

House of Representatives, 64th Cong., 2nd Sess. *Decision of Justice Sessions in Case of Steamship "Eastland." Letter from the Secretary of Commerce, Transmitting Transcript of the Decision of Justice Sessions, of the District Court of the United States for the Western District of Michigan, Southern Division, in Case Relating to Steamship "Eastland." Report No. 1247.* Hereafter, "Sessions Ruling." 1916.

Huffman, Alan. "Surviving the Worst: The Wreck of the *Sultana* at the End of the American Civil War." Mississippi History Now: An Online Publication of the Mississippi Historical Association. October 2009.

In re Petition of the St. Joseph-Chicago Steamship Co. for Limitation of Liability (US Circuit Court of Appeals for the Seventh Circuit, November 15, 1934).

——— (US District Court, Northern District of Illinois, October 20, 1933).

"In the Matter of the Petition of Joseph Mallings Erickson, to Be Admitted a Citizen of the US." Letter. January 12, 1909.

Interrogation of Joseph M. Erickson by Superintendent of Police. July 25, 1915. In file of *US v. Hull et al.*

Jones, W. Clyde, and Keene Addington, eds. *Reports of Cases Determined in the Appellate Courts of Illinois.* Vol. 117. Chicago: Callaghan & Co., 1905. 435–40.

Joseph Erickson to Florence Erickson. July 11, 1917.

——— to Hannah Erickson. November 19, 1917.

Journal of the Proceedings of the National Marine Engineers' Beneficial Association, Jan. 17–22, 1916. XIV, no. 1 (1916).

Kersten, Andrew Edmund. *Clarence Darrow: American Iconoclast.* New York: Hill and Wang, 2011.

Kogan, Herman. *The First Century: The Chicago Bar Association, 1874–1974.* Chicago: Rand McNally, 1974.

Kraus, Bea. *A Place to Remember: South Haven—a Success from the Beginning.* Allegan Forest, MI: Priscilla Press, 2003.

Kuntz, Tom, and William Alden Smith. *The Titanic Disaster Hearings: The Official Transcripts of the 1912 Senate Investigation.* New York: Pocket Books, 1998.

Leonard, John William. *The Book of Chicagoans, a Biographical Dictionary of Leading Living Men of the City of Chicago.* Chicago: Marquis, 1905.

Lewis, Lloyd, and Henry Justin Smith. *Chicago, the History of Its Reputation.* New York: Harcourt, Brace and Co., 1929.

"Ma" Reid to Florence Erickson. July 25, 1915.

Makinson, Randell L., and Thomas A. Heinz. *Greene & Greene: The Blacker House.* Salt Lake City: Gibbs Smith, 2000.

Maloney, Martin. *The Forensic Speaking of Clarence Darrow.* Diss., Northwestern University, 1947.

Marquis, Albert Nelson. *The Book of Chicagoans; a Biographical Dictionary of Leading Living Men of the City of Chicago, 1911.* Chicago: A.N. Marquis, 1911.

————. *Who's Who in Chicago: The Book of Chicagoans: A Bibliographical Dictionary of Leading Living Men and Women of the City of Chicago and Environs; 1926.* Chicago: Marquis, 1926.

Mary Field to Irving Stone. August 29, 1940. Clarence Darrow Papers, 1894–1941; Collection of the Manuscripts Division, Library of Congress, Washington, DC.

Masters, Edgar Lee. *Across Spoon River; an Autobiography.* New York: Farrar & Rinehart, 1936.

Mitts, Dorothy Marie. *That Noble Country; the Romance of the St. Clair River Region.* Philadelphia: Dorrance, 1968.

"My Friend Clarence Darrow." Letter from James Barbour. Clarence Darrow Papers, 1894–1941; Collection of the Manuscripts Division, Library of Congress, Washington, DC.

The New Grand Rapids Art Museum, Commemorating the Dedication. Grand Rapids, MI: Grand Rapids Art Museum, 1981.

Paananen, Eloise, and Arnold S. Lott. *America's Maritime Heritage.* Annapolis, MD: Naval Institute Press, 1975.

Parsons, Earl. *Stories of the Great Lakes.* S.l.: S.n., 1964.

Pennington, Rochelle. *The Historic Christmas Tree Ship: A True Story of Faith, Hope and Love.* S.l.: Pathways Press, 2004.

Plowden, David. *End of an Era: The Last of the Great Lakes Steamboats.* New York: Norton, 1992.

Portrait and Biographical Record of Kalamazoo, Allegan and Van Buren Counties, Michigan. Chicago: Chapman Bros., 1892.

Ratigan, William, and Reynold H. Weidenaar. *Great Lakes Shipwrecks & Survivals.* Grand Rapids, MI: Eerdmans, 1960.

Reber, L. Benjamin. *History of St. Joseph.* St. Joseph, MI: St. Joseph Chamber of Commerce, 1928.

Regular Menu. 1907. Chicago Athletic Association, New York Public Library, New York, NY.

Reid, Robert. *Hull Inspector's Report.* June 7, 1915. Steamboat-Inspection Service Inspection of the *Eastland.*

"*Report of Material Inspection of USS.* Wilmette,"US Navy, Bureau of Construction and Repair, Record Group 19, Box 351, File I-GX-13-3. Hereafter, "Wilmette Inspection." October 23–24, 1923. National Archives, Washington, DC.

Robert Reid to Florence Reid, Muskegon Business College, Muskegon, MI. March 4, 1912.

————. September 25, 1912.

Roper, Stephen. *Use and Abuse of the Steam-boiler.* Philadelphia: Claxton, Remsen & Haffelfinger, 1876.

Sandburg, Carl. "Looking 'Em Over." *The International Socialist Review* 16, no. 3 (September 1915).

Scott, James A. *The Law of Interstate Rendition, Erroneously Referred to as Interstate Extradition; a Treatise on the Arrest and Surrender of Fugitives from the Justice of One State to Another; the Removal of Federal Prisoners from One District to Another; and the Exemption of Persons from Service of Civil Process; and with an Appendix of the Statutes of the States and Territories on Fugitives from Justice*. Chicago: S. Hight, 1917.

Silver, Morris, and Thomas Confare, writers. "A Sail in the Summertime." Recorded 1905.

Sinkevitch, Alice, and Laurie McGovern Petersen. *AIA Guide to Chicago*. New York: Harcourt Brace, 1993.

South Haven a Pictorial Review, From the Collection of Richard W. Appleyard. 1976.

State of Michigan. Dairy and Food Commissioner of Michigan. *Annual Report*. 1904.

Steele, Walter. *St. Joseph-Chicago Steamship Co. 1914 Annual Report*. July 28, 1915. State of Michigan, Berrien County, MI.

Stieve, Jeanette. *By the Big Blue Water: Post Cards of the Past from South Haven, Michigan*. South Haven, MI: Stieve, 1977.

———. *Captain James Donahue; Paperbound History with References, Undated*. South Haven, MI.

———. *South Haven Ship Captains*. South Haven, MI: Michigan Maritime Museum.

Stone, Irving. *Clarence Darrow for the Defense: A Biography*. Garden City, NY: Doubleday, Doran, 1941.

Stonehouse, Frederick. *Great Lakes Crime: Murder, Mayhem, Booze & Broads*. Gwinn, MI: Avery Color Studios, 2004.

———. *Great Lakes Crime II: More Murder, Mayhem, Booze & Broads*. Gwinn, MI: Avery Color Studios, 2007.

———. *Haunted Lakes: Great Lakes Ghost Stories, Superstitions, and Sea Serpents*. Duluth, MN: Lake Superior Port Cities, 1997.

"The Story of July Twenty-Fourth." *Western Electric News* IV (August 1915): 1–9.

Sutcliffe, Andrea J. *Steam: The Untold Story of America's First Great Invention*. New York: Palgrave Macmillan, 2004.

Tariff Hearings before the Committee on Ways and Means of the House of Representatives, 60th Congress, 1908-1909. Washington: US Government Printing Office, 1909.

"Thirty-four Hours at the Switchboard." *Western Electric News* IV (August 1915): 21.

Thomas, Henry F. *A Twentieth Century History of Allegan County, Michigan*. Chicago: Lewis Pub., 1907.

Thompson, Mark L. *Steamboats & Sailors of the Great Lakes*. Detroit: Wayne State University Press, 1991.

Thompson, Merwin, Capt. "Just What Was the Cause of the Steamer *Eastland* Disaster?" *Inland Seas: Quarterly Journal of the Great Lakes Historical Society* 15, no. 3 (Fall 1959): 200–206.

Thompson, Merwin Stone. *An Ancient Mariner Recollects*. Oxford, OH: Printed by Typoprint, 1966.

Tierney, Kevin. *Darrow: A Biography*. New York: Crowell, 1979.

Transcript of Testimony before the Coroner's Jury July 24, 25, 26, 27, 28, 29, on the Body of Kate Austin and All Others Lost by the Overturning of the Excursion Steamer Eastland *While Tied to the Dock at Clark and S. Water Streets in the City of Chicago, July 24, 1915*. Hereafter, "The Coroner Hearing." Chicago: Clohesey, 1915.

Twain, Mark. *Life on the Mississippi*. Toronto: Bantam Books, 1981.

Uelman, Gerald. "Fighting Fire with Fire: A Reflection on the Ethics of Clarence Darrow." *Fordham Law Review* 71 (2002): 1543–565.

United States Department of Commerce. Steamboat Inspection Service. *General Rules and Regulations Respecting Bays, Rivers and Sounds*. 1914.

United States Department of Commerce and Labor. *Transportation By Water, Great Lakes and St. Lawrence River, 1906*. 1908.

United States War Department. *Annual Reports, War Department*. Washington: US Government Printing Office, 1904.

US Congress. House. Committee on Merchant Marine and Fisheries. *Investigation of Accident to the Steamer "Eastland."* Hereafter referred to as the "Redfield Hearing." H. Bill. Washington, DC: US Government Printing Office, 1916.

———. Committee on Ways and Means. *Tariff Hearings before the Committee on Ways and Means of the House of Representatives, Sixtieth Congress, 1908–1909*. By Sereno Elisha Payne. H. Bill. Washington: US Government Printing Office, 1909.

US v. William H. Hull, George T. Arnold, Harry Pedersen, Joseph M. Erickson, Robert Reid, and Charles Eckliff, in US District Court, Western District of Michigan before the Hon. Clarence W. Sessions, typescript transcription of evidence, National Archives and Records Administration, Great Lakes Center, Chicago, Record Group 21, CR 1628, file 358,803. The "Criminal Transcript."

Van der Linden, Peter, Rev. "The Jenks Ship Building Company of Port Huron." *Telescope: Great Lakes Maritime Institute* 25 (1967): 91–97.

Van Vulpen, James. *Grand Rapids Then and Now*. Grand Rapids, MI: Grand Rapids Historical Association, 1988.

Viskochil, Larry A., and Grant Talbot Dean. *Chicago at the Turn of the Century in Photographs: 122 Historic Views from the Collections of the Chicago Historical Society*. New York: Dover Publications, 1984.

Wachholz, Ted. *The Eastland Disaster*. Charleston, SC: Arcadia, 2005.

Walsh, Frank J. *Court Summons*. October 9, 1918. Harry Pedersen called for trial before Judge George Kersten, 10:00 a.m. in Criminal Court Building, Criminal Court of Cook County, Chicago.

Weinberg, Arthur, and Lila Shaffer Weinberg. *Clarence Darrow, a Sentimental Rebel*. New York: Putnam, 1980.

Wendt, Lloyd, and Herman Kogan. *Give the Lady What She Wants!: the Story of Marshall Field & Company*. Chicago: Rand McNally, 1952.

"What the Survivors Tell." *Western Electric News* IV (August 1915): 22–25.

Whitehead, George G. *Clarence Darrow, the Big Minority Man*. Girard, KS: Haldeman-Julius Publications, 1929.

Will of W.H. Hull. March 24, 1934. Probate Court, County of Berrien, Michigan, St. Joseph, MI.

Wright, Richard. "A History of Shipbuilding in Cleveland, Ohio, Part II." *Inland Seas* Spring (1957): 29–37.

NOTES

The single best repository of information on the *Eastland* disaster is the 1,549-page criminal trial transcript held by the National Archives.

Aside from that, there were four other inquiries into the disaster, one by the Chicago coroner, one by the Commerce Department, one by a state grand jury, and one by a federal grand jury. What records have survived amount to thousands of pages of information ranging from hearsay and misguided lines of inquiry, to useful, but often mind-numbing, technical specifics. One must pan for the nuggets.

The personal letters and primary records the author relied upon were generally located in probate, business, and criminal court archives spread throughout Michigan and Illinois.

The eyewitness accounts of the *Eastland* disaster, some hours after the disaster, are varied and sometimes conflicting. To keep the narrative as factual as possible, the author disregarded accounts that seemed sensational or otherwise unreliable. Newspaper reports on the *Eastland,* particularly in their first days in the summer of 1915, slipped into exaggeration as the nation was riveted with the coverage.

The text, therefore, does not relay the *New York Times* report of a "gloomy man who was out of work and contemplating suicide in the river" and who, on seeing the *Eastland* tip over, found a reason to live and rescued nine persons. How on earth would a reporter know what was churning in his mind?

The *New York Herald* quoted an eleven-year-old girl at the disaster site as saying: "I was in the water and next thing I knew, I was standing on the smokestacks. I looked around and there was Papa standing on the smokestacks, too." Photographs and later testimony made it clear that at least one of the *Eastland*'s smokestacks broke off immediately and sank when the ship went over.

Alexander Graham Bell, father of the telephone and early investor in the Western Electric Company, reportedly visited the Hawthorne Works factory to console survivors after the disaster. If true, the author was unable to verify it.

The tragic story of the *Eastland* needs no fabrication, no gloss.

Prologue

xv. The account of the *Eastland* mutiny is based on news reports including *Chicago Daily Tribune*, August 14, 15, 1903; *Kalamazoo Gazette*, August 19, 1903; *Grand Rapids Press*, October 7, November 2, 1903; *Jackson Citizen-Patriot*, November 7, 1903.

xv. *the captain pointed his pistol:* *Chicago Daily Tribune*, August 14, 1903.

xv. *Mothers and children took shade on settees:* *South Haven Daily Tribune*, May 5, 1903.

xv. *On either side of the towering smokestacks:* Ibid.

xv. *"What's the matter with you:* *Chicago Daily Tribune*, August 14, 1903.

xv. *"suitable food:* *Kalamazoo Gazette*, August 19, 1903.

xvi. *"This boat has already been delayed:* *Chicago Daily Tribune*, August 14, 1903.

xvi. *"We'll get nonunion men:* Ibid.

xvi. *not serve them mashed potatoes:* Ibid.

xvi. *"An awful cold:* *US v. William H. Hull et al.*, hereafter, Criminal Transcript, 1065.

xvii. *aboard the steamer* North Point: Erickson, Petition for Naturalization.

xvii. *sang tenor in the church choir:* Hannah Erickson to Florence Erickson.

xvii. *Erickson had gray eyes:* Draft registration card.

xvii. *worked on ocean steamers:* Criminal Transcript, 1065.

xvii. *"Perhaps nature has not been as kind:* Joseph Erickson to Florence Erickson.

xvii. *on a steamer bound for . . . Havana:* Criminal Transcript, 1065.

xvii. *Erickson took a junior crewman's job:* Ibid.

xvii. *He then checked the correct boxes:* Erickson, Petition for Naturalization.

xviii. *One woman strolling:* Jones, 435–40.

Part I: Ahead Strong

Chapter One

3. *He had served in the Civil War:* Stieve, *South Haven Ship Captains.*

3. *He descended from French shipbuilders:* Ibid.

3. *take . . . his personal yacht:* *South Haven Messenger*, January 11, 1901.

3. *the Clifford had traveled five thousand miles:* *South Haven Daily Tribune*, May 21, 1902.

3. *Leighton came to the small town:* Stieve, *South Haven Ship Captains.* In the old home of the one-legged lighthouse keeper in South Haven, Michigan, resides the Marialyce Canonie Great Lakes Research Library, which contained several booklets, some without page numbers, written by researcher Jeanette Stieve. Some years ago, she hand-copied accounts of South Haven captains and ships with meticulous references, which included personal journals, census records, and cited newspaper reports.

4. *he constructed the Leighton Opera:* Appleyard, 80.
4. *"Quick Sales and Small Profits:* Kraus, 248.
4. *In 1902, South Haven's business scene: South Haven a Pictorial Review,* foreword.
4. *Snobble's Restaurant:* Ibid., 39.
4. *passenger traffic . . . to 150,000:* Annual Reports, War Department, 1904, 3058.
4. *Vast new groves:* Ibid., 3064.
5. Hattie B. Pereue, *filled with a cargo: South Haven Daily Tribune,* September 3, 1902.
5. *the* Hattie B. Pereue *sank again: South Haven Daily Tribune,* October 16, 1902.
5. *The crew on the . . .* William E. Corey: *American Marine,* June 1907, 17.
5. *too many As . . . thirteen letters:* Stonehouse, *Haunted,* 67.
5. *Changing the name:* Ibid. Stonehouse has done an impressive job with scholarly research into a topic, superstition, that others might easily dismiss. He documents each irrationality with newspaper reports or oral accounts, revealing how Great Lakes sailors were additionally afraid of whistling, women and priests aboard, rats' fleeing, even the word "Erie" within a ship's name.
5. *The ship's contract, dated October 7:* Criminal Transcript, in exhibits for the case, Exhibit 17, 1.
6. *would pay Jenks twenty-five hundred dollars:* Ibid., 3.
6. *the seventh article:* Ibid.
6. *The ninth article:* Ibid., 4.
6. *habit of doodling: Grand Rapids Press,* January 31, 1916.
7. *the river was only seven feet:* Annual Reports, War Department, 1904, 3065.
7. *the* Petoskey *. . . dragged on the bottom:* Ibid., 3063.
7. *"I felt I had gotten off cheaply:* Ibid.
7. *To get around the problem:* Ibid., 3066.
7. *very fine sand:* Ibid.
8. *it had to load very lightly:* Ibid., 3063
8. *"Owing to the shallow water:* Ibid.
8. *"The increase in the passenger:* Ibid.
8. *on the wall in his office: South Haven Daily Tribune,* January 26, 1903.
8. *"We are ready to place:* Annual Reports, War Department, 1904, 3064.
9. *Against sharp opposition: Muskegon Chronicle,* March 18, 1903, and *Benton Harbor News-Palladium,* June 23, August 25, 1905.

Chapter Two
10. *Dunkley-Williams met on a Saturday: South Haven Daily Tribune,* October 13, 1902.
10. *Crary wrote back to General Gillespie:* Annual Reports, War Department, 1904, 3064.

10. *they wired a telegram: South Haven Daily Tribune,* October 13, 1902.

10. *The loser would have to select: South Haven Morning Sentinel,* December 6, 1902.

11. *almost impossible to sink": South Haven Daily Tribune,* November 29, 1902.

11. *Crary rushed out to Toledo: South Haven Daily Tribune,* January 26, 1903.

11. *Demand was enormous:* Van der Linden, 91–97.

11. *When the Smith Thompson was launched: American Marine,* July 1907, 31.

12. *In 1901, it was Ship Owners Dry Dock:* Van der Linden, 91–97.

12. *William died suddenly: Port Huron Daily Times,* December 13, 1902.

12. *with crosscut saw:* Ibid.

12. *Sidney Jenks . . . studied engineering out east: Camden* (NJ) *Courier-Post,* December 14, 1965.

12. *he repeatedly went out to visit:* Investigation of Accident, 229–30. Hereafter, "Redfield Hearing."

12. *"He was huffy at my attitude:* Ibid.

13. *it had a lot of material on hand: South Haven Daily Tribune,* October 13, 1902.

13. *"We will give the person who suggests: South Haven Daily Tribune,* January 21, 1903.

13. *the envelopes arrived at Citizens State Bank: South Haven Daily Tribune,* February 6, 1903.

14. *"DEAR SIR: I read in the paper: South Haven Daily Tribune,* February 19, 1903.

14. *plans to . . . offer telephone connections: South Haven Daily Tribune,* March 3, 1903.

Chapter Three

15. *"His experience and recognized conservatism: South Haven Daily Tribune,* March 3, 1903.

15. *"There will be a bar: South Haven Daily Tribune,* March 18, 1903.

15. *any glitch in a launch:* Stonehouse, *Haunted,* 65.

16. *"Took my first plunge: South Haven Daily Tribune,* March 24, 1903.

16. *their ship would be called the* Eastland*: South Haven Daily Tribune,* April 25, 1903.

16. *"No parent watched with more pride:* Mitts, 132.

16. *Students would be dismissed at noon:* Ibid., 133.

16. *the Stars and Stripes were winched: South Haven Daily Tribune,* May 6, 1903.

17. *"She dropped . . . then rolled over:* Criminal Transcript, 463–65.

17. *"And she came right back up:* Ibid.

Chapter Four

18. *she hired a horse-drawn coach:* South Haven Daily Tribune, May 6, 1903.
18. *the whistle at the pumping station:* South Haven Sentinel, June 26, 1903.
19. *Pereue personally took the wheel:* South Haven Tribune-Messenger, July 18, 1903.
19. *the fire whistle at the pumping station:* Ibid.
20. *Hundreds came aboard:* Manistee Daily News, July 18, 1903.
20. *At a ceremony aboard:* Kalamazoo Gazette, July 18, 1903.
20. *Pereue, still learning how:* South Haven Tribune-Messenger, July 18, 1903.
20. *an immense flower arrangement:* Ibid.

Chapter Five

22. *In their first . . . race:* South Haven Daily Tribune, July 21, 1903.
22. *President Dunkley crowed:* Ibid.
22. *The two ships did race again:* South Haven Daily Tribune, August 3, 1903.
23. *He ordered Pereue to step down:* Manistee Daily News, August 28, 1903.
23. *he had run the* Eastland's *stern:* South Haven Daily Tribune, July 22, 23, August 1, 1903.
23. *the mayor of Manistee:* American Lumbermen, 208.
23. *Captain Dority, an experienced master:* Manistee Daily News, August 28, 1903.
23. *Jenks agreed to install:* South Haven Daily Tribune, May 12, 1904.
23. *the grand jury had a busy docket:* Grand Rapids Press, October 7, 1903.
23. *"For some time:* Ibid.
24. *"meals were gleanings:* Ibid.
24. *jurors decided to issue no indictment:* Jackson Citizen-Patriot, November 7, 1903.
24. *new wooden letters:* South Haven Daily Tribune, May 27, 1904.
24. *The* Eastland *struck the bar:* South Haven Daily Tribune, May 12, 1904.
24. *on a wooden leg and crutches:* South Haven Tribune Messenger, May 12, 1905.
24. *Donahue crawled out to the light:* South Haven Messenger, January 17, 1890.
24–25. *"my Wife Died this Afternoon:* Stieve, Captain James Donahue.
25. *The tug* Mentor *was dispatched:* South Haven Daily Tribune, May 12, 1904.
25. *"The danger to this valuable vessel:* Ibid.
25. *made its fastest crossing:* South Haven Tribune Messenger, July 1, 1904.
25. *People lined both piers:* Kraus, 107.
25. *"This way for Variety Fruit Farm:* Ibid.
25. *The town sold a one-dollar badge:* Ibid.
26. *"We'll be on the bottom:* Criminal Transcript, 436.
26. *"would strike a rock or anything:* Ibid.
27. *Six-inch pipes would suffice:* Ibid.

Chapter Six

28. The account of the *Eastland*'s near-capsize in 1904 is based on news reports in the *Grand Rapids Press*, July 18, 1904, and the *Chicago Evening American*, July 17, 1904, as well as testimony before the Redfield and Coroner hearings in 1915.

28. *"We expect to receive satisfactory:* Redfield Hearing, 239.

28. *"This condition absolutely must:* Ibid.

28. *Eeles started running water:* Criminal Transcript, 28.

29. *"There was a terrifying sound:* Transcript Testimony; Hereafter, "Coroner Hearing," 117.

29. *"we must surely capsize:* Ibid.

29. *"For God's sake, captain,":* Chicago Evening American, July 17, 1904, and Coroner Hearing, 116.

29. *John Harrington . . . recalled the indignity:* Criminal Transcript, 1194.

30. *clinging to life preservers:* Grand Rapids Press, July 18, 1904.

Chapter Seven

31. *derogatory nicknames:* Hansen, 3.

31. *it might run north:* Ibid.

31. *the legendary slaughterhouses:* Hill, 103.

31. *chickens would prance:* Ibid.

31. *The stockyards, which accounted:* Chicago City Manual, 177.

32. *One man tried to pilot:* Chicago Daily Tribune, November 24, 1915.

32. *blue flames dancing:* Hill, 103.

32. *an island a mile square:* Lewis, 268.

32. *Crowds downtown watched:* Ibid., 272.

32. *Chicago dredged out freight tunnels:* Stonehouse, *Crime II*, 114.

32. *shadowy underground highway:* Ibid.

33. *Car-Barn Bandits: New York Times*, April 23, 1904.

33. *each would hang:* Ibid.

33. *When one customer refused: Chicago Daily Tribune*, November 29, 1903.

33. *one woman tried to defend:* Ibid., September 16, 1904.

33. *"night children" sold gum: Chicago Vice*, 35.

33. *set up bowling pins:* Ibid., 126.

33. *Leering men fondled:* Ibid., 249–50.

33. *Underfed, anemic children:* Ibid., 246.

33. *lookouts, also called "lighthouses:* Ibid., 123, 128.

33. *six perfumed parlors:* Lewis, 346–47.

33. *Prince Henry of Prussia:* Abbott, xxi.

33–34. *Masters . . . a frequent client:* Ibid.

34. *Harrison vowed to clean the city:* Lewis, 279.

34. *One woman, named Bertha:* Chicago Daily Tribune, January 20, 1907.

Chapter Eight
35. *three to four hundred tons:* Pennington, 16–17.
35. *once a bear, another time an eagle:* Ibid., 51.
35. *toy boats, rather than dolls:* Chicago Daily Journal, December 9, 1912.
35–36. *the two married in secret:* Daily (IL) State Register, July 18, 1903.
36. *Among his heroes:* Crandall, 21–22.
36. *the police arrested 32,800:* Altgeld, 217.
36. *"There should be no jails:* Darrow, Address, 24.
37. *As the city raged:* Farrell, 130–32.
37. *"This terrible tragedy:* Ibid.
37. *the company profited smartly:* Adams, 29.
37. *sales of more than thirty million:* Chicago Daily Tribune, February 16, 1904.
37. *Builders speculated:* Chicago Daily Tribune, October 11, 1903.
38. *James Novotny, a youthful cabinetmaker:* Chicago Daily Tribune, August 31, 1915, and "The Dead," 12.

Chapter Nine
39. *"On hitting the water:* Parsons, 63.
39. *Sailors joked:* Ibid., 48.
39. *the drowned bodies:* Bowen, 196–97.
40. *cribbage, their favorite off-duty pastime:* Grand Rapids Press, May 12, 1912.
40. *"Fury and snakes!:* Hallet, 104.
40. *"I am going ashore:* Joseph Erickson to Florence Erickson.
40. *Elephant Bill, Mother Lovely:* Wright, 29–37.
40. *the price for a roll with a hooker:* Chicago Vice, 392.
40. *The Wakefield monkey:* Havighurst, 213.
41. *"a species of wild men:* Gjerset, American Water, 67.
41. *$1.75 a day:* Gjerset, Great Lakes, 5.
41. *the "Norwegian Navy:* Gjerset, American Water, 215.
41. *By 1890, Norwegians threatened:* Gjerset, Great Lakes, 7.
41. *Over several decades, the people of Norway:* Ibid., 16.
42. *"In sailing on the ocean:* Gjerset, Great Lakes, 10.

Chapter Ten
43. *Most of Erickson's colleagues:* Grand Rapids Press, May 12, 1912.
43. *The job of oiler was dangerous:* American Marine, November 1915, 9–11.
43. *One surefire joke:* Plowden, 38.
43. *As the ship rolled:* American Marine, November 1915, 9–11.
44. *In the hold, there was gallows:* Ibid.

44. *Before he arrived in America:* Criminal Transcript, 1065.

44. *When they came up for fresh air:* Parsons, 77.

44. *"There were sounds of low thunder:* Hallet, 99.

44. *Worse, getting ground up: American Marine,* April 1919, 28.

44. *the typical lunch: American Marine,* November 1915, 9–11.

45. *With coal dust floating: American Marine,* January 1916, 11–16.

45. *The chief engineer: American Marine,* January 1910, 35.

45. *If he passed, he would be given: American Marine,* November 1915, 9–11.

46. *Sailing, Sailing isn't it joy:* Silver, 1.

46. *billboards for coffee, cheese and Quaker Oats:* Viskochil, 23.

46. *Later that summer, the* Eastland: The race account is based on news reports in the *Kalamazoo Gazette,* June 25, 1905 and, with local interest still humming three generations later, in the *Benton Harbor Herald Palladium,* July 14, 1976.

47. *"The* South Haven *will give: Kalamazoo Gazette,* June 25, 1905.

47. *he issued a warning:* Ibid., June 29, 1905.

47. *Off watch in the engine room:* Criminal Transcript, 1070. Erickson recalled in court testimony in 1916 precisely when he first saw the *Eastland,* in 1905 off South Haven.

Chapter Eleven

48. *caught shoplifting: Benton Harbor News-Palladium,* July 14, 1905.

48. *Erickson often used his time:* Joseph Erickson to Hannah Erickson.

48. *At Grand Haven's harbor: Evening News* (Sault Ste. Marie), July 25, 1905.

49. *The ports in cities:* Paananen, 204.

49. *By 1900, with shipments:* Ibid., 204.

49. *Six years later, the Great Lakes:* Commerce, *Transportation,* 121.

49. *"The wildest expectations of one year:* Havighurst, 222.

49. *While waiting for the lock: American Marine,* January 1914, 39.

49. *Having already made:* Thompson, *Steamboats & Sailors,* 25.

49. *He initially ordered:* Havighurst, 22.

49. *Andrew Carnegie:* Thompson, *Steamboats & Sailors,* 25.

50. *At one point, it was the world's largest: American Marine,* January 1909, 12–13.

50. *Bringing immense cargo freighters: American Marine,* October 1907, 15, and Thompson, *Steamboats & Sailors,* 45.

50. *In less than two decades:* Commerce, *Transportation,* 121.

50. *In the Chicago River: American Marine,* July 1908, 25.

50. *Knowing the turning basin: American Marine,* October 1908, 36.

50. *Erickson was one of a thirty-man: Grand Rapids Press,* May 12, 1912.

50. *It broke a rudder: Evening News* (Sault Ste. Marie), September 23, 1905.

50. *permission to stay out of school:* Ibid.

Chapter Twelve

51. *"The largest of yesterday's social affairs:* Chicago Record Herald, March 1, 1905.
51. *Born in rural Michigan:* Leonard, 547.
51. *Steele was a Republican:* Ibid.
51. *the prominent announcement:* Chicago Record Herald, March 1, 1905.
51. *The previous May, Blair:* Chicago Daily Tribune, May 2, 1904.
51. *The day after his daughter's wedding:* Chicago Record Herald, March 2, 1905.
52. *twenty-eight propeller blades:* Redfield Hearing, 322.
52. *Expenses were running up:* Hilton, *Eastland,* 50. George Hilton's *Eastland: Legacy of the Titanic* is the first book-length treatment of the disaster and is an amazing compendium on the ship, particularly its later history. Readers so interested will find much in that work, for instance, on the civil litigation, the *Eastland's* afterlife as a Navy vessel, and a full list of the disaster victims.
52. *"Although the Michigan Steamship:* Redfield Hearing, 244.
52. *it faced a claim:* South Haven Tribune Messenger, December 29, 1905.
52. *By late December 1905:* Ibid.
52. *Blacker . . . personally bought the* Eastland: Ibid.
52. *new home . . . would cost:* Makinson, 24.
53. *The fall after the* Eastland *was sold:* South Haven Tribune Messenger, September 26, 1906.

Chapter Thirteen

54. *The suction motors:* Muskegon Chronicle, May 30, 1906.
54. *Great Lakes transportation companies:* American Marine, March 1908, 22.
54. *Early investors in the* Eastland: Francis, "Eastland," Summer, 97.
54. *A fire broke out:* Ann Arbor Daily Times, March 28, 1907.
55. *There was more than four thousand dollars:* Ibid.
55. *Five days after the fire:* South Haven Tribune Messenger, April 1, 1907.
55. *Cedar Point was a sprawling newfangled:* Francis, "Eastland," Summer, 96–100.
55. *An early roller coaster, called The Racer:* Francis, Cedar Point, 41. This book has vintage photographs of, and little gems about, the early theme park, including that football legend Knute Rockne was part of the beach patrol in 1913.

Chapter Fourteen

56. *his chef quit:* Muskegon Chronicle, June 11, 1907.
56. *It wasn't unusual for one captain to swipe:* Parsons, 55.
56. *Port authorities in St. Joseph were puzzled:* Muskegon Chronicle, July 13, 1907.
56. *Fireman William Morton had just been paid:* Ibid., September 7, 1907.

57. *John McCourt, a deckhand:* Ibid., October 5, 1907.
57. *the home of Captain William R. Loutit:* Ewing, 88.
57. *Captain Evans quit to study law:* Grand Rapids Press, October 10, 1907.
57. *swallowed the anchor:* Hallet, 95.
57. *About thirty-five miles:* An old-fashioned pirate in modern times generated lots of headlines. This account is built from the June 30, 1908 news reports in the Chicago *Inter Ocean, Chicago Daily Tribune, New York Times,* and the *Muskegon Chronicle.* Several years later, there was actually another, lesser-noted instance of piracy on Lake Michigan, when two sailors commandeered the *Foam* and were soon after captured in Michigan City, Indiana. The captain of the *Foam* notified the pirates that he would not press charges if they returned the boat to him in Chicago. They did so the next day. *St. Joseph Daily Press,* July 10, 1914.
58. *"We had a good description:* Chicago *Inter Ocean,* June 30, 1908.
58. *The new captain of the* General Gillespie*:* Grand Rapids Press, May 12, 1912.
58. *This is to certify that the bearer:* McDonald, in file of Erickson *Petition for Naturalization.*
59. *He wrote in looping, nearly effeminate:* Erickson, *Petition for Naturalization.*
59. *After all, as one Norwegian proverb:* Asala, 28.

Chapter Fifteen

60. *Passenger accounts suggested:* Criminal Transcript, 1152–53.
60. *"A Week's Pleasure in a Day: Chronicle Telegram* (Elyria, OH), July 24, 1907.
60. *"Won't Sink. Can't Burn:* Ibid., August 12, 1908.
60. *including "Little Egypt:* Francis, "Eastland," Summer, 100.
60. *It ran a lottery, handing out five thousand:* Ibid., 183.
61. *it released a thousand balloons:* Ibid.
61. *"I was interested in the* Eastland*:* Thompson, *Ancient,* 67.
61. *That Independence Day:* Ibid.
61. *Thompson, who kept a leather billy club:* Ibid.

Chapter Sixteen

62. *the* Moselle *was steaming away:* Brown, 1.
62. *Between 1825 and 1848:* Ibid., viii.
62. *The superheated boilers:* Roper, 244.
62. *When the boilers blew: New York Daily News,* April 13, 1852.
62. *In one account of the explosion:* Brown, 14.
63. *"Four of the eight boilers:* Twain, 106–7.
63. *Their life-coverage policies:* Brown, 63.
63. *But Aetna life-insurance policies:* Ibid.
63. *Convinced the danger was unavoidable:* Brockmann, 19.

63. *"Why sleep over a volcano:* Ibid.
63. *Under pressure to do something:* Brown, viii.
63. *Inspections were haphazard: American Marine,* September 1915, 5–7.
64. *To put an end to the boiler explosions:* Ibid.

Chapter Seventeen
65. *When Reid stepped aboard:* Redfield Hearing, 116–17.
65. *To inspect the wooden hull:* Ibid.
65. *He insisted so many repairs:* Ibid.
65. *Reid ordered other ships:* Ibid.
65. *Reid's father, also named Robert:* Ibid.; Thomas, 154–55.
66. *While the* Buttars *was tied up: Muskegon Chronicle,* May 11, 1894.
66. *During the Spanish-American: Grand Rapids Press,* May 12, 1912.
66. *would grill Erickson for seven days:* Criminal Transcript, 1066.
66. *He was licensed not in the typical:* Ibid., 1067.
66. *"The Dredge General Gillespie:* "In the Matter of the Petition of Joseph Mallings Erickson."

Chapter Eighteen
68. *The undercover detective stepped: Chicago Vice,* 216.
68. *He stood in place:* Ibid.
68. *Down the hall, in stateroom No. 61:* Ibid.
68. *One child, eight, was drinking beer:* Ibid.
69. *X1044 was "the worst: Chicago Vice,* 215.
69. *an investigator left Chicago: Chicago Vice,* 216.
69. *"I ain't no saint:* Ibid., 217.
69. *The new City Hall building:* Sinkevitch, 74.
69. *From the eleven-story building:* Lewis, 346–47.
70. *A city ordinance: Chicago Vice,* 249.
70. *A Morals Court:* Lewis, 351.
70. *"Something must be done about those fellows:* Ibid., 275.
70. *largest employment site in all of Chicago: Chicago Daily Tribune,* February 4, 1910.
70. *It opened Hawthorne Hospital:* Adams, 84.
70. *seven hundred thousand of them on order: Wall Street Journal,* August 13, 1909.
71. *Platinum, for telephone transmitters:* Casson, 162.
71. *"a mad waltz of spindles:* Ibid., 161.
71. *He managed to find a job: Chicago Daily Tribune,* August 31, 1915.
71. *He bought the home and started paying: Red Cross Report,* 165.

Chapter Nineteen
72. *"The material she is built of: Cleveland Plain Dealer,* August 9, 1910.

72. *Some four hundred thousand people had enjoyed:* Ibid.
72. *And one of the directors of a Cleveland bank:* Hilton, *Eastland*, 56.
73. *had to rename itself:* Grand Rapids Press, May 12, 1912.
73. *Joseph had summoned his . . . brother:* Criminal Transcript, 1080.
73. *"tipping ship:* Grand Rapids Press, May 12, 1912.
73. *"Are you sinking, captain?:* Ibid.
74. *"Ida Walter Steele, wife of Julius:* Chicago Daily Tribune, May 7, 1912.
74. *her bridge club and luncheons:* Chicago Inter Ocean, February 24, 1911.
74. *Steele shepherded a small delegation:* Chicago Daily Tribune, June 23, 1909.
74. *105 acres of rich farmland:* Farm Journal, 229.
75. *They married in September:* St. Joseph Evening Herald, September 19, 1911.

Chapter Twenty
76. *Four days before Thanksgiving:* Chicago Daily Tribune, December 5, 7, 1912.
76. *Within weeks, Captain Schuenemann's:* Chicago Daily Tribune, December 11, 12, 13, 14, 21, 23, 1912.
76. *Her radicalism developed:* Cowan, 63.
76. *"I shall not go back out east:* Clarence Darrow to Mary Field, November 28, 1912.
77. *Someone planted a suitcase:* Stone, 167.
77. *The explosion wasn't caused:* Cowan, 175.
77. *He ordered a replica:* Ibid.
77. *"Suppose you thought I was guilty:* Uelman, 1543.
77. *"Here is a contest between two:* Ibid., 1544.
78. *In his summations for other cases:* Maloney, 473–75.
78. *"I have committed one crime:* Stone, 215.
78. *Against overwhelming evidence:* Uelman, 1544.
78. *He needed to protect them:* Cowan, 439.
78. *"I suspected at the time:* Masters, 284.
78. *"As to his 'guilt':* Mary Field to Irving Stone.
78. *"What in the hell:* Clarence Darrow to Mary Field, July 14, 1913.
79. *"And the sea is death and annihilation:* Ibid.
79. *He had been paid handsomely:* Washington Times, May 18, 1915.
79. *At home in South Chicago:* Stone, 221.
79. *"Well, Rube," he finally said:* Ibid.
79. *"I have heard a good many literary:* Cowan, 285.
79. *"You must not:* Stone, 222.
79. *"But I have no practice:* Ibid.

Chapter Twenty-One
80. *There was an opening:* Criminal Transcript, 1067.

80. *The chief engineer asked Erickson:* Ibid.
80. *The news was all over Ohio: American Marine,* October 1913, 10.
81. *With twenty-five vessels, it was a formidable freight: Duluth News-Tribune,* February 18, 1914.
81. *After several days of questions:* Criminal Transcript, 1068.
81. *The Disaster Fund reached $68,149: Cleveland Leader,* November 23, 1915.
81. *Erickson donated five dollars:* Ibid.
81. *cute, but sickly:* Criminal Transcript, 1072.
81. *Ever cautious, the inspector:* Robert Reid to Florence Reid, March 4, 1912.
82. *"I am painting and fixing up:* Robert Reid to Florence Reid, September 25, 1912.

Chapter Twenty-Two
83. *arrested for allowing gambling: Duluth News-Tribune,* July 19, 1912.
83. *In the same sweep, deputy marshals: Cleveland Plain Dealer,* July 19, 1912
83. *About eight hundred passengers and seven hundred crewmembers:* Kuntz, 559. The official transcripts of the 1912 Senate investigation of the disaster report that 832 passengers and 685 crew perished on the *Titanic.*
83. *the Steamboat Inspection Service issued:* Commerce, *General Rules,* and Criminal Transcript, 136–37
84. *When Cleveland inspectors Thomas W. Gould:* Redfield Hearing, 86.
84. *"Be careful and tend to the water ballast:* Ibid.
84. *Using a wireless radio:* Francis, "Eastland," Summer, 101–2.
84. *the Eastland had run up losses: New York Times,* July 25, 1915.
84. *Only ten survivors of the steamer: Springfield Republican,* April 30, 1914.
84. *They were mostly Union:* Huffman.
84. *the Sultana was afire:* Ibid.
85. *Florence, who was working: Grand Haven Daily Tribune,* December 26, 1914.
85. *The pride of Grand Haven: Grand Rapids Press,* January 3, 1907

Chapter Twenty-Three
86. *Florence had found herself short:* Criminal Transcript, 1071.
86. Sultana *ran coal to Ashtabula:* This is a synopsis of the vessel's season from the shipping news reported in the *Cleveland Plain Dealer,* April 24, September 25, November 6, 7, 15, 1914; and the *Duluth News-Tribune,* June 12 and July 18, 1914.
86. *some crews paid bribes, "beer money:* Dutton, 113.
87. *When a freight ship occasionally ran:* Ibid.
87. *To the Hagwood company: Duluth News-Tribune,* June 4, 1914.
87. *Hundreds of people clutching: St. Joseph Evening Herald,* July 6, 1914.

87. *They had already advertised:* St. Joseph Daily Press, July 3, 1914.
88. *had just decided to defect:* Ibid., May 15, 1914.
88. *People in St. Joseph derisively called:* Reber, 32.
88. *St. Joseph sent a delegation:* Ibid., 34.
88. *Daughters of the American Revolution:* Ibid., 24.
89. *Hull went out to Cleveland:* Criminal Transcript, 989–90.
89. *"snowing and cold,":* Ibid.
89. *Steele immediately picked up three hundred:* Steele, 2.
89. *about twenty thousand dollars short:* St. Joseph Evening Herald, May 15, 1914.
89. *"Mass Meeting Tonight of Vital:* St. Joseph Daily Press, May 14, 1914.
90. *"The moral support of every citizen:* Ibid.
90. *"We are strictly up against it:* St. Joseph Evening Herald, May 15, 1914.
90. *"money, chalk or marbles:* St. Joseph Daily Press, May 14, 1914.
90. *"The name Eastland is a prestige:* St. Joseph Evening Herald, May 15, 1914.
90. *"Who in this meeting will subscribe:* St. Joseph Daily Press, May 14, 1914.
90. *"The acquisition of the steamer:* St. Joseph Evening Herald, May 14, 1914.
91. *rain and unusually warm weather:* St. Joseph Daily Press, May 29, 1914.
91. *Steele sent a telegram to Hull:* Ibid., June 17, 1914.
91. *The return to Lake Michigan:* Ibid., June 5, 1914.
91. *steering the Eastland closer to shore:* Ibid.
91. *Good-bye ev-'ry thing:* Hough.
92. *The first man off the ship:* St. Joseph Evening Press, June 5, 1914

Chapter Twenty-Four

93. *the Eastland was struggling:* St. Joseph Evening Herald, June 14, 1914.
93. *Captain Ennes reported daily:* Criminal Transcript, 194.
93. *Donaldson even overheard Steele:* Ibid., 272.
93. *he packed his suitcase:* St. Joseph Daily Press, June 27, 1914.
93. *Oddly, Hull had asked:* Criminal Transcript, 993.
94. *some mysterious accident:* St. Joseph Evening Herald, July 6, 1914.
94. *rock-solid iron, ten inches thick:* Criminal Transcript, 930.
94. *The Eastland, crippled, arrived:* St. Joseph Daily Press, July 11, 1914.
94. *Steamboat inspector William Nicholas:* Redfield Hearing, 270.
94. *the Eastland carried its largest crowd:* Criminal Transcript, Government Exhibit 51.
94. *Graham & Morton put its shiniest: Benton Harbor: The Metropolis,* no page numbers.
94. *the ship's seacock froze: Benton Harbor News-Palladium,* February 16, 1915, and St. Joseph Evening Herald, February 16, 1915.

Chapter Twenty-Five

96. *They exchanged vows at seven:* Grand Haven Daily Tribune, December 26, 1914.

96. *Florence continued to struggle:* Criminal Transcript, 1072.

96. *Erickson met with his mentor:* Ibid., 1071.

96. *"I heard the* Eastland *is open:* Ibid.

97. *"I wish you would make an application:* Ibid.

97. *"I wish to apply for the position:* Ibid., 1072.

97. *"The position must be filled:* Ibid., 1073

97. *"As the position I now hold:* Ibid., 1075.

98. *Hull asked Erickson to come:* Ibid., 1076.

98. *They discussed the steamers Erickson:* Ibid., 1077.

98. *The two went over to Benton Harbor:* Ibid.

98. *"Lots of work . . . to be done:* Ibid., 1080.

98. *"Have any objection:* Ibid.

98. *Erickson would be paid the $175:* Ibid.

Chapter Twenty-Six

99. *an unusual visit:* This pivotal account is based on Joseph Erickson's signed testimony before the Chicago chief of police on July 25, 1915, in front of five witnesses, "Interrogation," as well as Erickson's sworn testimony confirming and buttressing the details of this meeting between Steele and himself during the criminal trial in Grand Rapids the following year, Criminal Transcript, 1102–3. In surviving testimony, Steele was never asked to confirm or deny any specifics of Erickson's account.

Chapter Twenty-Seven

101. *two Chicago teenagers:* Rockford (IL) Republic, June 29, 1915.

101. *attorney didn't own an automobile:* Whitehead, 10.

101. *over coffee and cigarettes:* Stone, 222.

101. *Sissman opened a joint bank account:* Ibid., 223.

101. *He represented a woman who mistook:* Daily (IL) State Register, March 15, 1914

101. *an attorney charged with tampering:* Chicago Inter Ocean, April 16, 1914.

101. *Darrow won an acquittal for her:* Stone, 223.

101. *"My prolonged absence:* Darrow, Story, 204–5.

102. *"I can only speak for:* Clarence Darrow to Mary Field Parton.

102. *"I know that all my life:* Chicago Daily Tribune, May 11, 1913.

102. *the 1915 crime tally:* Chicago Daily News Almanac, 680.

102. *Fainting Bertha was caught:* Chicago Daily Tribune, May 24, 1914.

102. *"I will suppress crime:* Lewis, 371.

103. *invited striking streetcar men:* Ibid., 379.

103. *Thirty-seven whole states: Chicago Daily News Almanac,* 174.
103. *"To turn, a signal shall:* Ibid., 187.
103. *1,183 churches, and 7,006 saloons:* Ibid., 642.
103. *Thompson dared to issue:* Lewis, 380.
103. *"No. 1 A shape:* Criminal Transcript, 1080.
103. *he and Captain Pedersen took:* Ibid.
103. *only 146 passengers aboard:* Ibid., Government Exhibit 51.
103. *"Keep her straight and trim:* Ibid., 1082.
103. *Behind his back: Allentown Call-Chronicle,* July 25, 1965.
103. *The two . . . did not socialize:* Criminal Transcript, 1083.
104. *Ray Davis . . . routinely began riding:* "Interrogation," 12.
104. *Hull reached out to Donaldson:* Criminal Transcript, 998.
104. *Donaldson's appearance:* Criminal Transcript, 1072.
104. *"Please accept this as:* Ibid.
104. *He withdrew his resignation:* Ibid.
104. *That day, that sorrow:* Blegen, 219.

Part II: What Is Honest Never Sinks

Chapter Twenty-Eight
106. *Pedersen flicked the ashes:* Criminal Transcript, 962.
106. *Pedersen had just passed Erickson:* Ibid.
106. *After Michigan City, it had:* Ibid., 1088.
106. *his watch stopped at 7:33:* Ibid., 1106.
107. *By 6:30, five thousand people: Chicago Daily Tribune,* July 25, 1915.
107. *white gangplank, four feet wide:* Criminal Transcript, 1030, 1036.
107. *Arthur MacDonald looked:* Criminal Transcript, 1270.
107. *Erickson noticed:* "Engineer's Log," 1. The handwritten three-page letter, with occasional ink splotches, is a remarkably concise and lucid account for a man who had just nearly drowned then been arrested and questioned for hours.
107. *"Boys, steady her up: Detroit News,* July 25, 1915.
107. *continuously had reached sixteen hundred:* Redfield Hearing, 29.
108. *Bradfield's Orchestra, a five-piece:* Coroner Hearing, 88.
108. *Erickson started up the engines:* "Engineer's Log," 1.
108. *he ordered his men:* Ibid.
108. *You'll need to proceed:* Criminal Transcript, 1030.
108. *The crew pulled up . . . drew a chain:* Criminal Transcript, 1040.
108. *E. W. Sladkey, who was in charge: Detroit Free Press,* July 25, 1915.
108. *Davis, Steele's assistant, showed up:* "Engineer's Log," 2.
108. *Erickson told Davis:* Ibid.

108. *"I guess we got it:* Coroner Hearing, 115.
108. *signaled a "Stand By" order:* Criminal Transcript, 969.
108–9. *Erickson acknowledged the standby:* "Engineer's Log," 2.
109. *MacDonald came up:* Criminal Transcript, 1270.
109. *it was tipping an alarming twenty-five degrees:* Ibid.
109. *Erickson dispatched his first assistant:* "Engineer's Log," 2.
109. *Harbormaster Adam Weckler:* Criminal Transcript, 434.
109. *"All together—hey:* Chicago Daily Tribune, July 25, 1915.
109. *MacDonald, in the tugboat, noticed:* Criminal Transcript, 1273.
109. *"Don't pull on her at all, cap:* Ibid., 1274.
109. *MacDonald saw something he hadn't seen:* Ibid., 1275.
110. *began to dig their heels:* Chicago Daily Tribune, July 25, 1915.
110. *a chute . . . used to discharge ashes:* Criminal Transcript, 1299.
110. *MacDonald was alarmed:* Criminal Transcript, 1273.
110. *"Get off—the boat's turning over:* Chicago Daily Tribune, July 26, 1915.
110. *"Open the doors, and take people off:* Criminal Transcript, 981.
110. *A refrigerator tipped:* New York Times, July 25, 1915.
110. *Dishes slipped from their shelves:* Detroit News, July 24, 1915.
110. *People sitting in chairs:* New York Times, July 25, 1915.
110. *A dozen passengers tried to leap:* Ibid.
110. *Children tumbled with grown-ups:* "What the Survivors," 23.
110. *burst like a cracked whip:* Criminal Transcript, 1275.
111. *fruit crates, chicken crates:* Detroit News, July 25, 1915.
111. *A young woman was struggling:* Ibid.
111. *"It rushed along by the stairs:* Chicago Daily Tribune, July 25, 1915.
111. *MacDonald helped back:* Criminal Transcript, 1274–75.
112. *A man named Brown, who worked in Western:* "What the Survivors," 24.
112. *victims tore away cabin partitions:* Chicago Daily Tribune, July 25, 1915.
112. *Helen Thyer was pitched into:* New York Times, July 25, 1915. The newspaper misspelled the name as "Thoyer," but Western Electric corrected it in its reckoning of the lost: "The Dead," 14.
112. *William Raphael jumped in:* New York Times, July 26, 1915.
112. *Julius Behnke and his wife:* Chicago Daily Tribune, July 25, 1915.
112. *George Goyette grabbed a handkerchief:* "What the Survivors," 23–24.
112. *"men fight and tear the clothing:* Detroit News, July 25, 1915.
112. *His face was half-lathered:* Allentown Call-Chronicle, July 25, 1965. An account published fifty years and a day after the disaster.
113. *Erickson had stayed put in the engine room:* "Engineer's Log," 2–3.
113. *Seconds away from drowning:* Allentown Call-Chronicle, July 25, 1965, an eyewitness account published fifty years after the disaster, and "Engineer's Log," 2–3.
113. *Stretching his hand up:* Criminal Transcript, 1096.

113. *the* Graeme Stewart, *waited: Chicago Daily Tribune,* July 26, 1915.
113. *After catching his breath:* Criminal Transcript, 1096.
113. *"Get some ropes:* Ibid.
113. *rescued a little girl . . . more:* Ibid.
114. *Thompson was driving:* Thompson, "Just What," 200–201.
114. *"Are you Captain Merwin:* Ibid.
114. *"Did you know:* Ibid.
114. *"It seems to me impossible:* Ibid.
114. *large fishing nets: New York Times,* July 25, 1915.
115. *"Excursion boat upset:* "Experiences," 19–20.
115. *The trolley man tried to stop her:* Ibid.
115. *The captain of the nearby Missouri:* Ratigan, 65–66.
115. *"They were already pulling them:* "Experiences," 19–20.
115. *churning up the dirty water: New York Times,* July 26, 1915.

Chapter Twenty-Nine
116. *"The bodies were laid out:* "Experiences," 19–20.
116. *"Isn't there some building:* Ibid.
116. *"dare go into the water:* Coroner Hearing, 36.
116. *Another man, the one who was:* Red Cross Report, 144.
117. *"When I got to the Iroquois Hospital:* "Experiences," 19–20.
117. *"My sister," she screamed: Detroit News,* July 25, 1915.
117. *"My husband!:* Ibid.
117. *with strychnine: New York Times,* July 25, 1915.
117. *the worn awnings of the fruit-houses:* Viskochil, 25.
117. *Father John O'Hearn:* Hilton, *Eastland,* 123.
117. *The first: "Pulmotor: Detroit News,* July 25, 1915.
118. *only other word . . . was "Gone:* Ibid.
118. *seized with grappling hooks:* Ibid.
119. *As bodies were lifted: Eastland Disaster Photos,* ICHi-02049, ICHi-32996, ICHi-02048, ICHi-32997.
119. *could hear faint tapping: Chicago Daily Tribune,* July 25, 1915.
119. *who'd struck his head:* Criminal Transcript, 984.
119. *three-eighth-inch steel-plated bottom:* Reid, *Hull Inspector's Report,* report has no page numbers.
119. *"Here, stop that!" the captain shouted: Chicago Daily Tribune,* July 25, 1915.
119. *"My orders are to save:* Ibid.
119. *Go to hell:* Ibid. Rista, perhaps considering a newspaper the whole family might read, seems to have cleaned up what he actually shouted at the interfering captain. His exact quotation in the *Tribune* was, "I told him to go to a place that was hotter than any torch flame." The author chose to report,

outside the sanctity of quotation marks, what the torch man more plausibly shouted in that moment of life or death.

119. *"Drown him: New York Times,* July 25, 1915.
119. *a man managed to break through: Chicago Daily Tribune,* July 25, 1915.
119. *"When they were cutting through:* Ibid.
120. *"As soon as we could get inside: New York Times,* July 25, 1915.
120. *"I could tell by the pull:* Ibid.
120. *One girl, about ten, was pulled: Eastland Disaster Photos,* ICHi-30730.
120. *Leonard Olson, stared into the lens: Eastland Disaster Photos,* ICHi-30783.
120. *"I stayed until they began: Benton Harbor News-Palladium,* July 25, 1915.

Chapter Thirty
123. *boarded the first train: St. Joseph Daily Press,* July 26, 1915.
123. *policemen immediately arrested Steele:* Ibid.
123. *He wanted to drive to lunch:* Ibid.
123. *oysters including Blue Points: Regular Menu.*

Chapter Thirty-One
124. *Among the underwater body hunters: New York Times,* July 25, 1915.
124. *Charles Trogg: Chicago Daily Tribune,* July 30, 1915.
124. *"I left . . . for you the other: New York Herald,* July 25, 1915.
125. *"She was alive but the baby:* Billow, 192.
125. *"The woman, in a daze:* Ibid.
126. *"I saw that woman's arm: New York Times,* July 25, 1915.
126. *Keeping order on the streets: Chicago Daily Tribune,* July 25, 1915.
126. *With a revolver pointed at him: Chicago Daily Tribune,* August 23, 1918. Schuettler's obituary recounts that story and a later colorful exploit of the man who would succeed Healey as Chicago police chief. Schuettler solved the murder of the wife of a sausage maker, who was ultimately convicted of disposing of her body in a lime vat. With his suspicious eye, Schuettler spotted a ring and a bit of bone in the mysterious vat.
126. *A flotilla of small boats:* Dowling, 45.
127. *Schuettler's men controlled the surging: Detroit News,* July 25, 1915.
127. *fearing that it would buckle:* Ibid.
127. *"I was told in English: New York Times,* July 25, 1915.
127. *removed their hats when two baby: Detroit News,* July 25, 1915.
127. *a tiny baby, a year old perhaps:* Ibid.
127. *Rista, the salvager, had dragged forty: Chicago Daily Tribune,* July 25, 1915.
127. *"When I came out:* Coroner Hearing, 3.
127. *He quickly penned out a relief: Detroit News,* July 24, 1940. A twenty-fifth anniversary story.

128. *Rain and sweat streaking his face:* Chicago Daily Tribune, July 25, 1915.

128. *"We will get every fact:* Detroit News, July 25, 1915.

128. *still three hundred bodies in the ship:* New York Times, July 25, 1915.

128. *More than forty crewmembers:* Chicago Herald, July 26, 1915.

128. *"We will leave no stone unturned:* Chicago Daily Tribune, July 25, 1915.

128. *carry the dead on Marshall Field trucks:* "Hawthorne's Automobile," 17, and Wendt, 294.

128. *The body of Katharine Krebel:* New York Times, July 26, 1915.

128. *Reid-Murdoch warehouse:* Bicknell, 307.

128. *having their own company picnic:* Red Cross Report, 11–12.

129. *numbered and tagged:* Chicago Daily Tribune, July 25, 1915.

129. *fifty embalmers were working:* Ibid.

129. *"Just let me rest a little:* New York Times, July 26, 1915.

Chapter Thirty-Two

130. *installed a bank of free phones:* New York Times, July 25, 1915.

130. *hotline to the Western Electric:* "Story of July Twenty-Fourth," 4.

130. *broke the lock on the door:* Ibid.

130. *Margaret Condon, the head telephone:* "Thirty-four Hours," 21.

130. *"Some of them are so distracted:* Ibid.

130. *West Side undertakers were charging:* Chicago Evening Post, July 28, 1915.

131. *"Gallery of Horrors:* Chicago Herald, July 25, 1915.

131. *doors of City Hall were draped:* "Story of July Twenty-Fourth," 7.

131. *Major League Baseball cancelled:* New York Times, July 26, 1915.

131. *forgotten his tickets:* New York Times, July 27, 1915.

131. *"If it had not been for the nail:* New York Times, July 25, 1915.

131. *Frederick Willard, a chemical engineer:* Coroner Hearing, 106, and Criminal Transcript, 471.

131. *a stranger she never saw:* Chicago Stories, from an interview with Libby Hruby.

131. *WHO HAS LITTLE MARTHA:* Chicago Daily Tribune, July 25, 1915.

131. *they found a boy, about:* New York Times, July 25, 1915.

Chapter Thirty-Three

133. All the quotations here are directly from the signed testimony of Joseph M. Erickson, on July 25, 1915, questioned by Chicago police chief Charles Healey. The testimony, fifteen pages in typescript, is located in the exhibits file of *US v. Hull et al.* The document itself is Exhibit 25 and is hand-signed on the last page, "CSD," or the abbreviations for Clarence S. Darrow.

135. *What is honest never sinks:* Asala, 57.

Chapter Thirty-Four

136. *Commonwealth Edison Company strung:* "Story of July Twenty-Fourth," 18.
136. *BODIES AWAITING IDENTIFICATION: Chicago Daily Tribune,* July 25, 1915.
137. *sprayed with fly-repellants or covered: Chicago Health Dept. Report,* 242.
137. *bodies lined eighty-five to a row: New York Herald,* July 25, 1915.
137. *composing the features on faces:* Bicknell, 307.
137. *handkerchiefs over their faces: Eastland Disaster Photos,* ICHi-O2047.
137. *terror frozen on faces, fingers curled:* Ibid., ICHi-30728.
137. *Red Cross set up a nursery: Chicago Daily Tribune,* July 26, 1915.
137. *One man laid across the body: New York Times,* July 26, 1915.
138. *An elderly woman dropped: New York Herald,* July 25, 1915.
138. *"Our work is being hindered: New York Times,* July 26, 1915.
138. *No. 396—Boy, 11 years old: Chicago Daily Tribune,* July 26, 1915.
138. *Willie Novotny, who was in fact: Chicago Daily Tribune,* August 1, 1915.
138. *twenty-two whole families were wiped out:* Red Cross Report, 17.
138. *More than five thousand people attended: Chicago Daily Tribune,* August 1, 1915.
138. *"The hearts of all Chicagoans:* Ibid.

Chapter Thirty-Five

139. *Kate Austin, a cook:* "The Dead," 9, and *Chicago Daily Tribune,* July 25, 1915.
140. *"Let us take a walk:* Coroner Hearing, 69.
140. *"Are you familiar:* Ibid. The questions and answers are truncated a bit for readability, but appear in their entirety between pages 69 and 87.
143. *"I was the angel: Chicago Daily Tribune,* July 28, 1915.
144. *Shirts, rompers, pants and dresses: Chicago Health Dept. Report,* 243.
144. *Steele wrote letters to salvage:* Hilton, *Eastland,* 144–45; *Chicago Daily Tribune,* August 17, 1915.
144. *$36.06 in cash on hand:* Steele, 1.

Chapter Thirty-Six

145. *After Erickson was sworn:* Coroner Hearing, 95–97. The quotations from the brief appearance of Erickson appear on the cited pages.
146. *"What was said between you:* Ibid., 125.
146. *"He told me to tell the truth:* Ibid.

Chapter Thirty-Seven

147. *"Men, women and children, trapped:* Sandburg, 132.
147. *"Grim, industrial feudalism:* Ibid., 135.
147. *Commerce secretary telegraphed:* Redfield Hearing, 7.
147. *Redfield took a train:* Ibid.

148. *"From the very fact:* Redfield Hearing, 152.

148. *"You were lucky in Cleveland:* Ibid.

148. *The opening of the hearing was delayed:* Chicago Evening Post, August 3, 1915.

148. One letter writer vowed: New York Times, August 3, 1915.

148. *investigation was a "farce:* Rockford Republican, July 30, 1915.

149. *Redfield was incensed:* Redfield Hearing, 9.

149. *slammed down his phone:* Chicago Daily Tribune, July 27, 1915.

149. *came to a verdict at 1:00 a.m.:* Coroner Hearing, 136–38.

149. *Hull hired armed guards:* Chicago Daily Tribune, July 30, 1915.

149. *the two company executives met:* St. Joseph Daily Press, July 28, 1915.

149. *Nicknamed "The Admiral:* Kogan, 52.

149. *and a lecturer:* Marquis, Who's Who, 501–2.

150. *Behind guarded doors:* St. Joseph Daily Press, July 28, 1915.

150. *"The captain is an autocrat:* Chicago Daily Tribune, July 30, 1915.

Chapter Thirty-Eight

151. *won the young judge wide:* New York Times, November 26, 1944.

151. *a group of twenty or so men standing:* Eastland Disaster Photos, DN064973.

151. *Landis became so impatient:* St. Joseph Daily Press, August 13, 1915.

151. *swinging a small walking stick:* Eastland Disaster Photos, DN064924.

151. *"It is not because he has anything:* St. Joseph Daily Press, July 30, 1915.

152. *"The instability of this vessel:* Chicago Daily News Almanac, 680.

152. *Steele had his . . . brother:* Application, Barbour.

152. *"I haven't done anything:* St. Joseph Daily Press, July 30, 1915.

152. *arranged for a saloon owner:* Application, Miller.

152. *Florence, arrived from St. Joseph:* "Ma" Reid to Florence Erickson.

153. *"Maybe you know that the crew:* Chicago Daily Tribune, August 6, 1915.

153. *A corpse was trapped:* Red Cross Report, 44.

153. *"From newspaper accounts: Journal of Proceedings,* 207.

154. *a one-thousand-dollar defense fund:* Ibid., 88.

154. *an 1895 barn:* Application, Clark.

154. *The charges were conspiracy:* Chicago Daily News Almanac, 680.

154. *Barbour and Kremer petitioned:* Chicago Evening Post, August 3, 1915.

Chapter Thirty-Nine

155. *He was defending a lawyer:* Chicago Daily Tribune, September 21, 1915.

155. *pardon for a confessed forger:* Chicago Daily Tribune, November 17, 1915.

155. *defense of Frank Lloyd Wright:* Chicago Daily Tribune, November 5, 1915.

155. *Reading a pamphlet or a book:* Feinberg, 396.

155. *She had been harassing him:* Chicago Daily Tribune, September 6, 1915.

156. *"I cannot believe that:* Wilkes-Barre Times, November 30, 1915.

156. *"I had an invitation to go:* Clarence Darrow to Mary Field, December 6, 1915.

156. *He had asked for a one-thousand dollar: Journal of Proceedings,* 215.

156. *donations as little as $1.75: American Marine,* February 1916, 33.

Part III: Trial and Error

Chapter Forty

159. *The federal prosecutors . . . would first have:* Scott, 323–26.

159. *The judge's father was a Presbyterian: Grand Rapids Herald,* April 2, 1931.

159. *went to the Fountain Street Baptist: City of Grand Rapids,* 448–49.

160. *the Consumers League of Michigan:* Ibid.

160. *"She was manned:* Ibid.

160. *"had knowledge of these facts:* Ibid.

The Red Cross Toll

162. *A young wife was drowned:* Red Cross Report, 33. The efforts to distribute funds in this disaster-relief program were incredible and may well deserve a case study. The Red Cross scouted across Europe, in many instances, to find dependents who might need assistance following the death of their loved ones. In other cases, the agency offered small but critical relief, as in the case of the *Eastland* violinist, whose instrument and sheet music became water-logged. Without them, he could not make a living. The Red Cross paid him fifteen dollars to have the violin repaired (Red Cross, 171). Also remarkable in this disaster relief: the Red Cross disseminated donations totaling more than $375,000, with an administrative budget of less than five hundred dollars.

162. *The husband and little boy were drowned:* Red Cross Report, 50.

162. *A daughter . . . was drowned:* Red Cross Report, 55.

Chapter Forty-One

163. *And the effect of the extra lifeboats:* Days after the *Eastland* sank, A. A. Schantz, a shipping executive in Detroit, estimated that the additional life-boats and rafts added to the ship in July 1915 (to comply with the forth-coming law, called the "Seamen's Act") amounted to eight tons, *Detroit Free Press,* July 31, 1915. Hilton estimated the added weight could amount to as much as fifteen tons, *Eastland,* 82. Taking the lower estimate of Schantz, a contemporaneous shipowner, and, with the average passenger weighing 140 to 150 pounds, the added lifeboat/raft tonnage amounts to the weight of 107 to 114 passengers. A very small number, indeed. Consider that there

is documentation for the *Eastland*'s carrying three thousand passengers in 1906—five hundred more passengers than the twenty-five hundred it had aboard when the ship capsized. The shipping industry had already objected to the proposed regulations stemming from the *Titanic* disaster. Then, after July 24, 1915, it immediately blamed them, at least in part, for the *Eastland* tragedy. See "Seamen's Law Blamed for Accident by Ship Owner: It Causes Boats to be Topheavy by Adding Unnecessary Equipment, Says Detroit Man," *Chicago Daily Tribune*, July 25, 1915. For further reading on Hilton's work on the unintended effects of industry regulation, see "The Basic Behavior of Regulatory Commissions," *American Economic Review*, v62 n2, May 1972.

165. *two different pairs of horn-rim glasses:* Grand Rapids Press, January 31, 1916.
165. *"As we passed out:* Criminal Transcript, 27.
165. *"It would take us a good deal longer:* Criminal Transcript, 28.

Chapter Forty-Two
166. *No, he did not similarly warn:* Redfield Hearing, 245.
166. *"never should have occurred:* Ibid., 262.
166. *tragedy preyed on his mind:* St. Joseph Evening Herald, October 19, 1915.
166. *"I'm trying to forget:* Ibid.
166. *ship's cook:* Redfield Hearing, 260.
167. *"There wasn't much attention:* Criminal Transcript, 36.
167. *"A-1, first class:* Ibid., 32.
167. *"All boats will roll:* Ibid., 34.
167. *"In all your experience:* Ibid., 38.

Chapter Forty-Three
168. *"I remember that it was not:* Criminal Transcript, 62.
168. *"With permanent ballast:* Ibid., 55–56.
168. *Teacher Lou Wilson:* Grand Rapids News, January 21, 1916.
168. *"wanted to try . . . and push it down:* Criminal Transcript, 104.
169. *"she was undoubtedly a cranky:* Ibid., 106.
169. *the dated gray spats:* Grand Rapids Press, January 31, 1916.
169. *"as good a sea vessel:* Criminal Transcript, 174.
169. *Nack testified that the ballast:* Ibid., 208–9.
170. *"ash chute" under the water:* Ibid., 215.
170. *"I would overcome it:* Ibid., 219.
170. *"This thing that happened:* Ibid., 221.
170. *"If the passengers boarded:* Ibid., 237.
170. *"I never laid at the dock:* Ibid., 238.
170. *"Just as soon as I knew:* Ibid., 239.

171. *"By knowing that:* Ibid., 240.
171. *"She stood up,"* Nack testified: Ibid., 244.
171. *Nack agreed . . . was an accurate:* Ibid., 251.
171. *"It would,"* Nack replied: Ibid., 258.
171. *"as if I hammered my fist:* Ibid., 262.

Chapter Forty-Four
172. *"Would you begin putting water:* Criminal Transcript, 267.
172. *"You considered that a safe:* Ibid., 268.
172. *"That is all:* Ibid., 270.
172. *that Erickson "lacked system:* Ibid., 276.
173. *Hull then offered him Erickson's job:* Ibid., 275.
173. *Donaldson: "They had knowledge:* Ibid., 272.
173. *"It should have gone back farther:* Ibid.
174. *Q. You are certain that:* Ibid.
174. *"That is, she was a cranky boat?":* Ibid.
174. *Donaldson: They had knowledge of it . . . :* Ibid., 281.
174. *The testimony would be tossed out:* Ibid., 283.
175. *"The paint of the boat was scratched:* Ibid., 292.
175. *"What do you say?:* Ibid., 294.
175. *"I can't see it on that:* Ibid.

The Red Cross Toll
176. *The wife and the two eldest children:* Red Cross Report, 73.
176. *The only son . . . was killed:* Red Cross Report, 83.
176. *A daughter was drowned:* Red Cross Report, 75.

Chapter Forty-Five
177. *"In your conversations:* Criminal Transcript, 418.
177. *"When you designed it:* Ibid., 426.
177. *"We did not:* Ibid.
177. *"how many people you expected:* Ibid., 434.
177. *"We didn't expect the* Eastland: Ibid.
177. *"Listing is not a detriment:* Ibid., 441.
177. *"Isn't it a fact that if loaded:* Ibid., 444.
178. *"Yes, sir:* Ibid.
178. *"You can't answer that:* Ibid.
178. *"I think not, sir:* Ibid.
178. *"If you thought you had designed:* Ibid., 460.
178. *"Why surely, If I had ever thought:* Ibid.
178. *"That would all depend:* Ibid., 462.

178. *Hired by the company to do so:* Ibid., 477
178. *heavy winter flooding: Chicago Evening American,* January 22, 1916.
179. *"Extending back a great length:* Criminal Transcript, 478.
179. *"So that thing which was:* Ibid., 479.
179. *"I have not said a word:* Ibid.
179. *"That is true, it does not exist:* Ibid.
179. *"Does the Chicago River Exist?":* Grand Rapids News, January 24, 1916.

Chapter Forty-Six
180. *Frenchy dove into the Chicago:* Criminal Transcript, 532.
180. *They had been placed:* Hilton, Eastland, 169.
180. *He had been paid ten dollars a day:* Ibid., 571.
180. *worked for the* Eastland's *owners:* Ibid., 576.
180. *"sawed the pile off:* Ibid., 534.
180. *"Are those the ones:* Ibid., 535.
181. *"the same two:* Ibid., 537.
181. *the* Neptune, *had occupied:* Ibid., 550.
181. *"Captain" Deneau (though he was not:* Chicago Daily Tribune, February 23, 1916.

Chapter Forty-Seven
182. *he had already testified:* Criminal Transcript, 700.
182. *"smelling the bottom:* Ibid., 711.
182. *"I neither can say positively:* Ibid., 713.
183. *"Well, I see them every day:* Ibid.
183. *"I don't believe she was:* Ibid., 716.
183. *Lynn said he began to doubt:* Ibid., 720–21.
183. *He said he allowed:* Ibid., 806.
184. *He had never heard:* Ibid., 800.
184. *"If I live to be 10,000:* Ibid., 820.
184. *Sessions would later blurt out:* Ibid., 1547.
184. *"You mean you were satisfied:* Ibid., 820.
184. *"But he hasn't said it or anything:* Ibid., 821.
184. *"Nor anything that intimated:* Ibid.

Chapter Forty-Eight
185. *produced a miniature tin ship:* Criminal Transcript, 840.
185. *Attorneys, newspapermen: Grand Rapids News,* January 27, 1916.
185. *And as it tipped it swung:* Ibid.
185. *"Ever study marine engineering:* Criminal Transcript, 844.

Chapter Forty-Nine

186. *he publicly vowed not: Chicago Daily Tribune*, July 27, 1915.
186. *to suggest he was a learned man:* Criminal Transcript, 892.
186. *"Had you ever heard:* Ibid., 897.
186. *"Ennes told me:* Ibid., 898.
186. *"She listed a little bit:* Ibid., 899.
187. *"I am no engineer:* Ibid., 902.
187. *"He is a good man:* Ibid., 910.
187. *"I will go back on her tomorrow:* Ibid.
187. *"Witness," Walker began:* Ibid., 934.
187. *Pedersen listed a couple:* Ibid.
187. *"Never was down there:* Ibid., 936.
187. *"You knew," Walker asked:* Ibid., 941.
188. *"There is no question:* Ibid., 968.
188. *Q. Is it possible for that boat:* Ibid., 972.
188. *"Did you make that statement?":* Ibid.
188. *how nervous he was: Chicago Evening American*, January 31, 1916.
188. *read the question:* Some examples, in Criminal Transcript, 937, 938 (twice), 939.
188. *"I don't think so," Pedersen said:* Ibid., 972.
189. *"Water counteracts the rolling:* Ibid., 978.
189. *"to list her out a little:* Ibid., 979.
189. *Walker asked him if the* Eastland: Ibid., 952.
189. *the starboard shaft had been broken:* Ibid.
189. *the* Eastland *might have struck something:* Ibid., 971. At this point he corrects himself from moments earlier, when he said the accident occurred in the summer of 1915.
189. *only $36.06 in cash:* Steele, 1.
189. *ten-inch propeller shaft:* Criminal Transcript, 930.

Chapter Fifty

190. *"What time were you interrogated:* Criminal Transcript, 984.
190. *"Around 9 or 10 p.m.:* Ibid.
190. *"Have an attorney there:* Ibid.
190. *"Was there a single thing:* Ibid., 985.
190. *"No, sir. If the whole United States Navy:* Ibid.
191. *"out of his head" and "staggering around:* Ibid., 984.
191. *"hold of his breeches:* Ibid., 917.
191. *"We were all working to save:* Ibid.
191. *tears streaming down: Grand Rapids Press*, January 31, 1916, and *Chicago Evening American*, January 31, 1916.

191. *"It was stated publicly:* Criminal Transcript, 917.
191. *"It appeared to me:* Ibid.
191. *"I knew the inside of the boat:* Ibid., 918.

The Red Cross Toll
192. *A daughter . . . was drowned:* Red Cross Report, 128.
192. *A daughter, employed by the Western:* Red Cross Report, 104.
192. *Two sons and two daughters:* Red Cross Report, 132.

Chapter Fifty-One
193. *"Any trouble with* Eastland *in 1915:* Criminal Transcript, 997.
193. *"No trouble at all:* Ibid., 998.
193. *"The first time I heard:* Ibid.
193. *"Did you hear anything:* Each of the succeeding questions with responses "No," and "never," Ibid., 999.
194. *"When did you first learn:* Ibid., 1004.
194. *"In this courtroom:* Ibid.
194. *"I was led to believe:* Ibid.
194. *"I heard it in this courtroom:* Ibid., 1007.
194. *"Isn't it a fact it was published:* Ibid.
194. *"It might have been:* Ibid.
195. *"Do you remember ever:* Each of the succeeding questions with responses "No," appear in Criminal Transcript, 1017.
195. *Hull denied that, as well:* Ibid., 998.
195. *insisting he had no doubts:* Ibid.
195. *"I think I saw something:* Ibid., 1055.
196. *"You knew of the South Haven:* Ibid., 1058.
196. *"I did not:* Ibid.
196. *The caption reads, "President Arnold:* Detroit Free Press, February 2, 1916.
196. *"Am still here on the Eastland Case:* Clarence Darrow to Paul Darrow.
196. *It used to be called "Noah's Ark:* Van Vulpen, 29.
196. *Congress had earmarked:* New Grand, 29.
196. *But a congressman:* Ibid.
197. *three railcar loads of Vermont marble:* Grand Rapids Herald, August 21, 1910.
197. *black cigars and being drunk:* New Grand, 33.
197. *"I dedicate thee to the use:* Ibid.

Chapter Fifty-Two
199. *"I was born in Norway:* Criminal Transcript, 1062.
199. *"My home? At present I am staying:* Ibid.
199. *Darrow extracted his biography:* Ibid., 1062–68.

200. *never heard Erickson utter an obscenity:* Ibid., 822.

200. *"When did you become acquainted:* Ibid.

200. *"The first time I saw Captain Reid:* This and the other questions about Florence appear in Criminal Transcript, 1068.

200. *"Where were you in 1904:* Ibid., 1071.

200. *"I was on the Atlantic Coast:* Ibid.

200. *"My reasons for a change:* Ibid., 1072.

200. *What condition was the* Eastland: Ibid., 1080.

201. *"She was in No. 1 A condition:* Ibid.

201. *"I will ask you in all your experience:* Ibid., 1081.

201. *"The captain is usually master:* Ibid.

201. *"I have, in all boats:* Ibid.

201. *'Keep her straight, and trim her:* Ibid.

201. *as Erickson prepared to step off:* Ibid., 1086.

201. *"Now I want to ask you a little:* Ibid., 1091.

201. *"Now to get down into that place:* This and the other questions about the engine room appear in Criminal Transcript, 1093–98.

Chapter Fifty-Three

204. *He wore a light gray overcoat:* Grand Rapids Press, January 22, 1916.

204. *punishing "the crime of thought:* Cowan, 34.

204. *Biology Club in Chicago:* Weinberg, 278.

204. *defense partners, including Barbour:* "My Friend." In this short narrative of his relationship with Darrow, which began with the *Eastland* case, Barbour recalls seeing Darrow's address that night. He wrote: "Mr. Darrow covered himself in glory, not alone in his argument in that case, but in his wonderful address on social issues delivered at the opera house."

204. *"There is no difference in people:* Speech based on accounts in the *Grand Rapids Herald* and *Grand Rapids News*, February 2, 1916, and *The Observer* (Grand Rapids), February 4, 1916.

The Red Cross Toll

206. *The husband . . . was drowned, with the little girl:* Red Cross Report, 51.

206. *A man . . . was killed:* Red Cross Report, 40.

206. *A young man was killed:* Red Cross Report, 39.

Chapter Fifty-Four

207. *"Coming down to where:* Criminal Transcript, 1101.

207. *"This is all incompetent:* Ibid.

207. *"I will state to the court right now:* Ibid.

208. *arrested around 10:30 a.m.:* Ibid., 1102.

208. *"I was taken to Chief Healey's office:* Ibid.
208. *"You were under arrest all:* Ibid., 1103.
208. *"And what was your condition:* Ibid.
208. *"Nervous wreck:* Ibid.
208. *"went over the boat:* Ibid.
208. *"And I think he asked me if:* Ibid.
209. *"Was there anything said:* Ibid.
209. *"Nothing definite:* Ibid.

Chapter Fifty-Five

210. *"You could not feed:* Criminal Transcript, 1111.
210. *Sessions said, "Well, that is:* Ibid., 1112.
210. *"No, it is not large enough:* Ibid.
210. *"Isn't it a fact that it takes 20:* Ibid., 1116.
211. *"It may take 12 or 14:* Ibid.
211. *"That seacock is sufficient:* Ibid., 1117.
211. *"No sir, it is not:* Ibid.
211. *"Haven't you made that statement:* Ibid.
211. *"not free and voluntary:* Ibid.
211. *And then overruled the objection:* Ibid.
212. *Over repeated objections:* Ibid., 1117, 1120, 1123, 1124.
212. *tried to get Erickson to admit:* Ibid., 1120.
212. *"I didn't suggest it:* Ibid., 1121, 1122.
212. *to be installed in the fall:* Ibid., 1123.
212. *"No, it wasn't:* Ibid.
212. *". . . did you tell the facts?:* Ibid., 1124.
212. *Darrow objected:* Ibid.
212. *"You weren't under any compulsion:* Ibid., 1125.
212. *"Why, it seemed that way:* Ibid.
212. *"When you appeared before:* Ibid.
213. *"That I cannot recall:* Ibid.
213. *"Did you make any other recommendation:* Ibid., 1131.
213. *"No, sir:* Ibid.
213. *he was "cross-examining:* Ibid, 1142.
213. *"No, there is only one side:* Ibid.
213. *"I thought that the captain:* Ibid.
213. *"No, there are only two sides:* Ibid.
213. *"Had you ever experienced:* Ibid., 1144.
213. *"No sir, at all times:* Ibid.
214. *"Up to the time of this accident:* Ibid.

214. "*. . . I never would have gone on:* Ibid.
214. *Then the defense rested:* Ibid, 1150.

Chapter Fifty-Six

216. *"Did you notice at any time:* Criminal Transcript, 1153.
216. *"What is your purpose to show:* Ibid.
216. *"Is this man a seaman:* Ibid., 1154.
216. *Sessions . . . agreed to let him testify:* Ibid.
216. *the* Eastland *tipped about twenty-five degrees:* Ibid.
216. *He said he had to hold on to a post:* Ibid., 1155.
216. *He saw chairs slide:* Ibid., 1156.
216. *People became seasick:* Ibid.
216. *Moyer said that he became so frightened:* Ibid.
216. *he had been doodling: Grand Rapids Press,* January 31, 1916.
216. *Kremer handed the typeset man:* Ibid., 1160.
216. *"Yes, sir, I would:* Ibid.
217. *at the defense table burst out laughing: Chicago Evening American,* February 2, 1916.
217. *"Men's liberty cannot be put:* Criminal Transcript, 1167.
217. *"It listed first to port:* Ibid., 1193.
217. *"My recollection is that the [fire] hose:* Ibid., 1194.
218. *"I have noticed she has an awful:* Ibid., 1270.
218. *"If the boat was listing:* Ibid., 1295.
218. *He calculated, in painstaking detail:* Ibid., 1331, 1333.
218. *"Is it possible for the lowest:* Ibid., 1136.
218. *"No:* Ibid.

Chapter Fifty-Seven

219. *Hinton Graves Clabaugh:* Criminal Transcript, 1368.
219. *a confidential investigator:* Marquis, *Who's Who,* 177.
219. *The attorney general in Washington:* Criminal Transcript, 1369.
219. *the Justice investigator sent a diver:* Ibid., 1370.
219. *He had specific instructions:* Ibid., 1377.
220. *He made a mark on the valve:* Ibid.
220. *"It took about eight turns:* Ibid., 1393.
220. *"It took about 19:* Ibid., 1394.
220. *"How big is the wheel:* The back-and-forth between the diver and Darrow is found in the Criminal Transcript, 1398–1403.
221. *he did indeed find some cement:* Ibid., 1413.
221. *"Well, sir, it was pretty clean:* Ibid.
221. *the* Neptune *and other ships larger:* Ibid., 1441.

221–22. *the defense argued that the level:* Ibid., 944.

222. *The Chicago River was one-tenth:* Ibid., 1412.

222. *They had to haul away:* Ibid., 1424.

222. *"Your work is all done:"* The back-and-forth between the judge and Judson is found in the Criminal Transcript, 1424–25.

Chapter Fifty-Eight

223. *He arrived at his post:* Criminal Transcript, 1433.

223. *"I says to Captain Lynn:"* Ibid., 1434.

223. *"I don't know as I have ever seen:"* Ibid., 1438.

223. *"Whenever I have seen her:"* Ibid., 1440.

224. *eighteen feet versus thirteen feet:* Ibid., 1438, 1441.

224. *"One seacock would not be sufficient:"* Ibid., 1442.

224. *"That's normally accomplished:"* Ibid.

224. *"You can refuse to turn a bridge:"* The quoted back-and-forth between Barbour and Weckler is found in the Criminal Transcript, 1442–68.

Chapter Fifty-Nine

226. *President Wilson chose him:* "Sadler Obituary," 591.

226. *The University of Michigan reached:* Ibid.

226. *Sadler described a calculation:* Criminal Transcript, 1509–12.

227. *"not excessive:"* Ibid., 1513.

227. *Sadler was asked what changes:* Ibid., 1517.

227. *"It is a very different set:"* Ibid., 1519.

227. *"Personally, I would have recommended:"* Ibid.

227. *"Because it is foolproof:"* Ibid.

227. *"Do you consider the form:"* Ibid., 1520.

227. *"I object:"* Ibid.

227. *"I think it is unsafe:"* Ibid.

227. *"I think that a scheme:"* Ibid., 1526.

227. *ten minutes of questions:* The quoted back-and-forth between the judge and Sadler is found in the Criminal Transcript, 1520–23.

228. *"Doctor, I ask you what you assume:"* Ibid., 1524.

228. *"Sixty tons:"* Ibid.

228. *"Suppose there were a hundred there:"* Ibid.

228. *"Just a minute, to interrupt:"* Ibid.

228. *"We will show" Darrow said:* Ibid.

229. *"If there were 120 tons of coal:"* Ibid., 1535.

229. *"Yes:"* Ibid.

229. *Salvagers found most of the bodies: Chicago Daily Tribune,* August 15, 1915.

Chapter Sixty

230. *"I would ask that counsel: Grand Rapids Herald,* February 4, 1916. Closing arguments did not survive in the case file at the National Archives. An archivist suggested to the author that the stenographers' notes of the closing arguments may not have been transcribed and were discarded after the defendants won the decision. The two days of closing arguments, however, were more closely followed and reported in the Grand Rapids and Chicago newspapers than the rest of the trial. It could be that the editors of the newspapers in Chicago did not want to spare reporters to cover the trial in Michigan day by day, figuring they would devote more time, labor, and space in their newspapers once the men were extradited and the full trial took place in Chicago. Alas . . .

230. *"The government does not seek: Grand Rapids Press,* February 4, 1916.

230. *"puzzling feature:* Ibid.

230. *Walker replied that the term: Grand Rapids News,* February 4, 1916.

230. *Clyne followed Walker:* Ibid.

231. *"It is only natural: Grand Rapids Press,* February 5, 1916.

231. *"The two inspectors hopelessly failed:* Ibid.

231. *"The* Eastland *was inherently defective:* Ibid.

231. *"These men knew: Grand Rapids Herald,* February 5, 1916.

231. *"The officers and crew had nothing: Chicago Daily Tribune,* February 5, 1916.

231. *"Send does not mean* take: Ibid.

232. *"The statute does not contemplate:* Ibid.

232. *If any offense were committed:* Ibid.

232. *soundings . . . were fraudulent: Grand Rapids News,* February 5, 1916.

232. *"We do know: Chicago Daily Tribune,* February 5, 1916.

Chapter Sixty-One

233. The chapter title comes from a poem, "The Lawyers Know Too Much," in Carl Sandburg's wonderful collection, *Smoke and Steel,* published in 1920. One part of the poem reads, "Why is there always a secret singing/When a lawyer cashes in?"

233. *Darrow stood up to seal: Grand Rapids Herald,* February 5, 1916. The author had to arrange Darrow's closing argument based on five separate news accounts of the address. The order and the diction of the quotations in the accounts were fairly consistent, but absent a word-for-word transcript there is no assurance that the arrangement of words presented here is precisely as Darrow spoke them that morning.

233. *"To return these six defendants:* Ibid.

233. *"It is not a question as to:* Ibid.

233. *"But I submit, if you please:* Ibid.

233. *With the gallery filled: Grand Rapids Press*, February 5, 1916.
233. *"The law under which:* Ibid.
234. *"There is no evidence: Grand Rapids Herald*, February 5, 1916
234. *"It is laughable to assume:* Ibid.
234. *"His place was in the very bottom:* Ibid.
234. *"It would be a travesty: Grand Rapids Press*, February 5, 1916.
234. *"The government has said it had:* Ibid.
234. *"This awful calamity directly:* Ibid.
235. *"The feeling aroused:* Ibid.
235. *"These defendants have a right: Chicago Daily Tribune*, February 5, 1916.
235. *"I live in Chicago myself:* Ibid.
235. *"This case is an unusual one: Grand Rapids Press*, February 5, 1916.
235. *permitted . . . the six defendants:* Ibid.
235. *Attorneys on both sides: Muskegon Chronicle*, February 5, 1916.

Chapter Sixty-Two
236. *"The magnitude and far-reaching: Decision of Justice Sessions*, 6.
236. *"A large part of the testimony:* Ibid.
236. *"The undisputed evidence shows:* Ibid., 7.
237. *"By no fiction of law or fact:* Ibid., 8.
237. *"Engineer Erickson's . . . station:* Ibid.
237. *"It is alleged in the indictment:* Ibid., 9.
237. *"there is nothing to indicate:* Ibid.
237. *He then cited the twelve-year record:* Ibid.
237. *"A wicked combination:* Ibid.
237. *"After the event, it is always easy:* Ibid., 10.
238. *"The dead cannot be restored:* Ibid.
238. *Inside the Story & Clark piano:* Ewing, 42.
238. *He collapsed: Grand Rapids Press*, February 19, 1916 and *Saginaw News*, February 19, 1916.

The Red Cross Toll
239. *The only wage earner of four orphans:* Red Cross Report, 36.
239. *Two daughters . . . were drowned:* Red Cross Report, 99, 100.
239. *One daughter was killed and another injured:* Red Cross Report, 84.

Epilogue
240. *They buried him a month shy: Cemetery*, June 20, 1916.
240. *"I was Happy to receive:* Joseph Erickson to Florence Erickson.
241. *Lieutenant Joseph Erickson: Grand Haven Daily Tribune*, December 3, 1917.
241. *"Was very pleased to get:* Joseph Erickson to Hannah Erickson.

241. *Erickson was promoted: Grand Haven Daily Tribune,* April 4, 1919.
241. *Florence bore their second baby: Grand Haven Daily Tribune,* December 3, 1917.
242. *were afraid to return to Chicago: Grand Rapids Press,* February 19, 1916.
242. *five hundred rifles: New York Times,* February 11, 1918.
242. *There is one intriguing summons:* Walsh, *Court Summons.*
242. *Erickson began having severe: Grand Haven Daily Tribune,* April 4, 1919.
242. *All the while, Erickson . . . spoke:* Ibid.
243. *"Perhaps nature has not been as kind:* Joseph Erickson to Florence Erickson.
243. *Captain John Pereue sold off all: South Haven Daily Tribune,* April 23, 1931.
243. *Judge Clarence William Sessions: Grand Rapids Herald,* April 2, 1931.
243. *William Cox Redfield kept his: New York Times,* June 12, 1932.
243. *William Harvey Hull became a banker: St. Joseph Herald Press,* September 22, 1933.
243. *left all his earthly possessions: Will of W. H. Hull.*
244. *Walter Steele . . . flip-flopped: In Re Petition,* 1934, 19.
244. *Pedersen again perjured himself:* Hilton, *Eastland,* 193.
244. *chance to receive ten thousand dollars each:* Ibid., 191.
245. *not mentioning it in his memoirs:* Puzzled by the omission, the author checked Darrow's original typescript for *The Story of My Life,* which is in the manuscript collections at the Library of Congress. The typescript includes pen edits by Darrow, but, even there, there was no discussion of the *Eastland* in pre-publication drafts of his memoir. Given that, Irving Stone has a puzzling line in his biography on Darrow, *Clarence Darrow for the Defense,* published in 1941. It says: "The case in which he thought he did his most astute work was the *Eastland* case" (Stone, 225). Stone then recounts how Darrow questioned a university professor at length during the trial. True, that would be Professor Sadler. But then Stone quotes Darrow as saying during the trial, "If there are only two men on the face of the globe who know everything there is to know about ships, how could it be possible that the poor captain of a lake steamer could know what was wrong with the *Eastland*?" Stone continues, "It was this question that led the jury to acquit Captain Erickson" (Stone, 225–26). There are several problems with this account. First, Darrow never said those words at the trial. Second, there was no jury. Finally, Erickson was the chief engineer, not captain, and Stone previously named him John, not Joseph. The author raises all of this because Stone's account is the most widely circulated version of Darrow's activity in the *Eastland* case, and it is wrong.
245. *The marine engineers' union paid: American Marine,* June 1916, 26, and August 1916, 30.
245. *"World is made up of two:* Inside cover of a personal notebook in Clarence Darrow papers at the Collections of the Manuscript Division, Library of Congress, Box 3.

245. *Captain Harry Pedersen died: St. Joseph Herald Press*, September 22, 1933.

245. *Judge Kenesaw Mountain Landis died: New York Times*, November 26, 1944.

245. *The* Eastland, *itself, was reborn as: Report of Material Inspection*, 4.

246. *The ship's bow was removed:* Ibid.

246. *It had orders to destroy: Chicago Daily Tribune*, June 8, 1921.

246. *cut up for scrap metal:* Hilton, *Eastland*, 229.

246. *tanks had become corroded, rusted red: Report of Material Inspection*, 4, 15, 16

246. *Sidney Grant Jenks left shipbuilding:* Criminal Transcript, 417, and *Camden Courier-Post*, December 14, 1965.

246. *he was working for Theisen-Clemens:* "Application for Social Security."

246. *a painting contractor in the Sunshine State: Certificate of Death*, Steele.

246. *had a stroke: Benton Harbor News-Palladium*, October 4, 1960.

246. *Steele died in Tampa: Certificate of Death*, Steele.

246. *His remains were cremated:* Ibid.

247. *Florence Erickson would remarry: Bremerton Sun*, February 13, 1978.

247. *"It was a very nice letter you wrote me:* Clarence Darrow to Florence Erickson.

247. *Florence lived to be eighty-eight: Bremerton Sun*, February 13, 1978.

INDEX

About the Author

Michael McCarthy worked for the *Wall Street Journal* for twenty-two years, first as a reporter and then as an editor on feature stories. He is the author of *The Sun Farmer* and has been published in *The Southern Review*, among other publications. He learned to sail on Lake Michigan and spent twelve years researching the *Eastland* case. McCarthy has lived in Chicago and now lives in South Haven, Michigan—two ports of call in the *Eastland* story.